UTOPIA OF UNDERSTANDING

SUNY series in Contemporary Continental Philosophy

Dennis J. Schmidt, editor

UTOPIA OF UNDERSTANDING

Between Babel and Auschwitz

DONATELLA ESTER Di CESARE

TRANSLATED BY

NIALL KEANE

STATE UNIVERSITY OF NEW YORK PRESS

Published by
STATE UNIVERSITY OF NEW YORK PRESS, ALBANY

© 2012 State University of New York

For information, contact
State University of New York Press, Albany, NY
www.sunypress.edu

Production, Laurie D. Searl
Marketing, Anne M. Valentine

Library of Congress Cataloging-in-Publication Data

Di Cesare, Donatella.
[Utopia del comprendere. English]
Utopia of understanding : between Babel and Auschwitz / Donatella Ester Di Cesare ; translated by Niall Keane.
    p. cm. — (SUNY series in contemporary Continental philosophy)
Includes bibliographical references and index.
ISBN 978-1-4384-4253-2 (hardcover : alk. paper)
ISBN 978-1-4384-4252-5 (pbk. : alk. paper)
1. Hermeneutics. 2. Language and languages—Philosophy.   I. Title.

BD241.D425313 2012
121'.686—dc23   2011030211

10 9 8 7 6 5 4 3 2 1

In memory of Caterina Serafino

CONTENTS

PREFACE

Every philosophy book, no less than a novel, no more than a poem, is autobiographical. It has to do with the biography of the one who writes it, although it is difficult to say how in each individual case. Therefore, it is difficult even in this case. I could not say when I began writing it, or for how long I have been writing it, and only with difficulty can I write the date of its end.

After many interruptions, and as many resumptions, this book was born from a lecture given in Heidelberg at a conference organized by German and American colleagues. I was not sure of its title, and even less of its thesis: *Exiled in the Mother Tongue*. Later, after some reflection, I was convinced both of the thesis and of the title, but also of the need to write a much larger text. Thus, the fourth chapter of this book was born. But in the meantime, other ideas, simply collateral and parallel, or already intertwined and connected, had begun to emerge, and other theses had sedimented. In particular, I had the opportunity to return again and again to the question of understanding, which opens up between hermeneutics and deconstruction, and to revisit the text of the lecture held on this theme at the *Forum für Philosophie* in Bad Homburg, the proceedings of which were published by Suhrkamp in 2000. The initial thesis, rearticulated in light of the later events, forms the content of Chapter 7.

In every way, I consider this to be a book about the philosophy of language, a continuation of what I have been writing since the beginning. But it would be vain, although actually not unusual, to repeat the same things. Once repeated, they already become different. I have never believed in coherence. Curiosity, a well-known feminine flaw, has forced me, in my exile, to search for new stars and new constellations. Hence, although I am the same, I am also different, perhaps even very different than I was at first. I have learned to be so thanks to hermeneutics. And it goes without saying that this book has developed through an uninterrupted dialogue with Hans-Georg Gadamer, uninterrupted even after the interruption of his death. It is difficult to say what I owe him, because it is too much. Perhaps in a word: philosophy. Just as there is no method, so in hermeneutics there is no correct *dóxa*, no orthodoxy to defend. Hence, I assume full responsibility for what I say and the positions I take. First of all, for my openness to deconstruction, to which I do not want to hide my debt—a word that would not have pleased Derrida. Furthermore, I certainly would not have written these pages without the constant point of orientation, that is, without the orient, of the Jewish tradition, which is perhaps the text's guiding thread, almost to the point of obsession.

In this book, different philosophers appear who have reflected and written on language, speaking, and understanding: Plato, Aristotle, Hamann, von Humboldt, Schleiermacher, Hegel, Nietzsche, Buber, Rosenzweig, Benjamin, Jaspers, Merleau-Ponty, Wittgenstein, Heidegger, Gadamer, and Derrida. But the whole book moves, so to speak, toward a poet, Paul Celan, to whom the seventh, and final, chapter is dedicated. I did not dwell on interpreting Celan, and moreover, I did not want to interpret Celan. If I have, one should treat it as an accident along the way, essential to every way. And much less did I seek out a new language for philosophy in Celan's work—an undertaking that would be doomed to failure from the very beginning. Through many readings, and on different occasions, I have realized that his poetry is a setting to work of a reflection on poetry and of a reflection on language where it would be impossible to separate, or even to distinguish, between the setting to work and the reflection. Yet what matters most is that, with his reflections, Celan situates himself within contemporary philosophy of language, not only thanks to the themes he confronts, but also thanks to the anti-metaphysical or a-metaphysical way that he confronts them. Speaking of the affinities with Wittgenstein of the *Philosophical Investigations*, or even more legitimately, with Heidegger of *On the Way to Language* is almost obvious. Yet there is something more, a surplus, an excess, and also a beyond, which is his distinctive and chosen trait. Celan thinks of language starting from Auschwitz, after Auschwitz.

One might ask: What does this have to do with Auschwitz? One could easily respond to this question with another question: How can one continue to philosophize calmly about language after Auschwitz? How can one continue to philosophize after the anti-world of the world and after the anti-language of language? How can one continue to philosophize as if nothing had happened? If anything, it is starting from "what happened," from that limit situation, where the limit of the human condition became the center of the inhuman condition, and the exception became the rule, that philosophy must rethink language, must reflect yet again, once again, and more responsibly, on speaking and understanding. And it is precisely understanding that, starting from Auschwitz, after Auschwitz, demands to be understood anew. In this sense, I hope this book is a political one, not only because it speaks of utopia, or of the atopical and heteropical utopias, that is, of the tomorrows of the future, of the coming of the other, of the messianic promise *to come*, but because the question of language is an eminently political question.

I thank Jacques Derrida for having given me the permission to cite what was at that time a still unpublished essay, *Béliers. Le dialogue ininterrompu entre deux infinis, le poème*, Galilée, Paris 2003.

This book is dedicated to my maternal grandmother, Caterina Serafino, who has given me a great past and who believed in the utopias of the future.

Heidelberg, September 2003

ONE

BEING AND LANGUAGE IN
PHILOSOPHICAL HERMENEUTICS

I once formulated this idea by saying that being that can be understood is language. This is certainly not a metaphysical assertion. Instead, it describes, from the medium of understanding, the unrestricted scope possessed by the hermeneutical perspective.

—Hans-Georg Gadamer[1]

1. PHILOSOPHICAL HERMENEUTICS AND THE *LINGUISTIC TURN*

"Being that can be understood is language" is perhaps the most cited, and possibly the most famous sentence of *Truth and Method*.[2] Written as kind of a summative statement toward the end of the book, it testifies to the centrality of language in philosophical hermeneutics. On the other hand, this centrality echoes, albeit indirectly, the movement of language from the margins to the center stage of philosophy. It illustrates the linguistic turn that Humboldt and Frege had already set in motion in radically different and independent ways in German-speaking philosophy, and finds its major twentieth-century representatives in Ludwig Wittgenstein and Martin Heidegger. Language is destined to become the dominant—if not exclusive—theme on the philosophical landscape.

At the end of the 1950s, when Gadamer wrote the third part of *Truth and Method*, the turn had not yet been fully achieved, and language had not yet imposed itself, as it would a few years later, also thanks to philosophical hermeneutics. The most diverse philosophical currents will coalesce under the theme of "language": These include logical positivism and the *ordinary language philosophy* of Oxford, American pragmatism,

1

structuralism, and psychoanalysis, the late Merleau-Ponty and Derrida's deconstruction, Heidegger and philosophical hermeneutics, culminating in the transcendental pragmatics of Apel and Habermas.

When Gadamer sets about outlining his *hermeneutics of language*, he has neither important forerunners nor actual points of reference—other than the tradition that he will reassess in a careful confrontation. Obviously, Heidegger constitutes the only notable exception to this rule. But the connection with Heidegger is more problematic here than one might think. On the one hand, Gadamer largely knows the works Heidegger dedicated to the theme of language and poetry from 1935 onward, and, although he can be assumed to have found a source of inspiration therein, it is hard to say how much and to what extent. On the other hand, one cannot forget that Heidegger's *On the Way to Language* was published only in 1959, when *Truth and Method* had just gone into print. Even if many turns of phrase in Gadamer's magnum opus seem to emerge against the background of Heidegger's thought—not least the very sentence "Being that can be understood is language"—he never expressly refers to Heidegger's writings on language.

Thus, when he ventures out alone into what in many respects is still uncharted territory for philosophy, the difficulties of his paths are as entirely clear to him as the goal he had set out to reach: *the ontological turn of hermeneutics guided by language*. Gadamer does not know, nor could he have known, however, that his *Wendung* corresponds to the *linguistic turn* of Anglo-American and French philosophy. In a footnote added to the new edition of *Truth and Method*, Gadamer significantly writes: "I am not unaware that the 'linguistic turn,' about which I knew nothing in the early '50's, recognized the same thing."[3] And he goes on to refer to his essay *The Phenomenological Movement*.[4]

2. WHICH "TURN"?

It is worth noting that the word Gadamer uses for "turn" is not *Kehre*, but *Wendung*. Here, it is clear that the aim is to distance himself from Heidegger, who, by way of his *Kehre*, wanted to abandon the ground of hermeneutic philosophy so as to turn toward the mystery of language. From Gadamer's standpoint, the *Kehre* seems more like a *Rückkehr*, a return—which nonetheless also implies a radicalization—to the early hermeneutics of *Geworfenheit*, of "being-thrown," where language, the primary *pro-jection* of this "being-thrown," of this being-*there* in the world, is the *being-there*, in its original form, and is the first presence to Being. The significance Heidegger attributes to language resounds in the "ontological turn" of Gadamer who, by following the guiding thread of language, remains within the bounds of hermeneutic philosophy. This may shed light on some important differences between the two philosophers on this point—and not on this point alone.

Aside from the weakening in Gadamer's thought of notions that are absolutely central to Heidegger's—such as metaphysics, the forgetting of Being, and the ontological difference—what is more noteworthy here is the different and novel interpretation of the relationship between *Being* and *language* put forward by the founder of philosophical hermeneutics. With respect to this reading, Vattimo, borrowing an expression from Habermas, speaks of the "urbanization" of Heidegger's thought.[5] As previously mentioned, Gadamer takes up the Heideggerian identification—or connection—between Being and language, but decidedly shifts the emphasis onto language. Such a shift could be regarded as an act of unfolding, or even dissolving, Being into language.[6]

Irrespective of what interpretation is given to the shift from Being to language, which is already achieved in the third part of *Truth and Method*, the distance between the two philosophers truly stands out when the concluding statements on their respective reflections on language are read together. In the famous conversation with the Japanese scholar, included in *On the Way to Language*, Heidegger recalls the phrase he had already used with reference to language in the *Letter on "Humanism"*: "Language is the house of Being."[7] For his part, Gadamer writes in the closing section of *Truth and Method*, which deals with the *"The Universal Aspect of Hermeneutics,"* that "Being that can be understood is language."[8]

3. FROM HEIDEGGER TO GADAMER: LANGUAGE AS DWELLING, REFUGE, SHELTER, EXILE

The terms of the relationship between *Being* and *language* are clearly inverted in the following two statements: in the first, language is the subject and Being is the predicate, whereas in the second, Being is the subject and language the predicate.[9] But this is not all. Beyond the inversion of subject and predicate, the terms, which mediate the relation, are different. More specifically, the metaphor of the "house" disappears in Gadamer—not just in this context, but also deliberately in all his reflections on language.

Rather than the house [*Haus*] of Being, language is more the dwelling of man [*Behausung*] that often reveals itself as a casing or shell [*Gehäuse*], which is too suffocating and too closed.[10] Gadamer thus wonders at the end of the essay *Von der Warheit des Wortes* (*On the Truth of the Word*): "But who is 'at home' [*zu Hause*] in a language?"[11] If language is truly the most familiar and intimate place of being-by-oneself (or perhaps the only one), it is likewise true that an even more fundamental nonfamiliarity stands behind and comes before this familiarity. The intimate familiarity of language is something uncanny [*Unheimliches*] and immemorial [*Unvordenkliches*]. This disquieting intimacy, this disconcerting immemoriality of language—actually revealing itself so *unheimlich nahe* to thought[12]—would represent our "homeland."[13]

The best-known version of hermeneutics is that most reassuring and urbanized one, emphasizing familiarity. Indeed, hermeneutics is responsible for drawing attention to the urban and civilized side of language. Yet hermeneutics is unwilling to eschew the paradox inherent in that strange and uncanny "homeland." This explains the existence of the other version, the more disquieting one, which rather emphasizes unfamiliarity. However, the two versions cannot be torn asunder, for they indeed complement one another.

"What is the homeland for us, this place of original familiarity? What is this place and what would it be without language? Language is above all a part of the immemoriality of the homeland!"[14] *Heimat*, which is the fleeting and ephemeral homeland that language can offer, is only attained with effort, starting out from the most essential *Heimatslosigkeit*, the lack of homeland, which defines our finitude in language even prior to our finitude in the world. At a second glance, however, dwelling, the refuge of language, reveals itself to be a shelter, or rather an exile. Poets such as Celan have managed to give voice to this exile—which can even be an exile in the mother tongue.[15] In giving voice to the originary homelessness in language, Gadamer's hermeneutics, especially in his later works, seems to converge with Derrida's deconstruction.[16]

But what might that more fundamental and more original nonfamiliarity be, if not Being's resistance to language? This question maps out the context most suited to explain the presence of "understanding" that mediates the relation between *Being* and *language* in Gadamer.

4. "THE HISTORY OF A COMMA"

The most-cited, but also the most misunderstood, sentence of philosophical hermeneutics already has its own *Wirkungsgeschichte*, its history of effects, a history of its reception, which has taken a troubled—and thus all the more interesting—path in Italy. Vattimo revisits this issue in his article "The History of a Comma."[17]

As so often happens, the problem stems from the translation, whose creative role in the *Wirkungsgeschichte* can never be overemphasized. The German sentence reads: "*Sein, das verstanden werden kann, ist Sprache.*"[18] In Vattimo's Italian translation, the sentence is rendered in the following way: "*l'essere che può venir compreso è linguaggio.*"[19] The two commas, present in German for grammatical reasons, are left out in Italian for stylistic reasons. Vattimo recalls that at the time he would rather have left the commas in, but the final decision rested with Gadamer. "I submitted the problem to Gadamer and he said that he did not agree, and that there was a risk that the sentence would be misunderstood."[20] Hence, the marginal aspect of a comma takes on a fundamental relevance for the translation and, therefore, also for the interpretation. In short, the necessary presence of the commas in German maintains the ambiguity of the sentence; the possibility of leaving the commas in or out in Italian, however, requires a choice that is more than just stylistic. More than simply style, it is the meaning that undergoes a transformation, or better, the "'ontological' weight" of the statement. Taken without commas, Vattimo maintains, it is a harmless utterance, which identifies the domain of beings that offer themselves to understanding with the domain of language; within commas it says that Being *is* language, and as such it is understandable.[21]

The chasm runs deep and perhaps leads to a crossroads not just in philosophical hermeneutics—or at least not just starting from there. As it stands, the hermeneutic difficulty of the statement raises the crucial question of the meaning to be attributed to Gadamer's philosophy as a whole. If the second interpretative path—the one indicated by Vattimo—is chosen over the first, one can find in philosophical hermeneutics the possibility of a "weak ontology," namely, a kind of "ontology of actuality."[22]

In the latter case, it follows that Being is identified with language. In Vattimo's view, this "ontologically more radical" reading would rid hermeneutics of a metaphysical residue that it would otherwise retain, and that might compromise its position with regard to ontology, from which it nonetheless seeks to take leave. Hence, one is faced with the necessity of going beyond Gadamerian hermeneutics that is locked in a sort of realism where the Being of the world is still identified with the objects as they present themselves, in space and time, to the subject describing them. Such a form of realism would ultimately expose hermeneutics to the suspicions of traditionalism and, above all, relativism.

Yet, in a bid to move beyond Gadamer, Vattimo's path returns to Heidegger. Vattimo's legitimate intention is to further the discussion with Heidegger that Gadamer never actually broke off.[23] Nevertheless, by taking up the Heideggerian discourse on the authenticity of Being, and recalling the metaphor of language as the "house of Being," Vattimo reads Gadamer with Heidegger, or better, on Heidegger's terms. Gadamer's sentence "Being, which can be understood, is language" is thus regarded as a *"translation"*[24] of Heidegger's sentence from *Being and Time*: "Being (not beings) [*Sein, nicht Seiendes*] is something which 'there is' [*gibt es*] only in so far as truth is [*ist*]. And truth *is* only in so far as and as long as Dasein is."[25]

Vattimo underlines the importance of the *nicht*, the "not" that separates Being from a being: There is Being only insofar as there is not only a being, and wherever there is Being, and not just a being, there is truth. Far from having a merely descriptive meaning, the "not" has a teleological meaning.[26] And thus Heidegger's sentence—but Gadamer's too—becomes an indication that somehow refers to the difference between the authenticity and inauthenticity of existence: For there to be Being, there cannot be—or cannot just be—a being in its beingness, namely, in its everyday objective "reality." In other words, Being is language precisely because it is not a being, precisely because it is not—authentically—a being.

By identifying Being and language, one grasps the ultimate meaning and, at the same time, the starting point of Vattimo's ontological and nihilistic radicalization of hermeneutics.

5. GADAMER'S SELF-INTERPRETATION

What kind of self-interpretation does Gadamer offer? If one of the principles of hermeneutics is that the interpreter understands the author better than the author understands himself, and if consistency is a criterion that must always be upheld when interpreting an author, since we are dealing with a sentence that somehow sums up philosophical hermeneutics as a whole, it might be fitting to listen to the author, who nevertheless will have the same difficulty as others in interpreting himself.

Certainly, Gadamer chooses the first interpretative path that does not identify Being with language. This not only applies to the early Gadamer of *Truth and Method*, but also and above all to the late Gadamer, who dedicated numerous essays to language. Conversely, the second interpretative path is carefully and willfully intentionally avoided. What Gadamer does *not* want is precisely to say that Being, all Being, can be understood insofar as it is language.[27] Even in the 1971 essay entitled "The Idea of Hegelian Logic," in distinguishing his own position from that of Heidegger's, Gadamer writes: "But Being itself, which has its abode there [in language], is not disconcealed as such, but keeps itself as concealed in the midst of all disconcealment as, in speaking, language itself remains essentially concealed."[28] And, in a retrospective interview about his work dating back to 1996, he warns: "Absolutely not, I have never thought or said that everything is language."[29]

6. UNDERSTANDING AS MIDDLE TERM AND MEDIATION

A closer look at the German sentence shows that it is less ambiguous than it may seem: *Sein, das verstanden werden kann, ist Sprache.* The role of the relative clause, wedged between the two commas, must not be underestimated. In fact, it is a restriction, or better still, a delimitation.[30] One could rephrase it this way: *Sein, sofern es . . .* Being, *insofar as* and *within the limits in which* it can be understood, is language. The relative clause is not a surplus tacked onto the previous equation of Being and language just to highlight the character of comprehensibility that Being has insofar as it is language. Quite the opposite, the relative clause is essential in that it both delimits and mediates at the same time. This is why "understanding" was mentioned earlier as a middle term between Being and language, a middle term that becomes pivotal for the other two by mediating their relation. Being and language can relate to one another only *through understanding*.

Being that gives itself to *understanding* is language. Or also, a Being that presents itself with the character of comprehensibility will therefore also have the character of linguisticality. This is because "understanding itself has a fundamental relation to linguisticality."[31] Only that which becomes language can be understood and, vice versa, one can only understand that which has become language. This does not rule out, starting from the possibility of understanding, that there is always not-understanding. Hence, if one thinks of the centrality of understanding in philosophical hermeneutics, it should come as no surprise that understanding is the middle term in Gadamer's statement.[32] Already in *Truth and Method*, Gadamer uses those words to point to the actual field of hermeneutics which, as he will later declare, is in no way limited to the human sciences.[33] What is made understandable *for us* is such because it is given in language, and hermeneutics is concerned precisely with what is "understandable." Outside and beyond language (i.e., what has come into language), there is no understanding, and hence, no hermeneutics.

Therefore, starting from understanding, hermeneutics cannot but address the issue of language, for *"language is the universal medium in which understanding occurs."*[34] In other words, language is the condition of understanding, both of what is understood and the way in which understanding takes place.

7. LANGUAGE AND LINGUISTICALITY

One could object to such a thesis by arguing that what gives itself to understanding is not necessarily in a linguistic form, or that understanding does not necessarily occur linguistically. For instance, what would be the linguistic character of a piece of music or painting and, likewise, the interpretation of the former and the contemplation of the latter?

Yet, it is worth noting here that Gadamer also speaks of "language" in a metaphorical sense when, for example, he refers to the language of a figurative work that calls on and addresses its beholder. Within this metaphorical absolutization of language that may in some cases be misleading, Gadamer, however, clearly asserts the priority of spoken language, into which all the other "languages" ultimately let themselves be translated.

We must rightly understand the fundamental priority of language asserted here. Indeed, language often seems ill-suited to express what we feel. In the face of the presence of overwhelming works of art, the task of expressing in words what they say to us seems like an infinite and hopeless undertaking. The fact that our desire and our capacity to understand always go beyond any statement that we can make seems like a critique of language. But this does not alter the fundamental priority of language.[35]

It is not by chance, then, that Gadamer separates "language" from "linguisticality." Following this distinction, which will be increasingly clarified in his work, linguisticality is the virtuality of the not-yet-said, always remaining in the background of saying, and the not-yet-understood, always remaining in the background of understanding. Hence, linguisticality always refers to language or, better still, to its self-fulfillment in the linguistic event. By colliding with the boundaries of the linguistic event, however, it helps bring about their overcoming. Here, in the experience of its boundaries, one can better grasp, and more so than anywhere else, the universality of language because even what is "prelinguistic," "paralinguistic," or "ultralinguistic," is such only in relation to language.

8. SEARCHING FOR THE "RIGHT" WORD

The *limits of language* correspond to the delimitation made by the relative clause. The hermeneutic experience of language therefore becomes the hermeneutic experience of the limits of language. Within the context of a critical—or self-critical—reflection on the third part of *Truth and Method*, Gadamer, especially since the 1980s, has again insisted on this experience, which is not neglected in his main work. *Grenzen der Sprache* (*The Limits of Language*) is the revealing title of an essay from 1985.[36] The "limits" are not to be understood here as "lacks" or "flaws" of language, measured against the yardstick of reason's perfection, as it is conceived in the linguistic–philosophical paradigms of the seventeenth and eighteenth centuries.

Gadamer sums up the hermeneutical question regarding the limits of language in what he calls "the search for the 'right' word.'" Yet the "right" word is by definition never "right," for otherwise it would be a word adequate for a pregiven object, which would only need to be pointed at by the tool of language. In the hermeneutical experience of limits, which occurs in speech, language is far from a means of dominating and calculating the world. In every act of speaking, even when subconscious and self-oblivious, and, likewise, in every act of understanding, one experiences the *limit*: the limit of the word that has been heard and uttered, understood and spoken. As the limit of the said refers to the unsaid, so too the limit of the understood refers to the not-understood, and so on *ad infinitum*.

The limit *says* that there is more: Gadamer thus outlines phenomenologically the experience of the limit:

> Finally it is worth dwelling upon the most deep-seated of the problems inherent in the limit of language. I take a dim view of this phenomenon that has already played a major role in other areas of research—my mind goes to psychoanalysis in particular. I am talking about every speaker's awareness that, in every instant while searching for the right word—such is the word that reaches the other—this might never be fully attained. What is hinted at, suggested, or subtly implied always goes beyond that which reaches the other through language, and is spoken in words. An unfulfilled need for the right word—that is perhaps what amounts to the true life and essence of language. A strong link is established here between the inability to satisfy this yearning, this *désir* (Lacan), and the fact that our own human existence dwindles over time and with the onset of death.[37]

For human finitude, which after all is one and the same with the finitude of language, the search for the "right" word remains an infinite task.

9. "BEING" TWICE: THE SPECULATIVE PASSAGE FROM BEING TO BEING-LANGUAGE

Beyond the interpretative arguments emphasized above, it has not been noted thus far—as it should be—that Being appears twice in Gadamer's sentence: "*Being* [*Sein*], . . . *is* [*ist*]. . . ." Yet, the *is* of the abstract copula concretely marks the passage (*Übergang*) from *Being* to *being-language*. It follows that the *is* does not mark a mere identity in which a tautology takes hold, sinking it into nihilism.[38] Rather, the *is* marks at the same time *identity and difference*; it shifts and defers the discourse from tautology to the other, that is, to what is different from the predicate.

"The 'is' or copula of the statement has an entirely different meaning here. It does not state the being of something using something else, but rather describes the movement in which thought passes over from the subject into the predicate in order to find there the firm ground which it has lost."[39] The *is* means that the passage, the speculative movement from subject to predicate, must be meant as interpretation. Gadamer's sentence finally reveals itself as a *speculative statement* in the Hegelian sense.[40] By setting it apart from all propositional statements, Gadamer observes that "the speculative statement maintains the mean between the extremes of tautology on the one hand and self-cancellation in the infinite determination of its meaning on the other."[41] Therefore, the speculative statement does not pass from the concept of the subject to the concept of the predicate, but asserts the truth of the subject in the form of the predicate.[42] In the predicate the subject is unfolded, understood, and interpreted. Nevertheless, the subject *Being*—and it is not without significance that Being, not language, is the subject—is not exhausted by the predicate *language*. If it were, it would not only be identified but defined as well, and hence Being would be something defined and determined, the very reproach that Heidegger makes in his criticism of the "forgetting of Being."

Hence, when the finitude of the "linguistic event" is considered, one is likely to say that Being is more than language.[43] And this is the case even if language also enacts Being's possibility of being. In doing so, however, by enacting from time to time Being's possibility of being, language achieves in turn a statute of existence. This is the only sense in which the *is* has not only a copulative, but also an existential value. Gadamer's explanatory addition should be understood in such a context: "To come into language [*Zur-Sprache-kommen*] does not mean that a second being [*Dasein*] is acquired."[44] For the manner in which something presents itself—through language—belongs to Being (*Sein*). It belongs to it, yet does not exhaust it. So, on the one hand, "the word is a word only because of what comes to language in it"; on the other hand, "that which comes into language is not something that is pregiven without language [*sprachlos Vorgegebenes*]; rather, the word gives it its own determinateness."[45]

Within the speculative unity of language, Gadamer stresses the "distinction" between being and self-presenting: "a distinction that is not really a distinction at all."[46] One cannot say that Gadamer here forgets or overlooks the ontological difference.[47] Rather, focusing on the passage from Being to Being-language, where that distinction slips in, Gadamer also envisages the reverse passage, where that distinction should not be: He thinks of the capacity of the spoken word to reflect, like in a *speculum*, the infinitude of the unsaid. "Speculative"—in the sense in which language is speculative—is "everything [*Seiendes*] in so far as it can be understood."[48]

10. THE UNIVERSAL "THERE" OF THE WORD

The word is the universal "there" of Being that comes to Being-*there* through the word. Hence, it is the "valence of being" within the word that Gadamer emphasizes.[49] Written in fits and starts between 1971 and 1993, when it was finally published, this essay is important because it clarifies the statute of the word, perhaps more than any other. "The universal 'there' of being that resides in the word is the miracle of language, and the highest possibility of saying consists in catching its passing away and escaping and in making firm its nearness to Being. It is nearness or presentness not of this or that but of the possibility of everything."[50]

There is Being in the "there" of the word. Yet what is withheld in the "there" of saying refers to what escapes its grasp. The presence of the universal "there" of Being in the word is always an absence as well, precisely due to Being's continual dispersal and retraction. The same play of presence and absence that marks Dasein,[51] underpins the hermeneutics of language that reveals itself as the thinking of the "there," that "miracle of language" in which Being *presences* by making itself absent. This is because the experience of language, as the experience of the limits of language, carries in itself a reference to Being that *is not* yet in the "there"—that is always already *beyond*.

11. SELF-OVERCOMING: THE MOVEMENT OF HERMENEUTICS

Going back to the statement in *Truth and Method,* it is noteworthy that Gadamer does not just reaffirm the delimitation carried out in the passage from Being to language, nor merely re-emphasizes the boundaries of understanding—for what has come to language must, yet cannot, be fully understood. Instead, once again he stresses the importance of the limits of language.

> When I wrote the sentence "Being which can be understood is language," I implied that what is can never be completely understood. And this follows insofar as everything that goes under the name of language always refers beyond that which achieves the status of a proposition [*Aussage*]. What is to be understood is what comes into language, but of course it is always what is taken [*genommen*] as something, taken as true [*wahr-genommen*]. This is the hermeneutical dimension in which Being "manifests itself."[52]

What language involves, as it enacts itself, entails the movement of hermeneutics that must constantly overcome itself. This is so because to follow language is to overcome oneself, if overcoming oneself means overstepping each time the "there" of the finite word, which in the finitude of its self-presenting points to the absent infinity of the unsaid. Habermas rightly claims that hermeneutics "uses the tendency to self-transcendence that is inherent in the practice of language."[53] This does not cast doubts over the insuperability of the "dialogue that we are," within which, however, everything can be said differently. The hermeneutic dimension in which Being can be understood is marked by this uninterrupted linguistic movement from finite to infinite.

12. THE UNDERSTANDING OF BEING:
HERMENEUTICS FACING ONTOLOGY

In the passage [*Übergang*] from *Being* to *Being-language*, a passage that is destined to remain as such, that is, to enact itself infinitely, conceals the fundamental aspiration of hermeneutics to be a critique of ontology.

The difficulty with all ontology consists in wanting to say what Being is. In order to do this, it either passes from Being to difference and says what is other and different; or, it sticks with identity and says nothing, it renounces all saying. In its sticking with, in its lingering on the question of the meaning of Being—which remains uncomprehended—ontology reveals an inclination toward mysticism. In an exemplary way, Hegel, in the *Science of Logic*, interprets Being as the "indeterminate immediate,"[54] on condition that this interpretation, at least in the context in which it appears, does not require, in its turn, to be interpreted. One must therefore resist saying and thinking, together with Being, what is *other* than Being. *Interpreted in this way*, Being—and here we are dealing with the whole *Science of Logic*—indicates the difficulty of understanding it, if not in an immediate manner.

What, then, does understanding Being mean? Either one presumes to understand Being immediately, or better, in its immediacy; or one understands Being through its passing into language—where *through* already refers to the infinity of the process of understanding, of the transitory Being-language of Being that continuously escapes the immediacy of understanding. The passage [*Übergang*] of Being into language is here a progression [*Fortgang*] in understanding: from what is understood to what is still to be understood, because what is understood has nothing but the appearance of a definitive understanding, of a last word—it is such only in comparison with this provisionality of past words that comes to light at every turn. The progression in understanding always fulfills itself in a *now*, and always in new words that interpret those words, which, although once understood, are now found to have become somewhat incomprehensible. This is the perspective of philosophical hermeneutics. And it is, therefore, from this perspective that hermeneutics faces ontology with the aim of understanding Being that passes to language.

13. THE A-METAPHYSICAL DIMENSION
OF PHILOSOPHICAL HERMENEUTICS

It is then legitimate to ask—with Michael Theunissen—whether Gadamer's philosophy is an ontologization of hermeneutics, or whether it is not rather a hermeneuticization of ontology.[55] Certainly, hermeneutics does not aim to radically transform the way in which Being is thought. And neither can one say that it is a theory of Being. As has been pointed out, hermeneutics is an *understanding of Being*. Rather than *anti-metaphysical*, the trait that distinguishes it is *a-metaphysical*.

In this respect, Gadamer puts it as follows: "I once formulated this idea by saying that being that can be understood is language. This is certainly not a metaphysical assertion. Instead, it describes, from the medium of understanding, the unrestricted scope possessed by the hermeneutical perspective. It would be easy to show that all historical experience satisfies this proposition, as does the experience of nature."[56]

Hermeneutics looks away from Being in order to turn toward language as the medium of understanding. Thus, by looking away from Being, it takes leave of ontology. Taking leave means that it no longer advances—nor does it want to advance—the claim to provide the final and definitive *lógos* of Being.

From this perspective, the aim of hermeneutics is not Being, even if it were to identify it with language, and not because the identification proposed by the radical ontological reading would appear scandalous. The scandal could only be felt by a philosophy founded on—as a prejudice but not only as a prejudice—a metaphysical realism. Yet hermeneutics has indeed contributed, in a decisive way, to solving and dismissing the metaphysical prejudices about ontology by turning toward language and omitting that question in which Rorty sees the barrier of metaphysics: "to get beyond metaphysics would be to stop asking the question of what is or is not real."[57] If this question has lost its weight and value with the *linguistic turn*, then even philosophical hermeneutics can be included in contemporary philosophy's "turn" toward language.

14. A PHILOSOPHY OF INFINITE FINITUDE

Yet it is necessary not to let a fundamental difference slip by quietly: Hermeneutics does not claim to affirm that Being *is* language. Not only because it does not accept the nihilistic consequences of such an identification, and neither in response to the legitimate concern that it might fall back into historicist metaphysics—a concern that Gadamer's philosophical hermeneutics indeed shares with Derrida's deconstruction. It does so simply because that identification would amount to an ultimate assertion that would go against the spirit and the *habitus* of hermeneutics.

To all intents and purposes, hermeneutics appears—or presents itself—as a philosophy marked by the finitude of historical horizons, which are never enclosed or static, but may still always merge at a later point. Untranslatability reveals itself as still being translatable.

Yet the thrust of the hermeneutic movement of understanding is not the ontological difference as such, nor the gap between *Seiendes* and *Sein*, the resoluteness of *Dasein*, and nor is it the Heideggerian concern for authenticity. If there is a striving toward Being, it does not arise from a response to the call of Being, but from heeding to and understanding the voice of the other speaking from the past of historical tradition, in a dialogue that extends to the present-day diversity of cultures, and demands the response of a project that is both individual and shared. It is in this uninterrupted dialogue that Being manifests itself as a polyphony.

Still, there is no single moment when Being is fully understood or defined, let alone by identifying itself with the horizon of language. For the horizon that expands and changes constantly would cease to be a horizon, insofar as it would stop the hermeneutic movement and would bring about the end of dialogue. In this way hermeneutics is a *philosophy of infinite finitude*.

NOTES

1. Hans-Georg Gadamer, "Aesthetics and Hermeneutics," in *Philosophical Hermeneutics*, ed. David E. Linge (Los Angeles: University of California Press, 1977), 103.

2. Hans-Georg Gadamer, *Truth and Method*, trans. Joel Weinsheimer and Donald G. Marshall (New York: Crossroad, 1989), 474.

3. Ibid., 487.

4. Hans-Georg Gadamer, "The Phenomenological Movement," in *Philosophical Hermeneutics*, ed. David E. Linge (Los Angeles: University of California Press, 1977), 172–173.

5. Gianni Vattimo, *The End of Modernity*, trans. Jon R. Snyder (Baltimore: Johns Hopkins Press, 1991), 130. See also Jurgen Habermas, "Urbanization of the Heideggerian province" in Jurgen Habermas, *Philosophical-Political Profiles*, trans. Frederick G. Lawrence (Cambridge: Cambridge University Press, 1983), 190.

6. See Gianni Vattimo, *The End of Modernity*, 131.

7. Martin Heidegger, *On the Way to Language*, trans. Peter D. Hertz (New York: Harper and Row Publishers, 1982), 135. Martin Heidegger, "Letter on "Humanism,"" in *Pathmarks*, ed. William McNeill (Cambridge: Cambridge University Press, 1998), 239. See also Martin Heidegger, "What Are Poets For?" in *Poetry Language Thought*, ed. Albert Hofstadter (New York: Harper and Row Publishers, 1971), 132.

8. Hans-Georg Gadamer, *Truth and Method*, trans. Joel Weinsheimer and Donald G. Marshall (New York: Crossroad, 1989), 474.

9. On this meaningful inversion, see § 9 of this chapter.

10. This is how Gadamer objects to Heidegger in "The Diversity of Europe: Inheritance and Future" in *Hans-Georg Gadamer on Education, Poetry, and History: Applied Hermeneutics*, eds. Dieter Misgeld and Graeme Nicholson (Albany: SUNY Press, 1992), 221–236.

11. Hans-Georg Gadamer, "On the Truth of the Word," *Symposium* 2, no. 6 (2002), 132.

12. See Hans-Georg Gadamer, *Truth and Method*, 387.

13. See Chapter IV, § 4.

14. Hans-Georg Gadamer, "Leben ist Einkehr in die Sprache. Gedanken über Sprache und Literatur," *Universitas* 10 (1993), 923.

15. See Chapter IV.

16. For a comparison of hermeneutics and deconstruction, see Chapter VI.

17. See Gianni Vattimo, "Historie d'une virgule. Gadamer et le sens de l'être," *Revue Internationale de Philosophie* 213, no. 3 (2000).

18. Hans-Georg Gadamer, *Truth and Method*, 474.

19. This is translated into English as "Being that can be understood is language."

20. Gianni Vattimo, "Historie d'une virgule. Gadamer et le sens de l'être," 499.

21. Gianni Vattimo, "Historie d'une virgule. Gadamer et le sens de l'être," 499–500.

22. Gianni Vattimo, "Gadamer and the Problem of Ontology" in *Gadamer's Century: Essays in Honor of Hans-Georg Gadamer*, Jeff Malpas, Ulrich Arnswald, and Jens Kertscher (eds.), Cambridge: The MIT Press, 2002, 305.

23. See Gianni Vattimo, *The End of Modernity*, 121–137. Gianni Vattimo, *Beyond Interpretation*, trans. David Webb (Stanford, CA: Stanford University Press, 1997).

24. Gianni Vattimo, "Historie d'une virgule. Gadamer et le sens de l'être," 509.

25. Martin Heidegger, *Being and Time*, trans. John Macquarrie and Edward Robinson (San Francisco: Harper and Row, 1962), 272.

26. Gianni Vattimo, "Gadamer and the Problem of Ontology" in *Gadamer's Century: Essays in Honor of Hans-Georg Gadamer*, Jeff Malpas, Ulrich Arnswald, and Jens Kertscher (eds.), Cambridge: The MIT Press, 2002, 305.

27. Nevertheless one continues in general to attribute to Gadamer the identity of Being and language.

28. Hans-Georg Gadamer, *Hegel's Dialectic*, trans. P. Christopher Smith (New Haven: Yale University Press, 1976), 97.

29. Hans-Georg Gadamer, "Dialogischer Rückblick auf das Gesammelte Werk und dessen Wirkungsgeschichte," in *Lesebuch*, ed. Jean Grondin (Tübingen: Mohr (Siebeck) UTB, 1997), 286.

30. Gadamer himself speaks explicitly of *Begrenzung* in his self-interpretation: "Here [in the commented on sentence] there is an inherent delimitation [*Begrenzung*]." See ibid.

31. Hans-Georg Gadamer, *Truth and Method*, 396 [translation modified].

32. On this, see particularly Chapter VI, §§ 9–10.

33. See Hans-Georg Gadamer, "Aesthetics and Hermeneutics," 103.

34. Hans-Georg Gadamer, *Truth and Method*, 389.

35. Ibid., 401.

36. Hans-Georg Gadamer, "The Boundaries of Language" in *Language and Linguisticality in Gadamer's Hermeneutics*, ed. Lawrence K. Schmidt (Lanham: Lexington Books, 2000), 9–17. On this, see Jean Grondin, *Einführung zu Gadamer* (Tübingen: Mohr (Siebeck) UTB, 2000), 202.

37. Hans-Georg Gadamer, "The Boundaries of Language," 17. Translation modified.

38. Edmond Jabès warns against the risks of such a tautology in *The Book of Shares* (Chicago: University of Chicago Press, 1989), 70.

39. Hans-Georg Gadamer, *Hegel's Dialectic*, 18.

40. On the "speculative assertion," see Chapter II, § 10.

41. Hans-Georg Gadamer, *Hegel's Dialectic*, 95.

42. See Hans-Georg Gadamer, *Truth and Method*, 456–474; Gadamer, *Hegel's Dialectic*, 93–99.

43. Hans-Georg Gadamer, *Truth and Method*, 476.

44. Ibid., 475.

45. Ibid. Translation modified.

46. Ibid.

47. On this issue, see Hans-Georg Gadamer, "Letter to Dallmayr," in *Dialogue and Deconstruction: The Gadamer-Derrida Encounter*, eds. Diane P. Michelfelder and Richard E. Palmer (Albany: State University of New York Press, 1989), 94.

48. Hans-Georg Gadamer, *Truth and Method*, 477.

49. Hans-Georg Gadamer, "On the Truth of the Word," 152.

50. Ibid., 153.

51. And in this play Gadamer had already captured the fundamental trait of Heidegger's hermeneutics of facticity. See Hans-Georg Gadamer, "Letter to Dallmayr," 97.

52. Hans-Georg Gadamer, "Text and Interpretation," in *Dialogue and Deconstruction: The Gadamer-Derrida Encounter*, eds. Diane P. Michelfelder and Richard E. Palmer (Albany: State University of New York Press, 1989), 25.

53. Jürgen Habermas, *On the Logic of the Social Sciences* (Cambridge, UK: Polity Press, 1988).

54. G.W.F. Hegel, *Hegel's Science of Logic*, trans. Arnold V. Miller (Amherst, NY: Humanity Books, 1998), 79.

55. See Michael Theunissen, "Philosophische Hermeneutik als Phänomenologie der Traditionsaneignung," in »*Sein, das verstanden werden kann, ist Sprache*«: *Hommage an Hans-Georg Gadamer* (Edition Suhrkamp, Nr. 2183), Frankfurt am Main, Suhrkamp, 2001, 61–88.

56. Hans-Georg Gadamer, "Aesthetics and Hermeneutics," 103.

57. Richard Rorty, "Being That Can Be Understood Is Language," in *Gadamer's Repercussions: Reconsidering Philosophical Hermeneutics*, ed. Bruce Krajewski (Berkeley: University of California Press, 2003), 26.

TWO

THE HERMENEUTIC

UNDERSTANDING OF LANGUAGE

Thus assertion cannot disown its ontological origin from an interpretation which understands. The primordial "as" of an interpretation (*hermeneia*) which understands circumspectively we call the "existential-*hermeneutical* 'as'" in distinction from the "*apophantical* 'as'" of the assertion.

—Martin Heidegger[1]

Every discourse is semantic, not as it is for a natural tool, but rather . . . through tradition. However not all discourses are apophantic, but only those in which there is an assertion that is either true or false.

—Aristotle[2]

1. HEIDEGGER AND THE DERIVATIVENESS OF ASSERTION

Assertion as a Derivative Mode of Interpretation is the title of §33 of *Being and Time*.[3] The polemical thrust of Heideggerian phenomenology turns against the tradition of logic in order to demonstrate the derivative status of assertion (*Aussage*). It is noteworthy that the derivative status has to do with assertions and not with language as such. Heidegger's aim in demonstrating the derivative status of assertion is to achieve a more hermeneutic understanding of language.

Differently from the widespread idea in traditional logic, language is for Heidegger not reducible to the entirety of what is asserted or to the sum of assertions. When looked at more closely, one can see that assertions derive from an originary experience of meaning about which logical assertions keep silent. "The hammer is heavy" is the example of an assertion provided by

Heidegger.[4] In logic, the "meaning" of what an assertion asserts is taken for granted: The quality of "heaviness" is attributed to the "hammer." It is *as if* what is asserted in this "theoretical judgment" had no bearing on the Being-there (*Dasein*) of the one who utters it. But behind this assertion, which derives from the abstracting fiction of the *as if*, there is a multiplicity of interpretative forms that springs from Being-there: "The hammer is too heavy." "It is too heavy!" "Hand me another hammer!"[5] These interpretative forms do not have the impartiality of a theoretical judgment, but give expression to the suffering of the worker because of the hammer, his rejection of the hammer, his search for help, and finally the need to take a break. The interpretation of the worker does not exhaust itself in assertions with a definite meaning. In fact, it is not exhausted in manifold interpretative forms and may also not be expressed in words. "From the fact that words are absent, it may not be concluded that interpretation is absent."[6]

Assertion is *derivative* in comparison with this "understanding" interpretation, which precedes, motivates, and grounds it, without ever being reduced to it. Heidegger calls the originary "pre-predicative" interpretation "hermeneutic."[7] The hermeneutic–existential interpretation, which originates and unfolds in Dasein's self-understanding, appears as distinct and even opposed to the apophantic abstraction peculiar to assertions. The opposition between hermeneutics and apophantics is implicitly the opposition between "authentic" and "inauthentic."[8] The passage from hermeneutics to apophantics is a "derivation" that is to be understood as a flattening out and an impoverishment. Hermeneutics, in its own affective-semantic richness, is impoverished or utterly lost in the derivative abstraction of the assertive predication. The impoverishment is linguistic, logical, and ontological: If the roots of hermeneutics are in the existential analytic of Dasein, then apophantic logic or rather "logistics" is based on the ontology of simple presence. Therefore, Heidegger justifiably speaks of the "derivative mode" of assertions.

As regards the variety and plurality of all forms of speaking—of all "language games" according to Wittgenstein's well-known expression[9]—in which our Being-in-the-world is articulated, assertion for Heidegger reveals itself as *one* form among others, and not even the primary one. However, if following Heidegger's own suggestion, the Aristotelian analysis of *lógos* is taken into consideration, it will be evident that assertion is the result of a derivation even for the founder of apophantics.[10]

2. ARISTOTLE'S LESSON

Ultimately, the passage from hermeneutic experience to assertion is the passage from *lógos semantikós* to *lógos apophantikós* described by Aristotle. The famous passage from *Perì hermeneías* reads:

Every discourse [*lógos*] is semantic [*semantikós*], not as it is for a natural tool, but rather—according to what is said—through tradition [*katà synthéken*]. However not all discourses [*lógoi*] are apophantic [*apophántikoi*], but only those in which there is an assertion that is either true or false. Such an assertion is surely not present in every discourse: prayer, for example, is a discourse, but it is neither true nor false.[11]

Every discourse originates from a conjunction or separation of its parts, and it is in the conjunction or separation that its truth or falsity may reside. Herein, moreover, lies the difference between discourse and noun because—as Plato had already seen—the noun only signifies as such, but can be neither true nor false.[12] However, discourse too, before being true or false, signifies, albeit in a different and additional way from the noun and the verb, which are its composing parts. And its *signifying* precedes its possibility to be true or false. Following Aristotle in this fundamental distinction, it is possible to claim that every *lógos* is semantic, but not every *lógos* is apophantic.

In everyday language, discourses are semantic because they simply signify, without requiring a verification of their truth-value. It would certainly be very strange if our daily discourse needed such verification. If this were the case, communication would end up being hampered, if not completely paralyzed. It would be enough to think of cases in which one speaks of nonexistent objects, that is where, in analytic-logical terms, the referent is lacking. Let us take as paradigmatic Aristotle's example of "hircocervus" (goat-stag).[13] Yet, everyday language, which is merely semantic, is replete with such examples. In short, the apophantic *lógos* is a specific case of semantic *lógos*. However, they are not substitutable for one another. As a further determination, apophantic character is added to the originary semantic character of the discourse.

Thus, apophantic *lógos* stands out not only because it has a logical function, but also and above all because it is engaged with the alternative between truth and falsity. This alternative is not implicit in its semantic or in its the apophantic character. The criterion of truth or falsehood exceeds *lógos* and situates itself outside of it. A judgment that affirms or denies must be verified in reality. The ontological reference gains a determining value in the apophantic *lógos*, not because it determines it, but because it constitutes the necessary criterion of verification. Things are rather different for the semantic *lógos*, which is neither reduced to the content of logical thought, nor requires an ontological reference.

Therefore, apophantic *lógos*, that is assertion, is understood by Aristotle to be "derivative," dependent and secondary, even before Heidegger and Gadamer.

3. HERMENEUTICS BETWEEN SEMANTIC *LÓGOS*
AND APOPHANTIC *LÓGOS*

Gadamer follows Heidegger's lead in denying the dominance of assertions. However, whereas Heidegger, by hinting at something beyond assertion, seems to evoke an understanding free from *lógos* (*lógos-frei*),[14] that is, an almost immediate seeing of things, Gadamer conceives the originary experience of understanding as *linguisticality*. Therefore, in *Truth and Method*, an assertion appears in clear contrast not to an a-linguistic perspective but to linguisticality itself. "The concept of the assertion . . . is antithetical to the nature of hermeneutical experience and in general to the linguisticality of the human experience of the world."[15]

Because the antithesis is not between assertion and a beyond-language, but rather between assertion and linguisticality itself, hermeneutics can avoid a frontal opposition to apophantics. Thus, it preserves the critical weight of the Heideggerian position, but avoids the difficulties ensuing from the dichotomy between authentic and inauthentic. In this sense, hermeneutics is not an invitation to exit from assertions, but is rather an invitation to enter them in a corresponding way. And "corresponding" means in a way that would correspond to the complexity of language and its movement in everyday praxis. Just because assertion is a reduction of language, it still has its roots in it; these roots are not to be severed, but should rather be strengthened. The aim is not only that of opening a passage from *semantic lógos* to *apophantic lógos*, but also the other way round. Without this last passage, apophantic logic that, above all in the most recent versions of analytic philosophy, wants to hide and even severs its semantic roots, would lose all legitimacy. On the contrary, apophantic logic gains its legitimacy, if it recognizes itself to be a reduction, that is, a logical abstraction from language. And by recognizing itself as such, it would leave room and right for the multiplicity of human *lógoi*.

4. THE LOGIC OF LINGUISTIC PRAXIS

But that the roots of language should not be severed is shown not only and not so much by the theoretical argument, namely, the complexity of language that cannot be reduced to a set of assertions, but above all by the practical argument, that is, the daily praxis of language. How is the understanding of language practiced in everyday life? This is a question that hermeneutics asks with the aim of welcoming the most elementary linguistic experience. Moreover, by responding to such an experience, hermeneutics simply wishes to give voice to the reflection on language, which is already nascent in this experience. Hence, the suggestion to go beyond assertions is brought to pass.

What then is an assertion? How should it be conceived in the praxis of understanding, namely, in the hermeneutic experience? One of the fundamental assumptions of philosophical hermeneutics—as Gadamer claims—is that every assertion must be considered as an answer to a question.[16] Thus, understanding an assertion means understanding the question to which that assertion is an answer. Moreover, the question to which every assertion constitutes an answer is, in turn, justified and hence every question is already an answer in itself. This means that each question is an answer to a solicitation. And so on endlessly. Therefore, every assertion, being an answer to a question, is always introduced in the movement of questioning. Only within such questioning, only starting from the question to which it is an answer, does an assertion acquire its meaning and can it be understood as a justified answer.[17] Hence, the assertion should be always located or relocated in the logic of question and answer, which, having dialogue as its peculiar dwelling place, can be called dialogical. The dialogic of question and answer is the logic of everyday linguistic praxis that searches for the sense of assertions, recognized as answers, until they reach the motivational context of the questions, namely, the dialogue from which they have sprung.[18]

5. AS IF "ASSERTIONS FALL DOWN FROM HEAVEN . . .": THE ANALYTIC ARTIFICE

The first step of hermeneutic endeavor, especially the requirement of going back to the motivating questions when understanding assertions, is not a particularly artificial procedure. On the contrary, it is our normal practice. If we have to answer a question and we cannot understand the question correctly . . . , then we obviously have to understand better the sense of the question. And so we ask in return why someone would ask that.[19]

Hence, it is not contrived to reflect on the implicit presuppositions of a question, like in the everyday understanding of language that hermeneutics intends to bring to further reflexivity. Rather, it is contrived not to reflect on such presuppositions. "It is quite *artful* to imagine that assertions fall down from heaven and that they can be subjected to *analytic* labor without once bringing into consideration why they were stated and in what way they are answers to something."[20]

Gadamer's remark against analytic philosophy, which he otherwise rarely mentions and only criticizes in an indirect and implicit way, resounds clearly here. It is precisely in such a context that the gap between hermeneutics and analytic philosophy is clearly defined. On the one hand, hermeneutics is open to the infinity of everyday dialogical practice by referring to the originary dialogical horizon where every saying evokes an unsaid, and every answer a question. On the other hand, analytic philosophy, abstracting itself from such a horizon, restricts itself to the logical, and yet derivative, positivity of the assertion. The respective attitudes toward language are rather different and even contrary: One is entitled to consider hermeneutics as a listening to language in its full complexity, whereas analytic philosophy can be considered as usage and mastery of language reduced to a mere formality. Regarding the latter, Gadamer observes: "The development of such grammars represent fascinating achievements of insight and logic. Admittedly, however, they limit themselves to the formal and the functional dimensions, regardless of the richness of content which is communicated through language. In so-called analytic philosophy, for example, the different dimensions of speech are only covered from a particular aspect."[21]

What hermeneutics disputes is the presumed autonomy of assertions. As an assertion is derived, through logical abstraction, from the motivational context in which it is produced, it cannot be separated and rendered autonomous if not by force. However, in such a way one does violence to language in whose concreteness of speaking and understanding one surely never comes across the abstraction of apophantic *lógos* and the assertion that abstracts itself from all that it does not say explicitly. And therefore Gadamer, not without irony, asks himself: "*Are there such pure assertions? When and where?*"[22]

6. ASSERTION, METHOD, AND THE POWER OF TECHNOLOGY

However, on closer inspection, there emerges a further philosophical issue. It is not enough to oppose the hermeneutic experience of dialogue to the logic of assertions. It is also necessary to uncover the causes that led to the dominance of assertions in the philosophical tradition. This dominance is the result of "one of the most consequential decisions made by our Western culture."[23] Behind this there lies the supremacy of modern science, supported by the ideal of method and methodical knowledge that has "changed our planet by privileging a certain form of access to our world, an access that is neither the only nor the most encompassing access that we possess."[24] The method consists in isolating facts and particular fields insofar as they can be perfectly known, dominated, and controlled. The experiment that has determined the success of the mathematical sciences of nature, from the mechanics of Galileo up to the present culture of technology, is nothing other than an accomplishment of this method. Assertion is that formalized object that results from the process of abstracting, isolating, and experimenting. Therefore, it can be exactly analyzed, mathematically described, and controlled by the human subject once and for all. Considered from the perspective of propositional calculus, as it is to be found in mathematical logic, this type of assertion turns out to be indispensable to the method of modern science. "For it is the very nature of scientific methodology that its assertions are like a kind of treasure house of methodically assured truths."[25]

However, here lurks one of the most relevant problems of modern science; namely, the fact that it can perfectly dominate its own assertions but not its own ends—the ends toward which science is directed, starting from the practical application represented by technology. Technology does not let itself be dominated and science does not limit itself. The limit, if there is one, ends up being entrusted to human and political capabilities. Although perhaps legitimate, the isolation of the truth-value of an assertion demands too high a price if an unlimited practical use of such pure propositional knowledge is to be made. Thus there arises the question whether the power of technology is the most incontrovertible evidence against the isolation and the separation of the assertions from any motivational context.[26] Hence, Gadamer asks: "Does it not appear to be true here that every assertion is always motivated by something?"[27] And he answers by observing that "in any case, the extreme example provided by our modern scientific and technological culture seems to show us that the isolation they accord to the assertion, the total detachment from any kind of context of motivation, becomes very questionable when one looks at the whole of science."[28]

The complexity of language therefore allows Gadamer to openly take a position against the method and its related culture of technology. In short, without the domination of assertions, there would be no primacy of method and no power of technology.

7. THE TRIBUNAL OF ASSERTIONS

The question of the autonomy of assertion is not merely a logical or a linguistic one. Looked at more closely, it acquires a broader frame of reference and reveals itself as a philosophical, ethical, and political question. Gadamer puts assertion on trial in order to expose its caricaturing trait, which emerges when, just like in an interrogation, one is forced to make statements without motivation or answer questions that are decontextualized and therefore nonsensical. The "pure" meaning of the registered assertion, the statement minuted, inserted into other contexts, is always already a distorted one.[29] The tribunal's violence, in turn, sets the measure of violence that can be perpetrated against language, denatured, and reduced to a series of randomly chosen assertions.

Everyone who has been either a witness or a victim of an interrogation knows how dreadful it is when one has to answer questions without knowing why one is asked them. The fiction of a 'pure' assertion apparently corresponds in this kind of witness testimony to the no less fictitious pure determination of factual statements, and it is precisely this fictitious restriction to the factual that then gives the attorneys their opportunity. So this extreme example of the assertion that is made in court teaches us that one speaks with motivation, and does not just make a statement but answers a question. Answering a question, however, entails grasping the sense of the question and therewith its background motivation. . . . It follows from this that an assertion never contains the full content of its meaning solely within itself.[30]

With this in mind, Gadamer speaks of "occasionality," a theme of the logical tradition taken up by Lipps and, in an analogous way, by J. L. Austin in British analytic philosophy.[31] "Occasional expressions" are those whose meaning is saturated only by the *occasion*, by the circumstance in which they are said. However, because it is a part of saying, the *occasion* is not occasional in the sense of accidental. On the contrary, the particular question of "occasional expressions" extends to the point of appearing in the general question of every said, which through the saturation of sense, always refers to an unsaid.

8. *HERMENEÍA*: FROM THE SAID TO THE UNSAID

It is not only an assertion in the more restricted meaning of *lógos apophantikós* that is at stake here, but also an assertion in the wider sense of *what is said* and its detachment from what it does not explicitly say. Hermeneutics further radicalizes its own position. "Language reaches its fullest potential *not in assertions*, but *as dialogue*, as that unity of meaning that constitutes itself beginning from the word [*Wort*] and from the word-answer [*Antwort*]."[32] The accomplishment of the meaning of the assertion itself requires hermeneutic labor that tries to recover the unsaid (*das Ungesagte*) by going beyond the said (*das Gesagte*).

In a now somewhat-dated and yet still important article, the theologian Wolfahrt Pannenberg criticized Gadamer, accusing him of condemning the assertive nature of linguistic experience too harshly.[33] Pannenberg's criticism develops along two lines. In the first place, the unsaid can be understood starting from the said, namely, from an assertion; it would therefore seem absurd to question the primary status of the assertion. In the second place, the unsaid must be articulated gradually through the said of assertions; therefore, the hermeneutic labor itself, which goes beyond an assertion, would nevertheless take place within the order of assertion.[34] In short, as the meaning of what is said stands out against the background of the meaning of what is not said, for Pannenberg there is not, nor should there be, a fracture between one and the other, all the more so because the unsaid can be understood only on the basis of the said.

But Pannenberg's critique seems to have a bearing on Heidegger's thought rather than Gadamer's. It is in Heidegger that one can discern the fracture between the logical universe of assertions and the understanding free from *lógos*. Things are different in Gadamer's hermeneutics, where, by outlining the relation between the said and the unsaid, continuity is presupposed and even needed. Within this context of continuity, Gadamer does not overlook the phenomenon of assertions, and nor does he wish to do so. If he did, hermeneutics would have devoted itself to a mysticism of the unsaid. On the contrary, starting out from an assertion, in order to understand its meaning, it does not abstractly take it up as an autonomous entity, but rather thematizes its indigence by recalling the infinity of the unsaid in which the finitude of that said is inscribed. It is here, in the originary dialogical horizon from which it derives, that the seemingly originary status of assertions turns out to be a secondary one. By emphasizing understanding, hermeneutics seeks to approach the speculative intent of language and to refer, beyond assertions, to linguisticality.

It is thus necessary to clarify what linguisticality (*Sprachlichkeit*) means. Evidently, it is not only a matter of the "linguistic character" of the hermeneutic experience, which in itself belongs to assertions as well. And it is not by chance that Gadamer distinguishes between "language" and "linguisticality."[35] According to this distinction, which gets increasingly defined throughout his work,[36] linguisticality is the virtuality of the not-yet-said that always remains in the background of saying, of the not-yet-understood that always remains in the background of understanding. It is the possibility of what is evoked and invoked having a voice in language. Thus, linguisticality always yearns for language. Ultimately, it is the yearning of our finitude that, entrusted to language, clashes with the limits of every assertion. But in such a clash, it is always the wanting to say which tends to overcome such limits.

Returning to linguisticality in a recent interview, Gadamer observes: "Hermeneutics is this: knowing how much of the un-said remains in what is said."[37] *Hermeneia* has not pursued any other goal since antiquity than to try to return from the said to the unsaid, proceeding from what is said so as to understand what still wants to be said, and thus to speculate, to attempt to understand.

9. *SPECULUM*: THE SPECULATIVE MOVEMENT OF LANGUAGE

It is precisely because the unsaid always remains in the background of what is said, and the not understood always remains in the background of what is understood, that the yearning peculiar to linguisticality will always be unfulfilled. Such a constitutive dissatisfaction of linguisticality corresponds to what Gadamer calls the "speculative structure" of language. The entire penultimate chapter of *Truth and Method* is dedicated to this theme and, in a certain way, it introduces the universality of hermeneutic experience at the end of the work.[38]

Speculum: The metaphor of the mirror brings to light the ability of the spoken word to reflect the infinity of the unsaid. Because every spoken word is finite, it discloses a beyond and offers us a glimpse of a further realm. Here a dialogue with Hegel and the Hegelian concept of the *speculative proposition* is opened up. The impulse comes from the intrinsic connection between the finitude of language and the finitude of man. To properly consider the finitude of human experience in its historicity, Gadamer chooses to follow the paths of language where the unity of this experience has been formed and reformed. In this sense, one can say that language "is the trace of our finitude."[39] Indeed, the *"medium"* (*Mitte*)—also intended as the "center"—of language is that from which all hermeneutic experience of the world takes shape.[40] Starting from this very "medium" of language, Gadamer conceives of a *hermeneutical dialectic* that distances itself profoundly from the *metaphysical dialectic* of Hegel. The distance, however, manifests itself within a nearness that is just as profound.

What is common to both dialectics is the *"speculative element"*[41] "Think of an object and of the mirror image of that object"—it is in such a way that Schelling describes the speculative opposition.[42] Here "speculative" refers to the mysterious relation of reflecting. "Being reflected involves a constant substitution of one thing for the other. When something is reflected in something else, say, the castle in the lake, it means that the lake throws back the image of the castle."[43] The mystery is the elusiveness of the reflected image that does not have a being for itself: It is an appearance that is not the object itself, but makes the object appear nonetheless. Yet, "speculative" has a further meaning within Hegelian philosophy: It indicates the one who, distrusting the apparent certainty of phenomena and the presumed evidence of ideas, knows how to reflect. However, there is also a speculative element in thinking that Hegel has grasped within the logic of philosophical proposition.[44]

What is a "speculative proposition"? In its exterior form, it appears to be a judgment in which a predicate is connected to a subject. But looked at more closely, it is not so. The speculative proposition does not pass from the concept of the subject to that of the predicate; rather, *it says the truth of the subject in the form of the predicate*. The highest example is: "God is One." Now, One is not an attribute that is predicated on God; One is the true essence of God. The subject is not determined, and there is no movement of determination, as occurs in representative thinking. On the contrary, the movement of determination in speculative thought—as Hegel claims in the *Phenomenology*[45]—undergoes a "counter-thrust" and is blocked. And this is so because it begins from the subject as if it were the foundation; however, because it is the predicate that is in fact the substance, it comes to learn that the subject has now become the predicate and is therewith removed. In short, the form of the speculative proposition destroys itself because it does not predicate something on something else but, oscillating between the two poles, it brings the unity of the concept to representation. Hegel compares this oscillation between the two poles to the rhythm that always results from the harmonic composition of meter and accent. "So, too, in the philosophical proposition the identity of subject and predicate is not meant to destroy the difference between them, which the form of the proposition expresses; their unity, rather, is meant to emerge as a harmony."[46]

10. BEYOND HEGEL: THE DIALECTIC OF FINITE AND INFINITE

For Hegel, however, the dialectical self-destruction of the proposition can and, indeed, must be clarified. The speculative movement of the proposition is clarified in the dialectical representation. The representation is not an external addition but is the way in which the speculative movement displays or rather demonstrates itself. At this point, Hegel introduces a distinction between what is speculative and what is dialectical—a distinction no longer considered from the point of view of absolute knowledge—thus granting a serious concession to the demands of philosophical demonstration, which are, after all, those of representative thought.

Yet Gadamer can no longer follow Hegel here because this concession implies a subordination of *language* to *assertion*.[47] After all, Hegelian dialectic is based on this subordination. It is true that Hegel grasps the speculative movement of language, but it is also true that he abstracts the relation of the reflexivity of conceptual determinations from language in order to lead it, through the mediation of dialectic, to the entirety of self-certain knowledge. Therefore, in the Hegelian conception, the speculative movement remains enclosed within the dimension of assertions and does not open itself up to the far more complex linguistic experience of the world. A different accent on this topic could have garnered Hegel a more contemporary relevance: Compared with all assertive propositions, which attribute a predicate to a subject, the speculative proposition "*is not so much assertion, as it is language,*" for being in the middle, between tautology on the one side, and the self-elimination in the infinite determination of its sense on the other, it claims to be the self-movement of thinking.[48]

But how can the speculative movement of language be outlined for hermeneutics? It is appropriate here to let Gadamer speak for himself:

Language itself, however, has something speculative about it in quite a different sense—not only in the sense Hegel intends, as an instinctive pre-figuring of logical reflection—but, rather, as the realization of sense, as the event of speech, of mediation, of coming to an understanding. Such a realization is speculative insofar as the finite possibilities of the word are oriented toward the meaning which manifests itself like something that points in the direction of an infinite. A person who has something to say seeks and finds the words to make himself intelligible to the other person. This does not mean that he makes "assertions."[49]

For Gadamer, the very process of speaking and understanding is speculative because an infinity of sense emanates from the finitude of a word. This is rendered possible as a result of the inherent capability of the word to indicate, from its own finite semantic latitude, the direction of the infinite horizon of meaning from whence it comes and to which it always refers. It is the horizon of meaning that interests Gadamer, and therefore words— "*singulare tantum*" as opposed to assertions[50]—turn out to be that mysterious image reflected in the mirror, the finite appearance of meaning, which is nevertheless capable of letting its infinity shine through. This is not the case with an assertion whose meaningfulness, which claims to be autonomous, is separated from its own horizon of meaning with methodic precision. *Assertion is this falling into the simple finite.*

To say what one means, on the other hand—to understand each other—means to hold what is said together with an infinity of what is not said in one unified meaning and to ensure that it is understood in this way. Someone who speaks in this way may well use only the most ordinary and common words and still be able to express what is unsaid and what is to be said. Someone who speaks is behaving speculatively when his words do not reflect beings, but express a relation to the whole of being.[51]

In this respect, Gadamer speaks of the word's "valence of Being."[52]

11. THE TRUTH OF THE WORD

If the word were reduced to a mere reflection of a being, it would be an empty, conventional label. This occurs when instrumental use is made of the word. The most striking example is that of logical-scientific language. However, already "in the most everyday existence of language,"[53] even prior to its givenness in poetic language, the word in its semantic fullness refers to the horizon of meaning. Put another way, given that the structure of Being is articulated in language, the word brings forth the connection between that particular being it indicates and signifies and the totality of Being.[54] Every word springs forth as if from the center of a totality by virtue of which it is, indeed, a word. As Humboldt says, every word "already attunes and presupposes an entire language" and brings the totality of the vision of the world articulated in language into view.[55]

It is here that Gadamer sees the "dialectic of the word" that "accords to every word an inner dimension of multiformity."[56] It is the dialectic of the infinite that discloses and unfolds itself time and again in the finite. "Thus every word, in the instant of its happening, carries with it the un-said, to which it is related by answering and summoning."[57] Therefore, the finitude of the word that cannot fully express itself, which evokes the unsaid infinity of meaning, is not a "casual imperfection of its expressive power,"[58] but is rather, in its speculative movement, the irrevocable witness to the fundamental finitude of our being.

Thus, by following the guiding thread of language, Gadamer deprives Hegel's dialectic of the idea of an absolute beginning. Because every word springs forth from the "medium" of language, which is also the "medium" of effective historical consciousness, hermeneutics, recognizing the radical finitude that originates from this middle, is not concerned with the problem of the *beginning*.[59] Because hermeneutics emerges from the happening of language, which is also the event of the word in its speculative truth, it is aware of the constitutive and permanent *openness* of this happening. Here there emerges the clearest difference with regard to the dialectical self-unfolding of spirit in Hegel. It is in this sense that Gadamer writes: "Dialectic must retrieve itself in hermeneutics."[60]

Hence, the speculative truth of the word is the cornerstone of hermeneutics. Apophantic logic admits that there are some implicit premises in every assertion to which it seeks to get back. And yet, confined to the positivity of assertions, it seeks out its truth beyond the horizon of meaning, beyond historical language, and beyond language itself. Hermeneutics conceives the truth of the word differently: In the finitude of words, one must always be able listen to the infinity of wanting to say, the infinity of wanting to understand.[61]

12. THE HERMENEUTIC LISTENING TO LANGUAGE

The hermeneutic listening to language means carefully lending an ear to the infinity of what is brought forth in saying. Sight, which is implied in the metaphor of the mirror, is almost imperceptibly substituted with the sense of hearing, which as a linguistic sense is also the hermeneutic sense *par excellence*. Even more than to the eighteenth-century tradition and to Herder who overturned the hierarchy of the senses, Gadamer refers directly to Aristotle who already affirmed the preeminence of hearing over all the other senses. In Aristotle, hearing, taken together with memory, constitutes the ability to learn: "It is hearing that contributes most to the growth of the intelligence. For rational discourse [lógos] is a cause of instruction in virtue of its being heard, which it is, not in its own right, but accidentally; since it is composed of words, and each word is a symbol."[62]

This preeminence is determined by the universality of lógos: Whereas all the other senses grant access only to their specific fields, the sense of hearing, due to its immediate participation in the universality of the linguistic experience of the world, is the "way to the whole."[63] Although the same is also true of sight, here an important phenomenological difference emerges: Whereas the one who sees can refuse to see by averting his gaze, the one who hears, when addressed, cannot stop hearing, whether he wants to or not. Given that language is the faculty of listening, the sense of hearing gains relevance in the context of linguistic experience and its universality. This is not only the case because there is nothing that cannot be given voice to through language, but also because there is nothing that cannot become accessible to hearing through language.

Nevertheless, the preeminence of hearing over sight takes on a new significance within philosophical hermeneutics. "The language in which hearing shares is not only universal, in the sense that everything can be expressed in it. The significance of the hermeneutical experience is rather that, in contrast to every other experience of the world, language opens up a completely new dimension, the profound dimension from which tradition comes down to those now living."[64] For Gadamer, the true essence of hearing and its close connection with the concept of "belonging," taken up in the hermeneutic sense, emerges here: "Belonging [zugehörig] is brought about by tradition's addressing us. Everyone who is situated in a tradition . . . must listen [hören] to what reaches him from it."[65] Therefore, the tradition's way of being is language, and the hearing that understands it thrusts its truth into its way of linguistically relating to the world. "This linguistic communication between present and tradition . . . is the happening that takes place in all understanding."[66]

The universality of hermeneutics finds its ground in the preeminence of listening.[67] "The art of understanding is, without a doubt, in every case the art of lending an ear."[68] Gadamer dwells on this theme until the very end—the 1998 essay "Über das Hören" published once more in his last book, Hermeneutische Entwürfe, written in 2000,[69]—in order to emphasize the "free opening to the dimension of the other" in the connection between listening and understanding, which is the foundation of every human bond.[70]

Moreover, the increased "inability to listen" is at the very root of the increased "inability to dialogue," in which Gadamer singles out a peculiar trait of the technological world and its strong monological thrust. On the contrary, becoming always more capable of communicating, that is, more capable of listening, is "the real elevation of man to humanity."[71]

NOTES

1. Martin Heidegger, *Being and Time*, trans. John Macquarrie and Edward Robinson (San Francisco: Harper and Row, 1962), 201.

2. Aristotle, *Peri hermeneias*, 17a 1–4.

3. See Martin Heidegger, *Being and Time*, trans. John Macquarrie and Edward Robinson (San Francisco: Harper & Row, 1962), 195–202.

4. Ibid., 199.

5. Ibid., 200.

6. Ibid. See also Martin Heidegger, *History of the Concept of Time*, trans. Theodore Kisiel (Indianapolis: Indiana University Press, 1992), 260–261; Martin Heidegger, *Basic Questions of Philosophy: Selected "Problems" of "Logic,"* trans. Richard Rojcewicz and André Schuwer (Bloomington: University of Indiana Press, 1994) 81–84.

7. Martin Heidegger, *Being and Time*, 201.

8. Martin Heidegger, *The Fundamental Concepts of Metaphysics: World, Finitude, Solitude*, trans. Will McNeill and Nicholas Walker (Bloomington: Indiana University Press, 1995), 29; Martin Heidegger, *Contributions to Philosophy (From Enowning)*, trans. Parvis Emad and Kenneth Maly (Bloomington: Indiana University Press, 1999), 251.

9. Ludwig Wittgenstein, *Philosophical Investigations*, trans. G.E.M. Anscombe, 2nd ed., rept. ed. (Oxford: Blackwell Publishers, 2000), §§ 65–71, 31–34.

10. Martin Heidegger, *Being and Time,* 201–203; Martin Heidegger, *Basic Questions of Philosophy*, 53–67.

11. Aristotle, 17a 1–4.

12. See Plato, *Sophist*, trans. Harold N. Fowler, vol. 123, *Loeb Classical Library* (Cambridge, MA: Harvard University Press, 1996), 259d–64b.

13. Aristotle, *Posterior Analytics*, 92b 7–8.

14. See Martin Heidegger, *Plato's Sophist*, trans. Richard Rojcewicz and André Schuwer (Bloomington: Indiana University Press, 1997), 388.

15. Hans-Georg Gadamer, *Truth and Method*, trans. Joel Weinsheimer and Donald G. Marshall (New York: Crossroad, 1989), 468 [translation modified].

16. See ibid., 370–373; Hans-Georg Gadamer, *Reason in the Age of Science*, trans. Frederick G. Lawrence (Cambridge, MA: MIT Press, 1989), 47.

17. See Hans-Georg Gadamer, "The Universality of the Hermeneutic Problem," in *Philosophical Hermeneutics*, ed. David E. Linge (Los Angeles: University of California Press, 1976), 11.

18. On dialogue, see chapters V § 8, VI §10, VII § 6.

19. Hans-Georg Gadamer, *Reason in the Age of Science*, trans. Frederick Lawrence (Cambridge, MA: MIT Press, 1989), 107.

20. Ibid. (My emphasis).

21. Hans Georg Gadamer, *The Enigma of Health: The Art of Healing in a Scientific Age* (Stanford: Stanford University Press, 1996), 166. Translation modified.

22. Hans-Georg Gadamer, "Language and Understanding," in *The Gadamer Reader: A Bouquet of the Later Writings*, ed. Richard Palmer (Evanston: Northwestern University Press, 2006), 102.

23. Ibid.

24. Ibid.

25. Ibid. See also Hans-Georg Gadamer, "What is Truth" in *Hermeneutics and Truth*, trans. Brice R. Wachterhauser (Evanston Ill.: Northwestern University Press, 1994), 33–46.

26. See Hans-Georg Gadamer, "Language and Understanding," 103.

27. Ibid.

28. Ibid.

29. See Hans-Georg Gadamer, *Truth and Method*, 476.

30. Hans-Georg Gadamer, "Language and Understanding," 104.

31. See Hans Lipps, *Untersuchungen zu einer hermeneutischen Logik* (Frankfurt am Main: V. Klostermann, 1938). John L. Austin, *How to Do Things with Words*, 2nd ed., The William James Lectures; 1955 (Oxford [Eng.]: Clarendon Press, 1975).

32. Hans-Georg Gadamer, "The Boundaries of Language," in *Language and Linguisticality in Gadamer's Hermeneutics*, trans. Lawrence K. Schmidt (Lanham, MD: Lexington Books, 2000), 16.

33. See Wolfhart Pannenberg, "Hermeneutic and Universal History," in *Basic Questions in Theology* (Philadelphia: Fortress Books, 1970), 96–136.

34. See ibid., 128.

35. See on this Chapter 1 § 7.

36. See Hans-Georg Gadamer, *Lesebuch*, ed. Jean Grondin (Tübingen: Mohr (Siebeck), 1997), 285–287.

37. Ibid., 286. Translation modified.

38. Hans-Georg Gadamer, *Truth and Method*, 456–474.

39. Ibid., 457.

40. Ibid.

41. Ibid., 465.

42. F. W. J. Schelling, *Bruno, or on the Natural and the Divine Principle of Things (1802)*, trans. Michael Vater (Albany: State University of New York Press, 1984), 137.

43. Hans-Georg Gadamer, *Truth and Method*, 465–466.

44. See ibid., 465–474. Hans-Georg Gadamer, *Hegel's Dialectic*, trans. P. Christopher Smith (New Haven: Yale University Press, 1976), 15–19, 91–99.

45. See G.W.F. Hegel, *Phenomenology of Spirit*, trans. A.V. Miller (Oxford: Oxford University Press, 1977), 38.

46. Ibid.

47. See Hans-Georg Gadamer, *Truth and Method*, 468.

48. Hans-Georg Gadamer, *Hegel's Dialectic*, 95.

49. Hans-Georg Gadamer, *Truth and Method*, 469.

50. Hans-Georg Gadamer, "Language and Understanding," 101. This is rendered as "singular only" in the English.

51. Hans-Georg Gadamer, *Truth and Method*, 469. Translation modified.

52. Hans Georg Gadamer, "On the Truth of the Word," *Symposium* 2, no. 6 (2002): 131.

53. Ibid.

54. See Chapter I, § 10; on the virtuality of the word, see also Chapter VI, §10.

55. Wilhelm von Humboldt, *Über das vergleichende Sprachstudium*, in *Gesammelte Schriften*, ed. Albert Leitzmann (Berlin: Behr, 1903–1936), vol. IV (1905), 14–15.

See also Wilhelm von Humboldt, *On Language: The Diversity of Human Language-Structure and Its Influence on the Mental Development of Mankind*, ed. Charles Taylor, trans. Peter Heath, *Texts in German Philosophy* (Cambridge: Cambridge University Press, 1988).

56. Hans-Georg Gadamer, *Truth and Method*, 458. Translation modified.

57. Ibid. [Translation modified].

58. Ibid.

59. See ibid., 472.

60. Hans-Georg Gadamer, *Hegel's Dialectic*, 99.

61. On this point, see Chapter VI, § 7.

62. Aristotle, *De Sensu*, 473a 10–15. See also *Metaphysics*, 980b 23–25.

63. Hans-Georg Gadamer, *Truth and Method*, 462.

64. Ibid., 462–463.

65. Ibid., 463.

66. Ibid. Translation modified.

67. "Reflections on My Philosophical Journey," in *The Philosophy of Hans-Georg Gadamer*, trans. Richard Palmer and ed. Lewis E. Hahn (Chicago Ill.: Open Court, 1997), 17. In this regard Manfred Riedel speaks of an "akraomatic dimension" of hermeneutics, deriving "akraomatic" from the Greek αχροαμαι, to lend an ear. See Manfred Riedel, "Die akroamatische Dimension der Hermeneutik," in *Hören auf die Sprache. Die akraomatische Dimension der Hermeneutik.* Suhrkamp, Frankfurt 1990, 172.

68. Hans-Georg Gadamer, "Europa und die Oikoumene," 274.

69. See Hans-Georg Gadamer, "Über das Hören," in *Hermeneutische Entwürfe. Vorträge und Aufsätze.* (Tübingen: Mohr (Siebeck), 2000), 48–55.

70. Ibid., 51. But Heidegger already had written: "Listening to . . . is Dasein's existential way of Being-open as Being-with for Others. Indeed, hearing constitutes the primary and authentic way in which Dasein is open for its ownmost potentiality-for-Being—as in hearing the voice of a friend whom every Dasein carries with it" (*Being and Time*, 207).

71. Hans-Georg Gadamer, "Die Unfähigkeit zum Gespräch," in *Gesammelte Werke 2: Hermeneutik II* (Tübingen: Mohr (Siebeck) UTB, 1999), 214.

THREE

TRANSLATION AND REDEMPTION

Speaking is translating.

—Johann Georg Hamann[1]

Everyone must translate, and everyone does.

—Franz Rosenzweig[2]

It is the task of the translator to redeem in his own language that pure
language which is exiled among alien tongues, to liberate it, imprisoned
as it is in the work, and to transpose it poetically.

—Walter Benjamin[3]

1. ". . . ONE SHALL NO LONGER UNDERSTAND THE LIP OF THE OTHER." BABEL

Confusion of languages, the punishment that God inflicts on humanity:
This is the most obvious and widespread interpretation of the myth of the
Tower that sticks out in the famous verses of *Bereshit* 11, 1–9. Persistently
repeated over the course of centuries, the interpretation has been crystallized
to the point of threatening the myth and its inexhaustible depth. The Tower,
which is the first record of a reflection on language, has run the risk of
becoming rigidified in an emblem of the never forgotten divine punishment,
that is, the confusion of languages. Nevertheless, Babel has always and will
always have a special appeal. This is hardly surprising because—going just a
little beyond the commonplace assumptions—there are many questions that
assemble around the Tower, around Babel, and around the myth of Babel.

First of all, Babel is a Jewish myth. There are no heroes, no heroines;
there are no leading roles or supporting characters. There are no individuals.

35

There are not even names. There is a community without a name that wants to make a name for itself. And it is precisely in the name, and not in the Tower, that the greatest sin consists. But if Babel is a Jewish myth, written and described in *Bereshit*, it is surprising that so little attention has been paid to the questions that have been posed in those complex passages by Jewish hermeneutics, from the teachers of the Talmud to the kabbalists. And all the more so, the blessing of Babel, the positive meaning of incompleteness and dispersion, runs throughout all Jewish hermeneutics.[4] Hence, it is necessary to start with this passage:

> All over the earth there was one language and the same words. Emigrating from the East, they arrived at a plain in the land of Shinar and settled down there. They spoke with one another: "Come here, let us make bricks and bake them well in the fire." Brick was their stone and pitch their cement. And then they said: "Come! Let us build a city and a tower whose chimney will touch the sky, and let us make a name for ourselves so that we will not be dispersed all over the earth." The Lord descended to see the city and tower that the children of man were constructing. He said: "Here they are one people and have one language, and this is only the beginning of their work—now what they have set out to do will no longer be impossible. Let us descend and multiply their languages, so that one shall no longer understand the lip of the other." The Lord cast them out from there over the earth and the building of the city was stopped. For this reason it is called Babel, confusion, because there the Lord multiplied the languages of the whole earth, and from there the Lord scattered them over the whole earth. (*Genesis* 11, 1–9)

Babel, Babylon, is the city where the most diverse languages are intertwined and confused. The Jews settled there after the exodus from Egypt. A rich and ancient market, the crossroads of trade, traffic, and intrigue, *Babel* became for the Jews, but not only for the Jews, the homonym and synonym of "confusion." In the Torah the whole myth is built around the name *Babel*, on the passage or translation from a proper name to a common name.[6] Furthermore, the translation arises from a false etymology: The Akkadian name *Bâb-Ilu* or *Bab-Ilani*, "Door of God" or "Door of the gods," is misinterpreted as *Babel* and brought back to the Hebrew verb *balal*, meaning "to confuse, to mix." Thus, if Babylon is for the Babylonians the "Door" of the revelation of the gods, for the foreigners, the Jews, it is the place of sacrilege, idolatry, and impiety.

The Torah does not dwell on language. There is, for example, no explanation of its origin. Hence, the attention given to the diversity of languages is striking.[7] But how is this diversity understood? In verse 11, 6, God observes with disconcert: *Here they are one people and they have one language*. But already in verse 11, 1, one can read: *All over the earth there was one language and the same words*. In Hebrew: *safah 'ekhat u-d*evarim* 'akhadim*. Not only do they have the same words, *d*evarim*, but they also have one שפה *safah*, one "lip," which in Hebrew is one of the words for language. From here the arrogant project emerges: one lip, one language, and one will. This linguistic uniqueness-unity will find its final expression in a great Tower. The Tower is therefore the immediate result of man's abuse of the one language. God intervenes. He does not let the Tower crumble—as is usually thought, even if nowhere is it written. Instead, he destroys the unity-uniqueness by creating the only insurmountable barrier: the linguistic barrier. However, the confusion does not merely produce a multiplicity of languages—this is, once again, the *lectio facilior*—and goes so far as to have an effect on individuals: The neighbor no longer understands his neighbor, can no longer perceive and read his lip. The diversity affects individual speech. What befalls them is the worst punishment that they could ever have imagined: *They can no longer understand each other*. This is the result of divine intervention in 11, 7: *Let us descend and multiply their language, so that the one shall no longer understand the lip of the other*.

But if God banishes the one language, and the possibility of understanding each other within that one language, He also prevents them from finishing their construction, from realizing and accomplishing the architectonic order that they had set as their task. One should not lose sight of the link between language and labor. *City, tower*, and *name* mark, in a growing idolatry, the undertaking of Babel. But why do human beings want to build a city for themselves? Why do they want to add a Tower to the city? And why do they want to top it all off with a name? From commentary to commentary—each commentator making fun of the other with the usual rabbinical irony—the questions multiply along with the answers. And hence more or less likely interpretations, more or less plausible clarifications, explanations that border on absurdity, are put forth. All in all, the construction of the city appears to be justified. The generation of division, the generation after the Flood, has but one goal: to *concentrate* itself in one city. The dispersion instills fear, and the vastness of the Mesopotamian plain does nothing but accentuate it. City and Tower must constitute the center and guarantee the security and the serenity that would be lost in nomadic dispersion. Less clear, however, is the purpose of the Tower, which could appear as a futile work. Yet—or perhaps just because of this—all commentators focus their attention on the Tower: "indicator" and "signpost," "sign" or "signal"—as Abraham Ibn Ezra claims[8]—so that the city will be easily recognizable and human beings will not lose their bearings. Very soon in Jewish hermeneutics, the Tower, as a mere signal for the city, ends up replacing what it stands for, that is, the city itself. But the purpose of the construction remains a mystery. There is no agreement among rabbis and kabbalists: The Tower might have been the product of pure and simple fear, it might have served to protect humanity from a second flood, it might have constituted the symbol of an idolatrous cult, it might have been the revolt of human pride against the one God, or it might reflect the desire to replace God with man. Yet on the following everyone agrees: The Tower was surely erected in the restless and troubled search for eternal fame, for renown, for a *name*.

Verse 11, 4, reads: *Let us make a name for ourselves*. Let us make a name for ourselves, in Hebrew שם, *shem*, to our glory, and not to the glory of God, *Hashem*. In Babel, human beings want to substitute the Divine Name with a proper human name. The name that they want to impose on and attach to themselves, which serves to achieve eternal fame, to ensure eternity, is the idol on the top of the Tower, is the crowning of Babel, the final challenge thrown down to God and His Name. Here is the idolatry that, according to the Talmud, has rendered idolatrous the entire generation of the division.[9] If God's Name must remain the eternal Name, which is handed down from generation to generation, then the name of man, which came yesterday, must be forgotten tomorrow.

In order to avoid dispersion, they could have used any other sign, or better signal. Alternatively, one must believe—but perhaps this is the case—that that *one name*, uttered in that one language by that one lip, is a conventional name, the result of convention and artifice, and is therefore artificial and, in its uniqueness, no less dangerous than the other two products that artifice devised in Babel: the city and the Tower.[10] Before the city and the Tower, the condition for the city and the Tower were bricks and mortar.[11] Two violent breaks, two ruptures with nature, mark the construction of Babel. The first gives rise to bricks and mortar, the second to the city and the Tower. Babel represents a double rupture in the continuity of nature, a double artifice, and a double affirmation of technology. And the first rupture in this enterprise is no less remarkable than the second, precisely because it marks the separation from natural conditions and declares the end of nomadic wandering. In verse 11, 3 we read the following: "brick was their stone and pitch their cement." The Hebrew leaves ample hermeneutic leeway for the understanding of this process by simply recognizing, by means of an opposition, the result: brick their stone; pitch their cement. Yet precisely because of this, a sense of the violence of this transition is conveyed. By means of an etymological game facilitated only by a vowel variation within the same schema of consonants, *chemar*, "pitch," becomes *chomer*, "cement." And the miracle of technology takes on unforeseen proportions. But the miracle turns out to be a mirage, a dangerous illusion, a trick, an error perpetrated against God and against man. Technology is then no longer a means, but becomes an end in itself. The enormity of the work required on the construction site that was Babel, where an incalculable number of people gathered, speaks already of the enormity of the error that was committed. Commentary, interpretations, and legends bloom from this. The fall of humanity, as abyssal as the abyss of the Tower, is described with striking mastery: "If a man were to fall down and die, no one was worried; but if a brick were to fall down, everyone became sad, cried and said: 'poor us! When will we haul up another one?' "[12] Such was the terror wrought by Babel.

The brick, the artificial stone for the construction of the metropolis, marks the beginning of the concentration. If God commands dispersion—*Be fertile and multiply and fill the land . . . (Genesis* 9, 1)—humanity chooses concentration. A single, universal metropolis, marked by a Tower that touches the sky, where everyone speaks one universal language: This is the ultimate end, the extreme result of the totalizing and totalitarian centralism of the Babelian venture. Yet, precisely Babel, the place of concentration, becomes the place of dispersion. God intervenes and scatters the humanity that has not obeyed His command. In order to realize His plan, it is not necessary to destroy the Tower. It is enough to undermine the focal point of the Tower and of the city, to pulverize that one name, opposed to His name. It is sufficient to melt, to mix and to multiply—*balal* means dissolving something solid with a liquid (*Exodus* 29, 2; Lev 2, 4)—that single language that wanted to be universal, that product of convention and artifice. God descends to confound that single language, and the confusion has, as its immediate effect, the destruction of the Tower and the dispersion of humanity.

The Torah tells the story of Babel, an undertaking that remained incomplete. That violent undertaking, the product of violence against God and against humankind, has to remain at least incomplete. And the remnant is there to bear witness to the pride that aimed at completion. Once again, interpretations abound. In the Talmud it is written: "One third was set ablaze, one third was swallowed up by the ground, and one third still remains."[13] That remnant—the *midrash* insists[14]—must remain as a warning to future generations so that they will not forget the terror of Babel. The Tower represents not only the irreducible multiplicity of languages, but also attests to the impossibility of completion and totalization. This monument to human pride that cost violence and blood—raised against God, insofar as it was raised against other human beings—has to remain at least incomplete. This is the punishment: *God condemns man to incomprehension, that is, to incompleteness.*

The fall of the Tower directs the human gaze, which had sought to take refuge in the closed verticality of the Tower, toward the open horizontality of the world. From the chimera of a single language, or of a single name, humanity falls from the Tower, falls with the Tower, and is dispersed throughout the individual diversity of languages, which are the fragments of that shattered Tower. The fall of the Tower of Babel is the fall of the universal language.

But the punishment turns into reparation. God destroys, or—as one could say with Derrida—"deconstructs."[15] Destruction reveals itself as deconstruction: with the confusion of languages and the dispersion that ensues, God prevents this totalitarian concentration in one city, around one Tower, under the banner of one idolatrous name, the artificial pillar of one language that allows for no differences within itself. Through Babel, God prevents the merciless tyranny that this totalitarianism would produce, because Babel is not only a proper name, but rather a divine event that repeats itself in time.

2. LANGUAGES IN THE DIASPORA

After the fall of the Tower, the dispersion of languages and the resulting incomprehension, translation is the thread that still binds speakers, whether of similar or very different languages, be they from afar or from near. Translation is the first response to the diaspora of languages after Babel. But this immemorial praxis nevertheless appears theoretically inexplicable. How is it possible to understand one another despite the incomprehensible abyss of that incomprehensibility, of that diversity of sounds that frequently reveals a diversity of thought?

Translation is the most eloquent witness of the dispersion and differentiation of languages and human speech. In order to dissimulate and pass over the former in silence, one dissimulates and passes over the latter in silence. Thus the history of translation is inextricably linked to the history of a reflection on language, on the semantic diversity of historical languages and on the individuality of speaking. Therefore, it is not surprising that in recent decades, after the linguistic turn, translation took on a novel centrality in contemporary debate. Hence, a *tournant philosophique* of translation has been correctly spoken of.[16]

In the as-yet-unwritten history of translation, with the exception of the chapters represented by Jerome and Luther, and the great interlude of the humanists who approached the Greek and Roman classical tradition with fidelity and responsibility, the question of translation never goes beyond the limits of sacred texts and is posed only much later in the late eighteenth century and the beginning of the nineteenth century. Still, for the entire duration of the Enlightenment, even though historical languages started to take on an increasingly prominent role in the epistemological process, and already with Leibniz, the idea that language is a *Vorstufe der*

Logik (a preliminary stage of logic) was thrown into crisis. Nevertheless, translation, by then so widespread as to have become almost a literary genre, did not constitute a philosophical problem. Indeed, it was not a problem at all. The rationalistic conception of language makes translation obvious and taken for granted. The mathematical model offered the old framework of equivalency, to which language could easily adapt when construed as a simple tool for designating and communicating objects and concepts that are the same for everyone. If the object is the same and, above all, if the concept is the same, then the sign in one language must be equivalent to the sign in another. The sign, which in the original language metaphysically "stands for" a concept that is identical for everyone, is substituted by an equivalent sign in the target language. Translation is nothing other than this substitution. "Languages," writes Breitinger in 1740, "are repositories of fully equivalent signs because they differ only on the exterior."[17] Just like garments, the signs of a language are outer and exterior wrapping. Translating is therefore *einkleiden*, "dressing up."[18] The diversity of languages, where possible, is downgraded, and reduced to the mere diversity of sounds, because it is perceived as an embarrassing obstacle that pure reason, which is dematerialized and totalizing, must eliminate and overcome.

3. "LOVE WITHOUT DEMANDS": TRANSLATION IN THE AGE OF ROMANTICISM

In German Romanticism, new metaphors begin to take the place of the increasingly worn-out metaphor of the garment. From Herder to Klopstock, from Klopstock to Voss, from the Schlegels to Goethe, to Schleiermacher, and to Humboldt, in artistic and literary versions that set out to render accurately even the meter, as well as in theoretical reflections that were to characterize the period, translation displays a new criterion, that of fidelity to the original. Hence, there is a break with the "beautiful infidels" who, uncontested, had for so long ruled the day. The new model of translation now aims to restore the color of the original by keeping the lexicon, grammar, and rhythm as unbroken as possible, and safeguarding the environment into which the work was born. This new model thus refers, more or less explicitly, to Herder's *Eigentümlichkeit*, that is to say, to the "peculiarity" of every language and, with it, of every culture, every epoch, every century, and also to the peculiar individuality of every text and every author. From this point on, translation tries to extend and empower *Weltliteratur*, intended as "a unique and single poetry that constitutes in itself an indissoluble whole, from the most ancient times to the most distant future."[19] In this way, translation means inviting the most diverse languages and literatures to enter into dialogue, yet without losing their peculiar character; it therefore sets out to "institute a cosmopolitan point of encounter for the human spirit,"[20] in line with what a *progressive universal philology* would require. This new historical and critical sensibility is echoed, however, in an awareness of the difficulty and the inexhaustibility of the task.

The question of translation could only really emerge within this new philosophical-linguistic context. Here language, on the one hand, constitutes the condition of possibility for knowledge, and is therefore not limited to restoring a prelinguistic thought by giving shape to it; and on the other, ever since the fall of the Tower, it manifests itself historically in an always fragmented and shattered form. The diversity of languages in which it manifests itself is not only a diversity of sounds, but also, and above all, a diversity of content. Thinking, which gives itself only through its linguistic articulation, will in turn be dispersed, disseminated, and fragmented into historical languages. Translation can acquire value only if the diversity of languages is meant as an irreducible diversity. And the philosophy that finally faces the former cannot avoid facing the latter.

The first to publicly advocate this new way of understanding translation is Schleiermacher, who on June 14, 1813, read the memoir entitled *Über die verschiedenen Methoden des Übersetzens* at the Academy of Sciences in Berlin.[21] From the outset, Schleiermacher draws attention to the hermeneutic vastness of translation that cannot be limited to the mere transposition of one language into another. As he notes: "We do not even have to go outside the domain of one language to encounter the same phenomenon."[22] A language reveals itself as a crossroads of differences, differences in the development of the language, in the dialects that run through it, and the differences that depend on social class and cultural formation. These are what linguistics labels as diachronic, diatopic, and diastratic differences.[23] But leaving such differences aside, translating is a phenomenon that also involves the linguistic praxis between one individual and another. Individual difference requires us to translate even within the same language, and translating strays into understanding. Furthermore, translating, that is, understanding, does not even spare the individual. "We must sometimes even translate our own words after a while, when we want to make them really our own again."[24] For this reason, each of us comes to translate and understand ourselves differently over time.[25]

Understanding, translating, and transposing, which are different aspects of one and the same phenomenon that opens up the very field of *hermeneutics*, are closely interwoven and therefore barely distinguishable. This notwithstanding, Schleiermacher makes the drastic decision to limit his inquiry to the problems posed by the transposition of one language into another. Translation, in all its other senses, is too closely tied to the demands of the moment to be able to give itself other rules than those that instill "a purely moral attitude." This allows the "sense" (*Sinn*) to "remain open to things that are less closely related," allows the "sense" to become *hermeneutic sense*.[26] Having left behind translating in its individual effects, but also in its broader effects for hermeneutics, and in so doing having given *hermeneutics* over to *ethics*, Schleiermacher concentrates solely on interlinguistic translation. For him, "irrationality," that is, the incongruence that pervades all the elements of two different languages, their irreducible diversity, which is not only phonic "for the ear" (*für das Ohr*), but is also the diversity of semantic contents and grammatical and syntactical relations (*Beugungen* and *Verbindungsweisen*), does not have the same impact on every linguistic production and therefore on every translation. In this way, Schleiermacher introduces a first distinction, and—as he himself admits, one with imprecise boundaries, between *Dolmetschen* and *Übersetzen*, between the oral translation of the interpreter (*Dolmetscher*) and the written translation of the translator (*Übersetzer*). The first of these does not pose theoretical problems because in practice it reveals itself to be "an almost mechanical affair" (*fast nur ein mechanisches Geschäft*) that in the "life of commerce" (*Geschäftsleben*) can ordinarily be resolved by anyone who has even an average knowledge of the two languages.[27] Here the increased instrumentality and signifying efficacy of the language, where meanings are defined with precision and dominate the things they designate, ensures that linguistic diversity is almost neutralized and understanding is almost immediate. Conversely, the "task of the translator," who has to measure up to texts written in the fields of art and science, is "infinitely difficult and complicated." What dominates in these fields is the "thinking" that "forms a whole with the discourse," while the thing withdraws, thus revealing that it is only there thanks to the word: "in the place of the thing there is only the word."[28] In the individual act of speaking, in discourse, the particular style of the author can stand out distinctly. Every discourse that carries the trace of individuality is born from the interaction between the speaker and the language. Hence, on the one hand, this speaker is "at the mercy" of the language that prescribes one's speaking and thinking, and on the other, one can, in turn, transform the language through speaking. The translator therefore faces a twofold difficulty, insofar as one must endeavor to render both "the spirit of the language" and the individuality of the speaker. Furthermore, one must also consider their reciprocal action from which the original springs. Once the key to the original is found, one must also reproduce it in one's own language, that is, in this case, German. But the term *reproduce* is unsatisfactory for Schleiermacher in so far as it recalls two traditional and by then established methods, that of the "paraphrase" (*Paraphrase*) and that of "reproduction" or "imitation" (*Nachbildung*).[29] The translator who paraphrases treats the elements of the two languages as "mathematical signs," and therefore as reducible to the same value, and, by searching in vain to establish equivalences, one resorts to periphrasis and additions, even in some cases taking the place of the commentary.[30] In renouncing from the outset all fidelity to the parts of the original, the reworking of the text aims at reproducing the overall impression, but ends up creating a completely different work.

But what then should translation be? For Schleiermacher, translation is disclosing to the reader the understanding of the original. But this disclosing is also mediating, and the mediations here are many. On the one hand, there is an author, with his or her distant and unfamiliar individuality, and there is the foreign language, and the way in which they have interacted to give life to the text. On the other hand, there is the translator's language and the translator himself or herself, with his or her more or less partial understanding. What will get through to the readers? And is translation not therefore "a mad undertaking"?[31] The two paths that Schleiermacher indicates are summed up in one sentence that is destined to mark a turning point in the reflection on translation and the object of numerous discussions: "Either the translator leaves the author in peace, as much as possible, and moves the reader toward him; or he leaves the reader in peace, as much as possible, and moves the author toward him."[32] This is clearly a matter of the two extreme paths contained in the *Verstehenskunst*, in the "art of understanding." The second of these is the most well worn, and consists in "translating an author in the way in which he himself would have originally written in German, had he been German."[33] In such a case, one's own language, the language of the translator, which is also that of the reader, has "nothing to fear" because in no way is its purity or integrity marred. But the aim here, the result of an abstraction that does not take into account the "formative capacity" of language, and believes that thought and language can be unbridled as one unbridles a pair of horses, is "empty and absurd."[34] The first of the two paths, instead, sets out to disclose the language of the original to the reader in the way the translator has understood and understands it; but however well the translator knows the language of the original, it will always be a foreign language for him or her, different from the mother tongue, and he or she will always be aware of this difference. In short, the translator, like every reader, will always feel a certain "sense of foreignness" (*das Gefühl des Fremden*) in the face of the other language.[35]

And it is precisely this ineliminable residue of foreignness that the translator must leave intact, so that the readers, even though they are reading a piece of writing in their mother tongue, are aware that before them lies a strange and foreign original.[36] The closer the connection to the original, the more foreign and strange the translation sounds—the more it presents itself as translation. One's own language, the mother tongue, prepares itself here to take on a "foreign appearance." But on this path, which Schleiermacher undoubtedly prefers to the other, the translator will need "art and measure" in order not to do too much damage to oneself or to the language. "The attempt seems to be the strangest form of humiliation [*Erniederigung*] a writer who is not a bad writer could impose upon himself."[37] The translator not only lowers and humbles himself or herself as an author, but also his or her own mother tongue, in front of the author of the original and the foreign language. By twisting the mother tongue to the contortions of the foreign language, and by wanting to preserve its intonation of strangeness, the translator exposes himself or herself to serious risks. Many will laugh and scoff at this undertaking. Who would not in fact want to beget children who represent the "paternal stock" rather than "illegitimate children"? The "illegitimate child" disgusts anyone who fears for the purity of the mother tongue.[38] But Schleiermacher puts forward two necessary conditions, namely, that the target language can support deviations and innovations, and that there is more than one illegitimate child, or, rather, that there is a large number of them. This will be the way for one's own language to extend and develop its potentiality, allowing the foreign languages and cultures to act within it, along with the works of the authors in their singular and strange individuality.

According to Schleiermacher, the German language is particularly well suited for just such an experiment. There are several reasons why this is the case. In addition to the "particular vocation" of the German people, compelled by circumstances to translate in large quantities, one would also need to mention the "mediating nature" of the German people and their particular "attentiveness to what is foreign." Even the German language already offers a linguistic space by permitting with its translations much more than is granted elsewhere. All of this seems to destine the Germans—Schleiermacher concludes in good faith—to reunite all the treasures of foreign science and art at the "heart of Europe."[39]

The translation, the beautiful infidel, who changes her garments so frivolously, is therefore presented by Schleiermacher in a completely different guise. Nonetheless, she remains absolutely feminine. And now, perhaps ugly—but only for those who consider themselves "masters"—yet faithful, extremely faithful, she does not hesitate to humble herself or even to give birth to illegitimate children for the sake of the stranger who is the author of the original text in another language. She even puts language at risk, even the mother tongue, together with the purity of its progeny. This feminine reading of translation finds a further, extreme metaphor in Humboldt. No matter how beautiful or ugly she is, the translation, which is always extremely faithful, is born from "*a love without demands*" (*eine anspruchslose Liebe*).[40] A love without demands is a love without requests, which asks for nothing, which does not ask for anything in return for what it gives, and does not even know that it gives—the *welcoming of receiving* which is the gesture *par excellence* of feminine *eros*. It is therefore a gift.

Humboldt's essay dates from 1816, three years after Schleiermacher's memoir and, in reality, it is the introduction—one of his many introductions—to his translation of Aeschylus' *Agamemnon*. The pages dedicated to a reflection on translation are relatively few; but they occupy a significant position in the complete work of Humboldt because they come between the aesthetic writings and those on the philosophy of language. There is no word in a given language—so Humboldt begins his argument—that is "completely equivalent" to that of another.[41] This is because the word is not a sign *for* a concept. "The word is so little the sign of a concept that the concept without the word cannot arise, nor could it even be held firm."[42] The concept is only given in the word and through the word—thanks to the word's sensible form. Hence, the concept cannot be untied or severed, as can happen in the case of the sign. In order to clarify this, Humboldt makes use of a comparison. The word, and the concept in it, is born in the same way that a cloud is born. "The indeterminate operating of the capacity to think thickens into a word just as soft clouds form in a clear sky."[43] Therefore thinking, by condensing itself, is concentrated in the word. The result of thinking, that is, the concept, gives itself in the form of the word, and the one is inseparable from the other. Inseparability is also simultaneity, the concept is not formed before the word, which would intervene only in a second moment so as to designate it. The formation of the one is at the same time the formation of the other. The comparison, however, also suggests further characteristics of both the word and the concept. That the word is like a "soft cloud" in the clear sky means that its contours are imprecise and vague, and that indeterminacy, first referred to in relation to the workings of thought, remains in the concept as it does in the word. It also means that the subsistence of both is as precarious as that of a cloud.

The difficulty of every translation springs from the impossibility of substituting a word from one language with one from another, while at the same time holding fast to the concept. Different languages cut out and articulate different concepts. Yet this should not deter us from translating. Translating is necessary and indispensable in the field of literature, both because it gives access, to those who do not know foreign languages, to forms of art and humanity that would otherwise remain foreign to them; and because it increases the expressive and semantic range of one's own language. Schleiermacher had already emphasized this. But as a linguist Humboldt adds something further: Languages, all of them, even the so-called idioms of "uncultured" peoples, which may appear as such only because one does not know them well enough, have the prodigious quality of always being sufficient for everyday use, but also of being able to infinitely rise to a higher and multiform use. It is here, against all racism and Eurocentrism, that Humboldt offers a theoretical legitimatization for the *equal dignity of all languages*: "Everything, from the most elevated to the most profound, from the most forceful to the most fragile, can be expressed in every language."[44] It would be enough—to use another metaphor—to reawaken in each one the tonalities that remain dormant, as if they lay at the bottom of an unplayed musical instrument.[45]

If through translation language is supposed to reach what it does not have or what it has in a different way, then fidelity will be indispensable. This fidelity must concern, however, only the "character of the original," which must not be betrayed for the details. Love without demands is an exclusive love, exclusively addressed to the original. In order to be faithful, the translation will therefore take on "a certain color of foreignness" (*eine gewisse Farbe der Fremdheit*).[46] It must, however, respect that limit by which, even if one senses that "the foreign" (*das Fremde*), the "foreignness" (*die Fremdheit*) does not dominate. In this latter case, the foreignness would turn into obscurity and would end up obscuring even the foreign. If the translator succeeds in finding such a risky and precarious balance, the translation will achieve its highest ends. The unbiased reader will easily single out the line of demarcation. Fidelity is therefore not mere imitation, or better still, it is not imitation at all, but rather respect for the foreignness of the original that one does not want to disguise and cross out through reworking. Even Humboldt refuses to follow the second path described by Schleiermacher, which consists in translating an author in the way he would have written had he been German. This would mean running counter to the principle by which all of hermeneutics abides, namely, the inseparability of thought and language.[47] According to Humboldt, the impossibility of reaching the peculiar beauty of the original often leads to grafting on to it a foreign adornment which alters it by transforming its color and its tone. Yet the obscurity cannot be an excuse for making unjust demands. On the contrary, only if it does not make demands can the translation reach its highest value. A translation that, instead of leaving space for the original, aims to become the protagonist, using the original only as an excuse for its own existence, would not even be a translation. It would be more of a commentary, or even an actual interpretation that, in order to explicate what the original only hints at, unraveling metaphors and adding logical passages where they have been left out, introduces a clarity that nonetheless obscures the text. One should not expect that what is sublime or unusual in the original language will become easily and immediately understandable in the translation. For Humboldt, translation, if it is to be such, cannot be a clarification.[48]

But translation's love without demands for the original does not stop here. Not only will it have to be content with not being particularly beautiful in order to be consistently faithful; not only will it have to put its own mother tongue at risk and, by humbling itself for love of the stranger and for the sake of welcoming the stranger, beget illegitimate children. Its "abnegation" (*Selbstverläugnung*) will also have to reach the point of sharing its love with others and, knowing itself as finite and mortal, much more so than the original, it will have to hope that others will take its place. The translation is less enduring than any other work, and for this reason it is destined to repetition. The more translations there are of a text, the more accessible that text will be to those who do not understand its language. Each translation renders what it has been able to conceive, whereas "the true spirit"—the masculine residue even in Humboldt—remains only in the original.[49]

Underlining the femininity of translation does not mean belittling its importance. On the contrary, precisely because it is feminine, translation is above all creative, albeit of a different creativity. It is in the welcoming of the text, strange and foreign as it is, that it unfolds its creativity. Friedrich Schlegel writes that translation does not translate a text, but translates "according to a text."[50] This is the goal but also the limit of translation because the original, historical, and individual act of speaking is, as such, irreproducible. Another metaphor that appears at this time, again in Humboldt, is that of the "bridge": Language is like a bridge that, thrown across the abyss of foreignness, "joins by isolating."[51] Although the bridge allows for "understanding," it accentuates the "difference" between one speaker and the other by bringing the individuality of each to the surface.[52] And that bridge made of air, which flows away and disperses, is there only as long as one speaks and understands. The bridge of understanding is then always at the same time a bridge of distance, just as every understanding is simultaneously always not-understanding.[53] But the *not* of not-understanding appears unavoidable in translation, which is thus revealed as the limit situation of understanding. This is the great novelty of the Romantic period, of its reflections, but also of the practice of translation. With its tint of strangeness, translation not only becomes aware that the original, which belongs to another world and comes from another author, cannot be appropriated, but also brings to light its own limit and, by setting it to work, enables one to experience the limit of translation. In *The Experience of the Foreign*[54]—the original French title reads *L'épreuve de l'étranger*—indicating both trial and suffering—the hermeneutic experience of translation is laid out before us. Here, the phenomenon of translation is expanded and deepened. And from here on the question is radicalized: Not only is *understanding translating*, but also the correlative act of *speaking is translating*.

At the sources of hermeneutics, translation reveals itself as the very movement of language. August Wilhelm Schlegel comes to the conclusion that "the human spirit can do nothing other than translate."[55] But behind these words there hides what Hamann, who was perhaps the first to speak of this, had written in his *Aesthetica in nuce*: "*Speaking is translating*— from a language of angels into a language of men, whether thoughts into words, things into names, images into signs."[56] Speaking, in its primary and poetic form—as Novalis says "after all every poem is translation"—is a continuous translating and self-translating in the mother tongue. Because not only understanding but also speaking is translating, the hermeneutic question becomes more urgent, insofar as translating is no longer just transposing between languages. The most obvious and manifest external or *inter*linguistic translation leaves room, beside itself, for the most hidden and unexpected internal or *intra*linguistic translation. One then discovers that even within what one considers *one's own* there is an ineliminable residue of an ungraspable and untranslatable *strangeness*. Those who speak the "same" language may not be foreigners but they remain, nonetheless, strangers. Even here understanding cannot be taken for granted. The specter of a mother tongue, which is anything but our own, begins to loom.[57]

4. FROM THE ORIGINAL TO THE ORIGINARY: ON HEIDEGGER

As is well known, the revival of Romantic hermeneutics by philosophical hermeneutics brings with it many innovations. The turn inaugurated by Gadamer takes shape primarily through a direct engagement with Schleiermacher. Schleiermacher conceives interpretation as a "reconstruction" that travels backwards along the path of the original work, and thus the interpreter appears as creative as the author—indeed even more so.[58] In the *Halle Notes* of 1805, Schleiermacher in effect writes: ". . . the interpreter can put himself 'inside' the author . . . understanding the author better than he understands himself."[59] To this famous sentence, which negates and suppresses "historical distance" while affirming the superiority of the interpreter over the author, Gadamer replies in *Truth and Method* with an equally famous sentence: "Understanding is not, in fact, understanding better [*Besserverstehen*], either in the case of superior knowledge of the subject because of clearer ideas or in the sense of fundamental superiority of conscious over unconscious production. It is enough to say that we understand in a *different way* [*anders*], *if we understand at all*."[60] Heidegger had already stated that an interpretation does not understand the text better than its author, but rather differently.[61] "Understanding in a different way," that is, understanding differently, takes the place of "understanding better," it becomes the trait, or at least one of the defining traits, of philosophical hermeneutics. What, then, will be the destiny of translation with regard to this understanding? Will it remain bound up with understanding? Will translating be an understanding differently?

Gadamer begins with the observation that language is the medium of understanding.[62] For this reason alone, every understanding must be, or should be, a form of translation. Gadamer, however, does not say this. Rather, by continuing to speak of understanding, he refers to those situations when understanding is found to be more difficult; here the conditions required for every understanding become apparent. The example he adopts is the dialogue that unfolds in two diverse languages. In this limit situation, translation will therefore be indispensable. And the question immediately hinges on "sense," on *Sinn*.[63] It is the sense that must in fact be translated, transposed, and transferred. The translator has the task of maintaining the sense and at the same time establishing its validity in a new way so that it could be understood in another linguistic world. By "establishing validity" (*zur Geltung kommen lassen*), the translator becomes an interpreter. Thus, every translation is an interpretation, and the "accomplishment" (*Vollendung*) of the interpretation.[64] Here the translation, from language to language, binds itself tightly to interpretation by distancing itself from the Romantic paradigm.

One can oppose the understanding–translating pairing of Romantic hermeneutics to the understanding–interpreting pairing of philosophical hermeneutics. In effect, translation already seems to lose its distinctiveness if, on the one hand, it is reduced to the condition of understanding, and for that very reason is separated from it, and, on the other, is almost resolved and dissolved into interpreting, of which it is the final result. The first supposition is confirmed soon after. In the case of translation, Gadamer adds, the linguistic mediation of understanding is not only evident, but is even produced "artificially" (*kunstvoll*). This means primarily that translation is not a limit case, but is rather an anomalous case, abnormal and irregular in respect to the norm, the "normal case" that is constituted by dialogue, even when dealing with dialogue in a foreign language.[65] In the second place, it means that translation, as an artificial and artful mediation, is considered in negative terms. Hence, one should refrain from translation. "Rather, having to rely on translation is tantamount to two people giving up their independent authority."[66] The *Selbstentmündigung* of which Gadamer speaks means "self-interdiction." Translation is therefore an interdiction, a self-interdiction on the part of the speakers who admit to being *inter-dicted*, of not being able to speak without the *inter-* and the *between* of an interruption, of an artificial intervention, of a trans-lation. This *between*, this *inter-* of the interdiction, is destined to negatively mark translation. Wherever translation is necessary, there is an *Abstand*, a "distance" to be crossed between the "spirit" of the original sound and the "spirit" of its rendering, namely, what one understands in the translation.[67] And so the *topos* of "the spirit and the letter" reappears, revisited according to the model of orality: spirit and sound. Elsewhere, with regard to "the despair of translation," Gadamer unsurprisingly defines it as "letters without spirit."[68] This reading, however, supposes that "spirit" is separable from sound and that, once separated, it can be rendered through the sounds of another language—a concession to the theory of language as instrument hardly attributable to the founder of philosophical hermeneutics who had, just a few pages earlier, completed "the ontological turn of hermeneutics guided by language."[69]

The following claim shows how Gadamer's position is far removed from that of Romantic hermeneutics and also, as we will see, from Heidegger's thinking: "Where there is understanding, there is not translation but speech."[70] Speaking is not translating. Rather speaking and translating are opposites and stand against each other. Speaking occurs in the everydayness of dialogue. Only where saying is interdicted by the encounter with the strangeness of the foreign language does speaking degenerate into translating. Thus, translating is not the primary modality of speaking. Coherently, and with a definite gesture, after having been set in opposition to speaking, translating is also separated from understanding. Understanding is not translating, and there remains neither continuity between one nor the other. "To understand a foreign language means that we do not need to translate it into our own."[71] That Gadamer stops at the boundaries between one's own language and the foreign language is symptomatic. And so translation, taken in its most traditional sense, which is less radical and less hermeneutic, is pushed toward interpretation. Translation therefore shares the same destiny as interpretation. Here Gadamer correctly distinguishes understanding from interpreting. In fact, there can be understanding *without interpreting*, insofar as understanding is an immediate "accomplishment of life" (*ein Lebensvollzug*).[72] Thus, one understands a language when one lives in that language. Incorrectly, however, Gadamer separates understanding from translating and turns the latter into a particular case of interpreting. Translating, which is rigorously interlinguistic, is thus only a "preliminary condition" of dialogue and understanding that can give itself in dialogue.[73]

Therefore, it is not surprising that, in addition to the process, even the product of translating bears a negative mark. No matter how the translator has empathetically accessed the author—here Gadamer speaks of *Einfühlung*—the translation will never be a reawakening of the original process that takes place in the soul of the one who wrote, but will only be a *Nachbildung*, a reconstruction, a reproduction of the text.[74] "No one can doubt that what we are dealing with here is interpretation."[75] Gadamer rejects the fidelity that, according to the traditional paradigm, turns toward the particulars, and therefore chooses, without hesitation, the translation that both Schleiermacher and Humboldt had carefully avoided. Gadamer comments that it is possible, when faced with the difficult choices that translation imposes, that one feels compelled to place more emphasis on a particular feature, omitting and eliminating others. In any case, it is a "new and diverse light" that is projected onto the text. "Translation, like all interpreting, is a highlighting."[76] The translator cannot leave any aspect of the work suspended, and must make a "decision" about the meaning of every nuance, also, and even more so, in the cases when the original remains obscure.[77] The translator must take responsibility for such a highlighting that will be clearer and more superficial than the original. However, this is not the responsibility of the translator, but rather of the author who must convey what he or she has understood and the way in which he or she has understood it. The problem of the original, on which the translation sheds some light, but also casts a shadow, is not even addressed here. The translation, dissolved and resolved in interpretation, is a new text that supplants the original. For this reason, Gadamer speaks of "renunciation,"[78] not because the translator renounces him or herself as author, but simply because *as author* he or she gives up the possibility of expressing every dimension of his or her text. But when translations are undeniably recreations, this "loss" is each time balanced by a "gain." The example that Gadamer refers to is the way Stefan George translated, or better recreated, Baudelaire's *Les fleurs du mal* into German. In this case, the "gain" is a new text.

Later, Gadamer partially adjusts his aim. He explains that just as the interlocutor in the dialogue must establish the validity of other and contrasting reasons, so too the translator, while preserving the "right" of the mother tongue (*das Recht der Muttersprache*), must establish the validity of what is strange and reluctant in the original—in the original, but not in the foreign language.[79] In the end, Gadamer recovers translation within hermeneutics: "The translator's task of re-creation differs only in degree, not in kind, from the general hermeneutical task that any text presents."[80] Thus, just as understanding may not be accomplished in a dialogue, so too translation may not be accomplished in a text. Dialogue and translation appear therefore as analogous. But the text only "speaks" through the interpreter.[81] And the translation gains new life in dialogue. "Translating is precisely a remainder of living dialogue, as mediated, divided, and broken."[82] Gadamer's position, therefore, does not change even in his later work. Translation, separated and detached from understanding, the leftovers of the act of interpreting, more than a limit experience, is an anomalous experience, one that, by remaining excluded, not so much at the limit but outside of it, seems neither to touch nor to be touched by hermeneutics. Heidegger's position differs in more than one way. Although there is no one text that is completely dedicated to this question, and references to it are few and far between, and at times seemingly marginal, it would be difficult, if not impossible, to imagine Heidegger's philosophy without translation. Moreover, his own philosophy is an act of translation. It is such in the way he reads texts, philosophical and poetic alike; it is such in the way he thinks, starting from the fragments of the pre-Socratics and working through the fragments. But, above all, it is such because the originary philosophical experience for Heidegger has the character of translation. What Heidegger says about translation is what he would be able to say about his own philosophizing. Thus translation stands out much more and the philosophical relevance of translating is discerned, above all, in the relation that it is able to establish with metaphysics. If metaphysics is the "forgetting of Being" because, according to a determinate formula, it forgets the possible, then translation is the attempt, within metaphysical thinking, to rediscover the possible, to recall that which has been forgotten and repressed. *Übersetzung*, translation, is then a modality of *Überwindung*, or better, of *Verwindung*, of the overcoming of metaphysics.

But what does Heidegger mean by translation? Undoubtedly the question of translation is informed by the question of language. And therefore the way in which Heidegger understands translation derives from the way he understands language. Perhaps for this reason there is not so much a reflection, but a setting to work of translation—above all through interpretation. In this way, translating reveals itself primarily as interpreting also for Heidegger. "Every translation is already an interpretation."[83] Nevertheless, the opposite also holds for Heidegger: "Every interpretation . . . is a translating."[84] Translation, as interpretation, is an emphasizing clarification and "can bring to light connections that indeed lie in the translated language but are not explicitly set forth in it."[85] The primacy conferred on interpretation, therefore, does not in any way hinder the peculiar relevance of translating, the fullness and depth of the phenomenon.

In a perhaps tacit (or perhaps voiced) continuity with the Romantics, Heidegger sees translating both as interlinguistic and as intralinguistic. One cannot limit translation to the transposition of one language into the other, from the foreign language to the mother tongue or vice versa. We "are already translating our own language, the mother tongue."[86] Heidegger not only refers to the limit situation of the interpretation of religious, literary, and scientific texts, but rather refers to speaking.

> *To speak and to say is in itself a translation,* the essence of which can by no means be divided without remainder into those situations where the translating and translate words belong to different languages. In every dialogue and every soliloquy an original translation holds sway. We do not here have in mind primarily the operation of substituting one turn of phrase for another in the same language

or the use of "paraphrase." Such a change in the choice of words is a consequence deriving from the fact that what is to be said has already been *transported* for us into another truth and clarity—or perhaps into obscurity. This *transporting* can occur without a change in the linguistic expression.[87]

The originary translating is intralinguistic translating, that is, speaking. So Heidegger, with a radicalization that has no equivalent in Gadamer, understands speaking and saying—the saying (*Sagen*) of the *Sage*, the saying in its poetic essence—as that originary translating that is an interpretive translating.

If it exists in its originary nature in speaking, then the interpretive translating is required as both *intra-*, in its own language, as well as *inter-*, between two different languages. The difference is one of intensity. In both cases translating uncovers something other and something new that in the translated language did not yet have any voice. For that very reason, translating makes this understandable, but not in the way that one normally means by making something understandable. The interpreting translation has a disruptive effect because it breaks, interrupts, and shatters the *Eigensinn* of common opinion, the blind "obstinance"—literally the *proper sense*, particular, particularistic, and egotistical—in such a way that the truth of a work can be unveiled.[88] In so doing, it shows that the difficulty of translation is not a technical difficulty; it is not a matter of finding a definite solution to a definite linguistic problem. Rather, the difficulty rests "in the relation of human beings to the essence of the word and to the worthiness of language."[89] If there is an ethos of translating, then this ethos is above all a recognition of the "worth" (*Würde*) of language that cannot be reduced to a mere instrument of exchange.[90] A better word for recognition is perhaps "listening" (*Hören*). The interpreting translation is possible only as a *listening to language*. "But how are we to hear without translating, translate without interpreting?"[91] Language is precisely a *Zuspruch*, that is, an "appeal to ourselves" without which we could not speak. In this appeal, to which we attune ourselves, the essence of the word manifests itself. This is much truer of the originary translating that dominates and imposes itself on all speaking. Translating, which is a listening to language, frees up that ontological reference to the essence of the word, that *Bezug* in its twofold meaning of relation, but also of purchase and profit, which it comes to acquire in its fundamental relation with Being.[92] Thus, in translating, even before than in speaking, one experiences language if one possesses the hermeneutic sensitivity, which in attuning oneself to it, respects the worthiness of language. What one is emerges from the ethos of translating.

As Heidegger writes, "Tell me what you think of translation, and I will tell you who you are."[93]

If translating is preparing and disposing oneself to listen to language, then one cannot follow the criterion of fidelity—at least not in the way that it is normally understood. Translation must set aside the dictionary,[94] because the dictionary is for Heidegger the tomb of language in which the treasure, the *Schatz*, that is the *Sprachschatz*, the lexicon of every language, seems buried forever. The dictionary implies an instrumental conception of language that reduces it to a pure means of exchange.[95] In the act of saying, the dictionary does not say what it should say, insofar as its powerlessness keeps silent about the "historical spirit" of the language.[96] Here the historical distance becomes relevant. Translating means listening to language, having an experience of the historical transmission (*Überlieferung*) that, even in its impenetrable spatio-temporal distance, can nonetheless come out into the open in the process of translating.

Heidegger distinguishes between two types of fidelity. There is a *wörtlich* translating and a *wortgetreu* translating. With the first, one usually means translating literally, that is, word for word. This "word-for-word" procedure, which Heidegger rejects, is nothing other than a technique for substituting one word for another that knows neither how to listen nor much less how to dialogue with the text. Translating that is "faithful to the word" is something else. It is neither a philological fidelity to the letter of the text, nor of a hermeneutic fidelity—as Gadamer thinks of it—to the meaning of the original. Fidelity is the fidelity to the "whole of what was said" (*zum Ganzen eines Spruches*), which has already imposed itself on the translation.[97] Starting out from this fidelity, and in this fidelity to the "whole," one completes the transition—or the leap, hardly translatable into English—from *Wörter* to *Worte*: from the words that, simply taken from the dictionary and from grammar, still lay isolated from the words that, tied and connected, already speak in the speaking of discourse. These words draw their naming power from the fidelity to the whole, together with their jointure. The translation that is faithful to the word is therefore one whose words (*Worte*) "speak out of the language of the matter" (*aus der Sprache der Sache*), which is none other than the matter of thinking itself.[98]

That there is even a "matter of thinking" at the center of translating, in the way it has been handed down in language as the historical transmission of language, bestows on translation a fundamental role in thinking. This is precisely because it is a matter of the happening of history, the *Geschehen der Geschichte*. Translating must open the path of thinking from its beginnings to the present in order to make available to experience what has hitherto remained "unthought." Translation is hence not a technical operation, nor does it amount to rendering "business documents" from one language into another.[99] To tell the truth, it is even more than a dialogical access to the text that is disclosed in the listening to language. The task of translation is an eminently philosophical task. The destiny of "the Land of the Evening," the destiny of the West (das Geschick des Abend-Landes),[100] depends on translating. For this reason, translating is not the result of a choice, of an option to which one can say, yes or no. Rather, there is a necessity and urgency to translating, to the Übersetzen that shows itself to be a Hinüber-setzen, a ferrying, a crossing, a passing beyond to the beginnings of thought and to the sources of the pre-Socratics.

It is in this extremely adventurous ferrying that the tragic nature of translating comes to light.

> There is a great necessity with regard to the translation of Heraclitus' words. Here trans*lating* becomes a *trans*lating to the other shore that is almost unknown and lies on the other bank of a wide river. There will most certainly be an odyssey that usually ends in shipwreck.[101]

Translating is therefore not a transition, or a gradual dislocation, but a leap, as if from one side of a river to another. The vastness of the river opens up an abyss. The risk is great; but the destiny of the West depends on it. And so translation, which wants to allow the most ancient saying of thinking to be said, must dare to take the leap. In its daring, translation will be violent. Without violence it would not be possible to attempt the "leap over the gulf."[102] Nonetheless, the riverbank remains unreachable and the abyss groundless. Translating, even in its eminent sense, in its eminently philosophical sense, is destined to founder. And this is because, at its intended destination, at the origin of historical transmission itself, of the history of every translation, there is no word, nor even a state of affairs, but once again only a translation, a narration, a story. At the origin, there is no original. The groundless abyss (Abgrund) is immeasurable because it lacks an initial ground (Grund). In this respect, the history of the translation of lógos down through the centuries is paradigmatic. For in its leaps, starting with ratio, it reveals its lack of foundation or precise derivation, because already at the beginning it had no ground. And hence one can say that Being, by being neither the first word nor the initial concept, is its transmission accomplished through the diverse epochal stages of its translation. One can affirm that Being is the history of Being, which ungrounded, nongrounded, can be experienced only as an abyss. Being is this abyss.[103] If Being has no ground, and is only ever a word, which exists in the process of historical transmission as translated, then the other riverbank will never be reached.

Nevertheless, the other riverbank remains the goal of this translation. And the translation remains the *trans-* of the crossing between the two banks. As Derrida observes,[104] the word *Übersetzung* can be translated only at the risk of losing many of its connotations. Heidegger emphasizes not so much the *Setzung*, the positional value of the positing, as he does on the *über*, the *trans-* of a movement that is discontinuous rather than gradual, which will also be a transformation in understanding. Suddenly, a word reveals a new meaning, or even just a new semantic nuance. As understanding is modified, so is the perspective, which is separated from the previous understanding by an abyssal difference. *Translating*, at the limit of understanding, brings forth an understanding that is always an understanding differently. Therefore, Heidegger overturns the principle of Romantic hermeneutics according to which the interpreter would understand the author better than the author understands himself. The experience of translating demonstrates the opposite: There is no author who understands himself because understanding—even of oneself—is an understanding differently. "How then could anybody else dare claim to understand a thinker—even to understand him better?"[105] This does not deny that the act of translating is also always a dialogue. The hermeneutic model of dialogue remains valid, but in another way. The interpreting translation, which is first and foremost a listening, must direct itself to the text—here Heidegger refers to texts which more than any other merit translation, namely the fragments of the pre-Socratics—as if that text had never been translated. Unconcerned with the interpretations offered by later philosophy, and springing from the *Fragwürdigkeit*, from the "question worthiness of thinking," the interpreter must attempt to enter into dialogue with the text.[106] Yet what matters in this dialogue is neither the author nor the translator. If it were the case, these would still remain the subjects. Self-abandonment is rather the "spirit of the dialogue," and therefore of the translation, which leads to the unsaid.[107] Translating is therefore a giving oneself over to a dialogue with the text, making way for the self-understanding of the text, allowing it to speak so that it can say its unsaid.

Thus a fitting translation is a paratactic translation that, compared with a "sense-by-sense" translation, has the merit of following the path of the question, leading us to the unthought and unsaid. By coordinating words in an apparently casual way, this translation brings their unreachable complexity of sense to light. The glossolalic stuttering of parataxis imitates the ruinous character of a centuries old sentence whose originary meaning has been lost forever by turning into a linguistic riddle, into a hieroglyphic whose deciphering must direct itself to that which is no longer legible but nonetheless audible. "For the saying *speaks* where there are no words, in the field between the words which the colons indicate."[108] But the translating that is *sprachgerecht*, which does justice to language, to the worthiness of language and to the essence of the word in all of its modes (and parataxis is an extreme mode, even though paradoxically eloquent), points to the other bank of the river, that place where one can experience what withdraws itself. *Trans*-lating is listening to everything that in the process of historical transmission is buried, obscured, and distorted. But even here the *trans*- implies the *inter*- of an interruption. Translating is interrupting. A translation that is "faithful to the word" breaks and interrupts the process of historical transmission by allowing those otherwise buried meanings of Being to manifest themselves. The translation is an excavation. By following the traces that words leave behind in the happening of language, where etymology again reveals itself to be the way—be it a side street or a main street—of ontology, it is possible to let the history of Being emerge. The destruction of metaphysics is the reconstruction of the history of Being, one that inaugurates a new understanding of language. In Heidegger's view, destruction (*Destruktion*), which is more than a mere interpretation, is this exhumation and disinterment, bringing to light the unthought and the unsaid in a way that recalls the authentic experience of the originary.

The relation between translation and tradition is one of reciprocal connection—in the sense of *Überlieferung*, transmission.[109] If transmission solidifies, it becomes a burden and an obstacle that degenerates into the opposite of what its name would indicate: *Überlieferung* refers to *Liefern*, that is, to liberate. The process of transmission brings to light the buried treasures of the past by liberating them, even if this is only the light of a reluctant dawn. This is only possible, however, thanks to the translation that, by interrupting the tradition, helps it to prepare itself for the future of a thinking that is reawakened to the beginning.

The step, or better, the leap of translation, in order to carry itself across the river, happens here and happens for a future that can be born from translating, that is, by revoking the word of the beginning. But it is precisely here that translation, while fulfilling the highest task on which the destiny of the West depends, inevitably ends up being shipwrecked. This is so because the word of the beginning is irrevocable. The authentic experience of the originary cannot be recalled, it cannot be repealed. In its differentiating movement, translation can indicate the possible that emerges in the unsaid and unthought by continually overcoming the determination of the said and the thought. In this respect, *Übersetzung* can already be understood as an *Überwindung* or a *Verwindung*, as an overcoming of metaphysics, if Being for Heidegger must be thought in terms of being possible. On the other hand, translation, when it is faithful to the word and respects the worthiness of language, limits itself, by revoking the language, to enabling the experience of the unthought and the unsaid of the beginning in its unattainability. Rather, it must keep it at a distance so that it might even be surprising in its foreignness.[110] Heidegger calls this "uncoveredness." More than this, translation cannot do. There is no immediate access, neither hidden nor counterfeit, to the originary sense of Being; nor much less can translation listen to what the process of historical transmission gives to thinking. If this were the case, the other riverbank would be easy to reach, and translation would await philosophy on the post-metaphysical shore. But translation, while revoking the originary unthought and unsaid also brings it to light, and also uncovers its irrevocable hiddenness. Translating is also stating the absence of that which one translates. The very need to translate what is said is a clue to its absence.

The antinomy in which translation is entangled now appears clear: On the one hand, it expresses the possibility of the unthought and unsaid of the beginning; and on the other, it simultaneously expresses the impossibility of re-evoking, recalling, and recovering it. The beginning, when it is re-evoked, revokes itself. It is forever lost. This impossibility of rendering the originary beginning, of restoring it through its translation, ends up obfuscating the translation, inevitably diminishing its value, reducing its role, and transforming it in the search for the lost origin. By attempting the leap each time, and by failing each time, translation shows its decline from the originary beginning. In deciphering the legibility of the world where its decline is always already inscribed, if what is legible can also be forgotten, then through the interpreting of the text of history, through translating the process of historical transmission, one can lay bare the lost beginning. In relation to such a beginning, both the future, in its being turned toward that beginning, as well as the present—issues forth but at the same time decays. This antinomy marks the act of translation for Heidegger and, through the connection that it makes, also marks tradition, the transmission of the Überlieferung. Tradition appears not as a succession of diverse and discordant translations of Being, but rather as a process of growing decadence from that lost Greek beginning. Translation itself, far from being just a differentiating movement, reveals itself as this decline and, in fact, it is this decline. Such is already the passage from Greek to Latin.[111] The absence of the foundation of Western thought begins with translating. From translation to translation, from leap to leap, it precipitates an inexorable restriction and withdrawal of Being. In the nihilistic blinding at the peak of modernity, Being withdraws altogether in the "chatter" of the technological age.[112] With such Sprachlosigkeit, with this waning of language, which is also a waning of Being, translation must now come to terms, once one concedes that there is still something left to translate in which the unthought and the unsaid of the beginning can be experienced. The antinomy that marks translation in the transition from the original to the originary therefore reveals itself as an antinomy of philosophy, as an antinomy of Heidegger's philosophy.

In the fundamental verticality which the movement of translating displays in Heidegger, over and against any horizontal tendency, there occurs a further adjustment, one that is no less foundational and no less eloquently definitive. The aim of translating is to follow the course of history back to its summit, to its "peak" (Gipfel), in those beginnings where it awaits a "dialogue" (Zwiesprache) from peak to peak.[113] But in the abysses that stretch out between the peaks of history (Geschichte) there is no historical mediation (Historie), there is no comparison that can serve as a bridge to connect diverse epochs and cultures. There is not even a hermeneutics that can mediate between styles, tendencies and situations, without risking the lapse into relativism or without attaching itself to an ideal of the classical sort. In this latter case, one does nothing more than reproduce ancient models. And one does not want to see that "the temples of the earth were left in ruin, the holy places abandoned and, populated only through blind habit, have become inessential for history [geschichtlich]."[114] If the horizontal movement of translating can only be followed at the cost of a leveling, there remains nonetheless a vertical movement that, lest it fall silent in a by now exhausted antiquity, will have to find a new direction. It will have to abandon the historicist mediation in order to enter decisively into the tradition of a people. The unthought and the unsaid of the beginning will be sought out in the "essence of the language of a historical people."[115] That this language is German is unsurprising. The only two thinking languages for Heidegger are Greek and German.[116] What is at stake here is "whether the German people will or will not remain the historical people of the West."[117] Along with the German people, and through the German people, what is at stake, for Heidegger, is the West, the destiny of the West, and with that the destiny of mankind on earth.

The metaphor of the peak, and of the climb toward the peak, returns a few more times in the 1940s. And it becomes the most important metaphor for translation, the way Heidegger comes to define it, but also to restrict it. The aspiration to push oneself toward the dawn of the origin, in order to bring the traces of Being back to light, appears legitimate and legitimated by a continuity with the origin that is nothing other than the identification of an identitical ethnic lineage. But does translation then reveal itself as a process of identification? And what is the relation between one's own and the foreign, the two poles of translating? How does the reappropriated identity of the German language relate to the foreignness of other languages?

Translation, in its authentic form, must be a dialogue between one's own language and a foreign language. Nevertheless, the greatest risk in the age of technology is that translation will be nothing more than a "detour" of "linguistic traffic."[118] The relation to the other language, the foreign language, is thus a relation motivated and dominated by technology—it is a technological relation. The paradigmatic case is obviously that of the Anglo-American language. For those who learn this language, like the Japanese and the Germans, the risk is great. Given that the other language no longer has the character of a language, reduced as it is to a mere instrument of exchange, one forgets its dialogical character in the act of translating. Translating, *Übersetzen*, does not mean *Ersetzen*, substituting the foreign language with one's own or vice versa.[119] In what does this transition of the *Übersetzen* consist? It is a matter of both a *Hinübersetzen* and a *Herübersetzen*. The transition is twofold: It is a transition over there, into the other language, and it is a transition back here, into one's own language. It starts out from what is one's own and familiar, and it makes a return by traveling through the foreign. Another word for *Übersetzen*, for translating, is *Heimischwerden*, finding a dwelling. One finds a dwelling and one returns home by crossing into the foreign, by passing through the foreign. The crossing of translation is not an appropriation of the foreign. In the transition the foreign remains foreign, and is cared for as such. The same thing happens to one's own language. But this does not exclude that in this passage one's own can become other, and the foreign become one's own. However, one faces the other as if there were no contamination. In short, there is no appropriation of the foreign here, nor is there an estrangement of one's own. The difference between this and the Hegelian transition is obvious, insofar as there is no appropriation of the foreign. And yet one still returns home, with oneself. In effect, what matters is always one's own. What then was that transition, that crossing over? What is translation? Translation "is an encounter with a foreign language for the sake of appropriating one's own language."[120] The encounter with the foreign language serves only to uncover again, to clarify, and to unfold what is properly one's own in one's own language. "What is one's own in this case is whatever belongs to the fatherland of the Germans."[121]

The manifestation of the foreign, of the strange, is at the service of what is one's own in such a way that through estrangement what is one's own can more knowingly take hold of its own identity from that distance. For the German language, to which the salvation of metaphysics is entrusted, there will be only this identificatory reappropriation, this identification of itself with itself. Thus it discovers and rediscovers its dwelling by sinking its roots more firmly into mother earth. Its self-translation will always be within its own history and the history of its own tradition. The movement is always vertical, from the original to the originary. But the originary at which one now aims is the unthought and the unsaid within the *Heimat*, within the only dwelling that still remains in the *Heimatslösigkeit*, in the homelessness of modern man, which is now more than ever exiled from Being. This dwelling is one's own mother tongue.[122]

5. GIVING VOICE TO THE FOREIGN VOICE: THE TRANSLATION OF THE TORAH

The manifestation of the foreign in Jewish hermeneutics is the other way round: There, the other's difference is no longer a passage made in order to return to oneself. In fact, here one begins to doubt the very possibility of such a return. Translation articulates itself as a movement toward the foreign—without return. And it seems to point to a new direction in philosophy.

As has been the case in the entire history of Europe, the body of Scripture is the text by which one measures the practice of translating and from which there springs a new reflection. As Derrida observes,[123] the translation of the Bible, which has always marked the development of languages, and their rooting and uprooting from that body of scripture, is destined to be an event once more. Recovered in its originality, the Hebrew text of the Torah, through the German version by Buber and Rosenzweig, opens up a new perspective on translating. The novelty rests not only and not so much on the practical outcomes that remain up for discussion and are today widely discussed in order to ignore the purpose of the work[124] starting from the criteria characterized by a hitherto unknown fidelity, Rosenzweig defines a completely new way of understanding the act of translating, one that encounters and sometimes even coincides with that of Benjamin.[125]

The reflections of Rosenzweig are concentrated almost exclusively on the Torah, and it is not a choice determined by his work as translator. The motive is much more profound and theological: The originary vocation of the Torah is that of being translated.[126] Scripture and translation are for Rosenzweig one and the same: Each refers to the other, and one cannot exist without the other. And both have an eschatological meaning because they prepare for the messianic advent. The revealed Word could not move toward the final days if it were not translated. Here one finds the messianic nature of translating and its value for redemption.

Even if the Torah is a text, clearly a text like others and translatable like others, because of its sacred nature it cannot be subjected to criteria that apply to the translation of other texts. In the field of Jewish hermeneutics itself, even the Talmud is not comparable to the Torah. The translator of the revealed Word takes on the greatest responsibility, the first of which is that the translation lives up to everything that is present in the original. Only in such a way can the translation be as valid, and it has been valid, as the original, as in the case of the *Septuaginta* and the *Vulgata*. From this limit situation, at the eschatological limit of translation, the need arises for a new fidelity that concerns every act of translating and turns it into a philosophical question central to the hermeneutics of Rosenzweig. Moreover, the question of translating coincides here with the whole of hermeneutics.

But what does *translating* mean for Rosenzweig? In line with Hamann, and with the Romantic's philosophy of language, Rosenzweig claims that, "all speaking is translation."[127] Meaning expands and deepens to the point that translating reveals itself as intralinguistic before it becomes interlinguistic. Speaking and understanding are two directions of the same movement, the movement of translating. And therefore from the beginning Rosenzweig identifies the fundamental movement of language in translating and, since spirit articulates itself linguistically, it is the fundamental movement of spirit. His proximity to the Romantics, on the one hand, and to Benjamin, on the other, cannot be underestimated. Whoever misses the act of translating also misses language. Only by starting from translating can one grasp the dialogical nature of language.

The one who speaks, translates, and the one who listens, translates. In linguistic praxis, the act of translating is neither optional nor derivative. Rosenzweig writes, "Everyone must translate, and every one does."[128] The one who speaks translates himself into the language of the other, which is not a generic other, but is "this very definite other" that one encounters. The one who listens translates the words while understanding them. In fact, understanding is brought back to translating, and Rosenzweig describes it as a passage from the ear to the mouth. Understanding therefore means translating, transporting, transferring the words that resound in one's own ear into the language of one's own mouth. Language is symptomatically brought back to the acoustical-phonetic organs—which are usually only ever employed as metonymies for referring to language—that is to the ear, but above all to the tongue and to the mouth (in Hebrew *lashon, safah*).[129] The passage of translating, and thus of understanding, fulfills itself in the articulation, or better, the rearticulation of the articulated sounds just heard. The rearticulation of sound carries with it a rearticulation of thought. Both exist individually. Thus, Rosenzweig reaches his first conclusion: "We all have our own individual speech."[130]

Nevertheless, if one were to stop here, language would end up being constituted by a multiplicity of monologues. But monological speaking is rather what logicians, "those would-be-monologists," claim for themselves.[131] Logic is by definition monological because it develops independently of grammar. Already in *The Star of Redemption* Rosenzweig criticizes idealism sharply in its attempt to rise above language, with a "logic foreign to language,"[132] and to choose, as this very foundation, a thought that "pushes further on the inclined plane of its '*pure*' logic, foreign to language, recessed behind man."[133] Because of its mistrust of language, logical idealism is "not of a mind to listen and respond to this voice, which resounds in man without apparent reason but all the more realistically for that."[134] Because idealism claims "reasons, justifications, calculability" that language cannot offer, it invents logic, that is, it reduces grammar to logic, the mastery of actual Being to that of possible Being, what is living in language to a "realm of shadows."[135]

Speech, in its phonic and acoustic reality, but above all in the real grammar of pronouns and verbs that bear the *other* and *time*, that are posited by language and constitute thought, is always *dialogical speaking*. Given that speech must decline and conjugate itself grammatically, it is speech, articulated in the past, present, or future, of a concrete "I" turned toward a "you," which is equally concrete, which has not only ears, but also a mouth—and that in turn will be the "I" that speaks to a "you."[136] Thus, if the verb makes it exist concretely, and the pronoun situates it in reality, speech is always that of an "I" to a "you," of a "you" to an "I," in its dialogical nature, the *speech of a concrete individual*. For this very reason, it is concretely individual, insofar as speaking is a translating which, in turn, requires a translating in the correlative act of understanding. It is here that speaking and understanding, in their irreducible individuality, both refer to the linguistic movement that holds them together, that is, translating.

Although it speaks, the "I" does not and cannot expect that the "you," which faces it and to which it turns, has the same ears and the same mouth. This empirical difference, which already emanates from the phonic-acoustic organs, marks speaking and listening. It opens up that *dia-*, that "between," "amongst," or "across," that difference which traverses every speaking and every listening, and by dividing them from within, and while disclosing them to their dialogical nature, also renders *trans*lating necessary.[137] If the "you" were to have the same ears and the same mouth as the "I," translating would be "unnecessary."[138] And what can be said for intralinguistic translation can also be said for the interlinguistic one. Furthermore, also in the case of the speaking and listening of peoples, translation would be unnecessary. But only "a foolish egoism" would want this, an egoism content and satisfied with its own personal and national Being-there. In its purest form, this foolish egoism is that of logical idealism. Rosenzweig insists, however, that there is no place for such an attitude in this world.[139]

But in light of what has been said, even if translating is necessary, it is nonetheless impossible. This *impossible necessity* and *necessary impossibility* of translating forces one to place it among those necessary and impossible compromises whose succession bears the name "life."[140] To the theoretical impossibility there responds a practical necessity. Because of this, translating is difficult to explain theoretically, while in practice everyone and anyone who is assigned this "task," without really knowing it, accomplishes it. Due to this theoretical difficulty, translating has eluded philosophical reflection and, by seeking refuge in praxis, has hidden and obscured the diversity of languages and the individuality of speaking. It is important, for Rosenzweig, that the theoretical impossibility and practical necessity of translating between one language and another can emerge only by starting from the *dia-* that traverses speaking and understanding, and which sheds light on that impossibility and necessity. In short, intralinguistic translating is neither a conquest nor a final recognition. On the contrary, from the *prius* of intralinguistic translating, from this unavoidable theoretical knot, one can find indications for interlinguistic translating which correspond to the *dia-* that traverses language and to its dialogical nature.

This path leads Rosenzweig closer to Romantic hermeneutics. It is not surprising that it is precisely the encounter with Schleiermacher which is the prelude to his argumentation. How does one translate, how can one translate, how should one translate from one language to another? Rosenzweig again takes up the antithesis defined by Schleiermacher: Either one leaves the author in peace and moves the reader toward the author, or one leaves the reader in peace and moves the author toward the reader.[141] For Rosenzweig, the antithesis, although perhaps "dazzling," is, in reality, "dazzling and nothing more."[142] For example, by taking Plato—who was brilliantly translated by Schleiermacher—this antithesis, taken at its word, would suggest, as ideal translations, "either the Teubner text or the *Critique of Pure Reason*."[143] Both are paradoxical in the solution they propose, and in the end, neither is a translation. In the first case, rather than a translation one offers a commentary to the reader so as not to spoil the text; in the second case, one recreates the original, and hence from a Platonic dialogue the work of Kant emerges. If it is not taken up as an antithesis, as a real *aut aut*, but only as a choice that one makes concretely again and again, this antithesis might be helpful in order to pose the question as to the proportions of what can be only a "mixture."[144] Thus, in certain cases one will have to move the reader, and in other cases, the writer. The two movements delimit each other reciprocally. The second is the dominant one and Rosenzweig immediately links it to the name of Luther. Luther's faith determines "the work of mediation," commanding him to take the text literally where, and only where, there is "the living word of God," where the Old Testament "practiced Christ." In all other cases, "the translator 'sends the Hebrew words packing, and speaks the meaning of them in the best German he can.'"[145] The first movement is the exception and, as with all exceptions, it is more controversial but also more interesting than the by now established rule. Hence, as one already saw with the Romantics, it is in the first move, where the reader is carried toward the original, that one finds Rosenzweig's preference.

Nevertheless, the preference here, as the name of Luther implies, has clear theological motivations. Luther, the model against whom Rosenzweig knows he cannot measure himself, had turned the translation of the Bible into a masterpiece of the German language. By inaugurating literary history, he had made it the foundational work of a new Christian faith, but at the same time erased the original and, with the original, severed Christianity from every Jewish root. For Rosenzweig, the translation of the Torah is above all a theological response and thus also a linguistic response. A *theology of translation* is born here, from the need to erase the erasure, to unearth those roots, to evoke the original, to give voice to the stranger that one wanted to keep silent. Rosenzweig's choice, the extreme choice that leads to extreme criteria, makes sense only starting from this need, one that is not literary, as it was with the Romantics, nor even philosophical, as it was with Heidegger, but absolutely theological. This is not to say that the need does not have literary or, above all, philosophical resonance. And in fact, in the very theology of translation, as put forward by Rosenzweig and Benjamin, the turning point that makes translation a philosophical question can be seen.

If the original—the stranger who for centuries was incorporated, assimilated, and devoured—has to take up the word again, then translation cannot mean appropriation, neither in the sense of appropriation of the strange, nor even in the sense of the appropriation of one's own. In what consists, then, the movement through which the translator carries the reader toward the original? Rosenzweig describes it in the Afterword to the hymns and poems of the great Hebrew poet Yehuda HaLevy, who lived in Spain between the eleventh and twelfth centuries. As with Humboldt in his Introduction to Aeschylus' *Agamemnon*, Rosenzweig takes up again his experience as a translator, an experience that is nevertheless informed by the Torah even prior to the text of HaLevy. And he immediately clarifies his objective: "These translations want to be nothing other than translations."[146] The way to respect the original in its foreignness and in its irreducible inability to be appropriated is to present the translation *as* a translation. In this way, and only in this way, can the original remain original. On the contrary, if the translation becomes a reproduction of the original, it covers, hides, and even erases the original. In a word, it incorporates the original. In translating, the translation intervenes *between* the reader and the original. The reader encounters the translation before reaching the original. The reader is pleased by it, and stops at the translation satisfied and rewarded. The reader goes no further. Behind his intention to make the original "more understandable," the poetic remaking barely masks the desire to replace it. In order to facilitate the reader, the translation becomes a work that stands in for the work, the translator becomes an author in the place of the author. But why, Rosenzweig asks, does not the translator write his own poetry? Why does he need a foreign poem for a poetic remaking? Conversely, Rosenzweig has no desire to take the place of Yehuda HaLevy in his translation; this would lead the reader to believe that these verses had been composed in German, that he had composed Christian hymns, and that he was a contemporary poet. Whoever reads his translation cannot and must not forget, not even for an instant, that these are *translations* of the poems of Yehuda HaLevy.

In order to avoid the "universally accepted" criterion of poetic remaking (which is nevertheless debatable), Rosenzweig refers to a criterion explicated many times for the translation of the Torah, that of literality. Yet what does it mean to translate to the letter? And what does it means to be *faithful* to the letter? For Rosenzweig, behind, before and anterior to fidelity, there is *faith*.[147] But, first and foremost, faith is faith in the Torah and in the letters of the Torah. It is therefore faith that prescribes the act of translation. The translator becomes altogether similar to the *sofer*, the scribe who must write the scroll of the Torah. The prescriptions that are valid for one are also valid for the other: One cannot leave out a word, nor even forget a letter, for the Torah would no longer be the Torah. The roll would no longer have value. And the Torah, according to the *Kabbalah*, is the score from which God draws the world by reading it "word for word," because "all of the words and all of the actions of all of the worlds are in the Torah . . ."[148] Whoever studies the Torah, whoever reads it, translates it, and interprets it, "allows the world to exist."[149] Reading, translating, and interpreting—in Judaism these are the creative acts *par excellence*. Faithfulness to the word, literality, does not mean exactness, equivalence, or conformity, but rather devotion, dedication, and respect for scripture, starting from the letters of the alphabet, because they are the letters that bear the world.

It is therefore a desperate undertaking. Above all in the case of the Torah's translation, as one sees clearly in the final work of Buber and Rosenzweig.[150] It is less so in the case of other texts. From this, however, there comes a reappraisal of literality and new instructions for the translator. It is not that Rosenzweig failed to recognize the semantic diversity of languages. On the contrary, with an observation that could easily have come from Wittgenstein, he writes:

> The aerial view of a language's verbal landscape seems at first glance severed and radically diverse from that of every other language; and even the maps of these landscapes, the dictionaries with their enumerations of various senses, only construct for each word in

the one language an environing circle of a certain diameter that intersects several circles surrounding words of the other language.[151]

Thus, one must not confuse literality with Scholastic literalism. As was the case for Heidegger some years later, also for Rosenzweig the dictionary is not the "highest authority" for the translator.[152] Noteworthy here is the proximity between these two philosophers: Both are turned, even if along different paths, toward the definition of criteria for a new translation that is *wortgetreu*, faithful to the word. Rosenzweig writes: "Language does not consist of vocabulary [*Wörter*] but of words [*Worte*] . . . [and] Words stand only in the sentence."[153] The translator must aim at the above connected words, at their "wavy flow" in the gravel bank of the sentence, at the contours that they assume while they are connected and that the dictionary, concentrated on the center of their gravity, can never restore. These contours "are what want to be and must be translated."[154] That, by such a way, one can follow the contours of a sentence's syntactical and grammatical construction is neither new nor complicated; it is more difficult to follow the contours of words, not only within sentences, but even more so—as Rosenzweig proposes and achieves in the act of translating—in the realm of etymology.[155] Literality means going down all the way to the etymological root of words, uncovering them through translation, and bringing them to light in a new language. Even for Rosenzweig, as for Heidegger, translation is an excavating activity, and etymology, the search for the *etymon*, for the originary truth enclosed in the word, is an integral part of a translation faithful to the word, and of this faithfulness it is in fact the highest form of bearing witness.

Here the translator distinguishes himself from the poet, because while the poet, by giving himself over to the word, can bring forth "words from words," the translator, following the words of another, must render it "word for word." In contrast to the poet, the translator is forced to choose words, and to this end he must know the place of the words in the horizon of his own language and in the horizon of the language of the poet. He must know if the word whose trace he follows has a near or distant origin, if it dwells at the center of the language or in its peripheral regions.[156] If the poet relies on the word, the translator relies on the word of the poet, and thus he submits himself to the poet. Nevertheless, Rosenzweig adds nothing more and does not touch upon the question of the poet's creativity and the translator's creativity, a problem that Benjamin instead addresses.[157]

What sort of translation would be faithful and literal, hence moving the reader toward the original? Rosenzweig's response is a strong, drastic radicalization both with respect to the considerations of the Romantics, and with respect to those of Heidegger. If Heidegger grants a validity to

strangeness, at least in the distance from the unthought and the unsaid of
the origin, Schleiermacher, and even more so Humboldt, are at pains to
give translation a tint of foreignness so as to grant space to the original. For
Rosenzweig, it is not simply a matter of a foreignness toward the original
or toward the originary that the translator brings to light, of which the
translator makes us aware. Rather, and much more so, "the translator makes
himself a mouthpiece of the *foreign voice*, which he makes audible over
the gulf of space or time."[158] And where the foreign voice has something
to say, and the translator makes himself into a spokesperson, the target
language will no longer be what it was before. The novelty, therefore, is that
translation brings about the transformation of one's own language.

"In point of fact, the task of translating is totally misunderstood if
it is seen as the Germanizing of what is foreign."[159] A *Verdeutschung*, a
Germanization, can be adopted for a "business letter"—an example that even
Heidegger uses. Thus, Rosenzweig clarifies, if while working in a business
I receive an order from Turkey, I quickly hand it over to the translation
department without much fuss. The letter will be accurately translated and
will be sufficiently German. But a letter from a Turkish friend would already
demand much more. Translated in the same way, it would be sufficiently
German, but would not be sufficiently Turkish. "I shall not hear the
person, his tone, his meaning, his heartbeat."[160] The voice of the friend is
covered and silenced by the layer of foreign words. But the Germanization,
the appropriation of the stranger, can be endured, and can even have a
semblance of legitimacy, where the stranger has no voice, does not have
a singular, unique, and unrepeatable voice, and speaks as if it had nothing
to say. And although this voice has nothing to say, it does not demand
anything of language. Here translation is reduced to a substitution that,
by replacing the stranger, appropriates it, and language is demeaned and
crystallized into a "tool." The translated language becomes a tool and so too
does the target language. Any kind of Esperanto could call the existence
of such a translation into question. And in the end, German "does not
have a new face."[161] The business translation, as with every Germanization,
leaves language intact because it occurs in a German that already exists.
Conversely, the task of the translator, the new task of the translator, which
here surprisingly coincides literally with what was outlined by Benjamin,
consists in "making that which is German, foreign."[162] This not only means
reproducing the foreign tone in all its strangeness, but even transforming the
target language that, by opening itself up to the foreign, and to what the
foreign has to say in a new way, by welcoming it, disposes itself to change.
One recognizes the work of the translator in this transformation. In fact,
it is impossible to imagine that the translation of Shakespeare, Isaiah, or
Dante leaves the German language unchanged, that it does not renew it

profoundly. One cannot ask the impossible of language. What would seem impossible is none other than the impossibility already possible in speaking, the necessity that creative speaking modifies language. All of the translator's creativity clearly emerges here, which can be nothing other than the fact that speaking itself is creative.[163]

More than just taking on a tint of foreignness, translation enforces the rights of the foreign language in one's own language, and requires a transformation in one's own language. It is like arriving at an extreme stage, but certainly not the final one, of a history, characteristically Eurocentric, marked by diverse stages, that—when looked at more closely—have as the protagonists "one's own" and "the stranger." When one no longer perceives the necessity of translation because one's own language is the language *tout court*, one replaces the estrangement of the stranger with the appropriation of the stranger, which for centuries had characterized European culture, and subsequently the appropriation of one's own language defended by Heidegger. In Jewish hermeneutics, of which Rosenzweig and Benjamin are both representatives, in a parallel and independent manner, translation understands itself as an *estrangement of one's own*.

6. THE DIALOGUE OF LANGUAGES: ON BENJAMIN

Yet the estrangement of one's own cannot be the final goal of the translator. The "task," as Benjamin outlines it, seems to have an even higher goal, and seems not to be able to stop at what is one's own, at the domain of one's own, no matter how estranged. On the other hand, the estrangement of one's own by no means amounts to renouncing, abandoning, and negating one's own. Rather, it means to allow one's own language to be broadened and deepened by the foreign language, that is, to be transformed by the encounter with the other language. This encounter is what is most important, because the encounter that exists in translation is like a dialogue between different languages. *Translation* is this *dialogue of languages*.

Benjamin speaks of the original and of translation, yet displacing, dislocating, and translating, in an original way, such a relationship that he studies and examines in poetic and sacred texts—the interlinear version of the sacred text is precisely, for Benjamin, the archetype of every translation.[164] What, then, is the relation between the original and the translation? First of all, translation is not a simple reception, even if it is able to contribute to it. But neither is translation communication. What precisely does a poetic text "say"? The demand of the original, and specifically of the poetic text, neither passes itself off as that which is said, communicated, enunciated, nor does it pass itself off as a so-called message. The translation, whose goal is to mediate, would mediate nothing other than communication, namely, something inessential.[165] On the other hand, between the original and the translation a representative or reproductive relation does not take place. According to Benjamin, in order to demonstrate this, one would need to take up the same arguments that the critique of knowledge uses: As with knowledge, if it were to be a copy of the real, there could be no objectivity, nor even the pretense of objectivity, so too, no translation would be possible if it were to aim at the reproduction of the original. If we leave out reception, communication, and reproduction, the following question needs to be asked again: What is the relation between the original and the translation?

This relation unfolds along the thread of "life" (*Leben*) and "survival" (*Fortleben*). "Translation is a form."[166] The "law" of this form, that is, of translation, is held within the original and its translatability. One can consider this law, following a suggestion from Derrida, as a "demand in the strong sense," as a "need" that orders, sends, and assigns.[167] Once this law is posited as a demand and a request, two questions emerge with regard to the translatability of the work. The first is whether the work will ever find among its readers a good enough translator. The second, and decisive, question is whether the work in its essence permits a translation and hence, on the basis of the meaning of this form, requires it. The decision regarding the first question—as Benjamin clarifies—is "problematic," because it is possible that a good enough translator is found, but it is also possible that he will not be found. Regarding the second question, the decision is rather "apodictic," because it is demonstrable by being contained a priori in the law of the original. The second decision is therefore independent of the first and only a superficial consideration would take them as equivalent. The original requires translation even if there is no translator capable of responding to this demand, to this injunction, to the tacit desire of the original. In order to clarify the need of the other, the demand of the translator, even in the absence of a translator, Benjamin makes a comparison. The need for translation is compared with an unforgettable moment in one's life. One could speak of this moment even if everyone had forgotten it. If, because of its essence, it requires not to be forgotten, the predicate "unforgettable" contains nothing false. Rather, it contains apodictically a need to which mankind is not equal, and at the same time a reference to a realm in which it would find its equal, to "God's remembrance."[168] Oblivion is only accidental for that which in its essence is unforgettable. The need of the unforgettable is not touched by the finitude of memory.[169] One can say the same for the need of translation. The translatability of linguistic works is *a priori*, it belongs to their essence and they are unaffected by the accidental nature of being translatable for mankind. On the other hand, they are untranslatable in the strong sense of the term. And here, too, there holds valid the reference to the realm in which only the need for translation, the desire of the other who translates, would be fulfilled, to "God's remembrance."

If survival is *a priori*, then death (i.e., the death of the work) does not change anything. Survival is nonetheless entrusted to translation. Hence, between the original and the translation an "intimate" connection begins to emerge, which Benjamin calls a "vital connection."[170] The translation proceeds from the original; in fact, it comes after the original, not however, from its life (*leben*), but rather from its survival (*Überleben*). Thus, a new meaning for translation comes to light: *Übersetzen* means to carry *über*, beyond the limit of life, rendering *Überleben* possible. But Benjamin, in order to avoid equivocation, dwells immediately on the concept of "life." The connection between life and survival is here to be taken in a "non-metaphorical" sense. More precisely, "life" cannot be limited to "organic physicality." Life determines itself according to history, not nature. Only when one recognizes life in everything that has a history, does one do justice to the concept of "life." The "task of the philosopher" is precisely that of understanding natural life on the basis of the broader life of history.[171] The case of translation, and of the survival of the original by means of translation, demonstrates that there is life when survival surpasses organic life and death. By inverting and radicalizing the perspective, one could add that it is starting from language and survival, through the act of translating in language, that one has access to a concept of life not limited by organic physicality, but broadened to history. This linguistic survival indicates precisely that life cannot be reduced to this organic nature. However, it is worthwhile and, in fact important, to ask what does Benjamin mean when, referring to translation, he speaks of *survival*, a term that corresponds to two German words: *Überleben* and *Fortleben*. Both help to clarify that survival is more than mere survival, it is not only a life *über*, further and beyond the original, but it is also *fort*, starting from, and a long way from the original. In the translation, the original does not only live longer, it also lives more and better. In short, survival means transformation. Transforming and modifying oneself is, after all, part and parcel of life.[172] "For in its survival—which could not be called that, if it were not a transformation and a renewal of something living—the original undergoes a change."[173] The original survives by transforming itself. This is possible thanks to the translatability that belongs *a priori* to its essence and is ultimately the very translatability of language. Language, in its translatability, renders the original translatable and allows survival. Survival, precisely because it is a linguistic survival, is not only a beyond, but is also something more. The original unfolds in a development that is always broader than its meanings. Even for words that seem to be fixed, there is a "posthumous maturation" (*Nachreife*).[174] This shows, yet again, that the translation is neither a copying nor a remaking of the original, and thus that it will be rendered neither as identical nor as something completely different, but as a moment of "growth" in which the original survives by transforming itself and fulfilling itself.

This is, however, only the first conclusion that can be drawn from the way Benjamin conceives the vital link between the original and the translation. It is the first step, but, from a theoretical standpoint, perhaps not the most important. There are at least three further steps, perhaps more. It is nevertheless worth emphasizing that the connection between life and survival marks a decisive turn in this writing, but not only in this writing. Such a turn is decisive with regard to the way translation is understood, not only in respect to the Romantics, to whom Benjamin is here close, if not extremely close, but also with regard to Heidegger as well as Rosenzweig.

If there is a posthumous maturity to the words of the original, and to the original itself, which in survival is elevated to a new, more comprehensive, and ultimately more expansive life, and if the original reaches its fulfillment in translation, it is because the original begins with a lack. The beginning of the original is a lack and a lacking. From the very outset the original is marked by the translatability of its "à-traduire," which is marked by the need for translation.[175] It requires it, claims it, and invokes it, starting with this nostalgia for translation, by imploring and begging for what it does not have, for what it lacks. And if it demands this complement, which is a completion, it is because at its origin it was not without a lack, without a blemish—it was neither whole nor complete, and nor was it identical with itself. The commencement was not a commencement, the beginning was not a beginning, and the origin was not an origin. From the very outset, there where the original originally begins, there are already privation and proscription, there is already exile. Thus, the original in exile awaits its translation. And, because the original lacks any essential qualities that define it, one would have to find—but Benjamin does not—another word for "original."

The original, which from the very beginning is not original, changes, and even grows, through translation. The latter, on the other hand, insofar as it is not a copy, nor much less a remaking, does not leave the mother tongue untouched; rather, it broadens and deepens it through the foreign language.[176] But how can the translator do this? By responding to this question one moves closer to the translator's task and the premises of a further and important conclusion are clarified.

In order to respond to the above question, however, it is necessary to define more strictly what Benjamin means by the act of translating, the praxis of translating. One can start with the example of "bread," in order to move toward the issue of "arcade," and finally to that of "tangent." These three examples, or these three metaphors, help us understand, under diverse yet complementary philosophical-linguistic perspectives, what for Benjamin ought to be the task of translation. Similarly to Rosenzweig, for Benjamin too the approach that the translator must take toward the target language should be such that it awakens the echo of the original.[177] Thus the translator must above all be aware of the incommensurable difference that exists between two languages. It is such a difference that assigns the task to the translator. If the translator were to have what Benjamin, in his 1916 essay "On Language in General and on the Language of Man," called a "bourgeois conception of language," if he were to think that language is a cluster of signs that serve to indicate things that are the same for everyone, and to convey them, if he were to have an instrumental and conventional conception of language, the translator's task would be annulled, or it would have been at the very least been drastically reduced to the mere substitution of signs.[178] However, after Babel, after that one language, there exist "so many translations, so many languages."[179] Since Babel, and the diaspora of languages, every language, now in exile, appears as a translation. The differences between one language and another, between one translation and another, "the differences between languages are those of media that are distinguished as it were by their density—that is, gradually."[180] If the difference in "density" between the "communicant" and the "communicable," between the "namer" and the "name" is still enigmatic, later on the difference is explicated with clarity, even if it is through the categories of a Husserlian scholasticism—intention, mode of intention, intended—which, in this case, are not necessarily the most helpful and the most efficacious. *Brot* and *pain* are, in the "bourgeois conception" of language, two words, one German and one French, which vary in their letters and in their sounds, words that stand for one and the same object, "bread." Benjamin explains this difference in quite another way, adding that, "this law is one of the fundamental principles of the philosophy of language."[181] In the intention, one needs to distinguish the way of intending (*die art des Meinens*) from the intended itself (*das Gemeinte*). In its supposed identity with itself, the intended is the same, because both languages designate the same thing, while the mode of intending it, that is, signifying it, is different. German and French designate the same thing but, signifying it differently, they appear not to be interchangeable and in fact they reciprocally exclude one another. The incommensurable difference between languages therefore lies in their semantic density. The translator, who has been assigned his task, by bracketing the intended object, stakes everything on the manner of intending. Therefore, translating has everything to do with the manner of intending.

If the echo of the original must be reawakened, the translator will have to embrace a principle of fidelity. As Heidegger and Rosenzweig had already done, Benjamin again proposes a notion of translation that would be *wortgetreu*, faithful to the word. Like Heidegger who opts for a paratactic translation, giving the word space by holding the syntax open, and like Rosenzweig, who prefers to follow the contours of the word, even going back to etymology, rather than following the contours of the proposition; so too Benjamin, in the translation faithful to its literality (*Wörtlichkeit*), gives primacy to the "name." And he does so by way of an architectural image. The proposition is like a "wall" erected in front of the language of the original. *Wörtlichkeit*, understood in the sense of *Wort für Wort*, word for word—the word taken in its highest value as "name," where the vocative and the performative are one and the same—is instead an "arcade."[182] One might ask, but why an arcade? The answer is simple: The arcade, while being a support, nonetheless lets the light shine through and allows us to see the original. And so the arcade responds to the need for translation to be "transparent" so as not to obscure the original. Hence, the "originary element" of the translator, that toward which the translator's work must aspire, is not the proposition, but rather the word.

As always, alongside fidelity one also finds the question of freedom. Once again, this freedom cannot be reduced to the reproduction of sense. It is rather from the new way of conceiving fidelity that a novel way of conceiving freedom emerges, which actually "furnishes a new and higher justification."[183] Freedom is nonetheless the freedom of the translator.[184] But it is not, and is no longer, the simple freedom to move at one's ease through one's own language at the other's expense. Freedom does not obey the law of appropriation, or even the law of estrangement. It is neither freedom from the foreign language, nor freedom from one's own. Freedom follows the movement of language, which is a movement of liberation. Here freedom is liberation, and to translate is to liberate. Translation liberates the foreign languages as well as one's own, because by making the original's way of intending enter "lovingly" (*liebend*) into one's own, both are seen in a new light. No longer one language against the other, each one in its monadic solitude, they are now parts of a greater language in whose light they appear as fragments of the fallen Tower. Once again, Benjamin captures in an image the fleeting encounter of the translation with the original, which is the image of the tangent that fleetingly (*flüchtig*) touches the circumference at only one point.

> Just as this touch, rather than the point, prescribes the law according to which it is to continue on its straight path to infinity, so too does a translation touch the original lightly and only at the infinitely small point of the sense, thereupon pursuing its own course according to the laws of fidelity in the freedom of linguistic flux.[185]

Derrida interprets this contact as a caress.[186] It is a gesture of extreme and cautious love. The translation does not render, restore, produce, or reproduce but rather brushes up against the original with a caress, and this fleeting contact between the body of one language and the body of the other is enough to liberate both of them.

The further conclusion that one can draw from this vital link between the original and the translation is that both languages change in the course of survival. The original, in exile from its very origin, renews and unfolds itself further; for the posthumous maturity of the words, implicit tendencies can emerge from the already formed text that have an impact on the life of the language. On the other hand, even the mother tongue of the translator, his or her own language, changes, already starting from the translation, from the first contact with the body of the other language, that is, from the entrance of the original into its body. It is the translator's task to let the mother tongue be powerfully shaken, and thus to break its limits, to broaden its confines, and to shed light on its as yet undeveloped potentiality. And so, Benjamin says, it is up to the translation, here almost in the role of a midwife, to assist in both "the maturing process of the original language and the birth pangs of its own."[187] Put succinctly, translation is not a neutral transition, an innocent and uncontaminated relation. It does not leave the two languages intact. It does not, however, restrict itself to acting on one, on its own language. It is neither appropriation of its own language, nor is it an estrangement. The translation—and this is the real shift of perspective in Benjamin—with its *between* (*trans-*), opens a passage between the two languages and changes their identity and self-understanding, even prior to their semantic or syntactic particularity. In this encounter, every language already transforms itself to the degree that it discovers itself to be different from the other, almost an idiom of the other. In the passing over into a superior realm, languages, elevated by translation, return to their affinity while experiencing their reciprocal strangeness.

What sort of affinity is this? "Affinity" (*Verwandtschaft*) cannot be brought back to a simple "similarity" (*Ähnlichkeit*), which is a much vaguer concept. Similarity does not necessarily correspond to affinity.[188] For Benjamin, who, in this case, is the heir of comparative linguistics, but above all of the linguistics of Humboldt, affinity shows its polyvalence and richness of meanings also and even more so in the realm of languages. Affinity certainly implies kinship, but its value is not exhausted by the idea of lineage. There is a historical kinship amongst languages. But there is also—as Humboldt pointed out—an affinity of languages that goes beyond this historical kinship, and that is hence a "suprahistorical affinity."[189] In this regard, Benjamin speaks of an "intimate relation" between languages, which is one of "convergence."[190] Before ever revealing themselves as being estranged, and "abstracted from all historical relations[191]," languages have an *a priori* affinity and are such "in that which they intend."[192] All languages have the same goal, and each one points to this goal with its own intention, traveling along its own way. None of them, however, in their singularity, can ever reach that goal because that goal is accessible only to the entirety of their intentions, which are reciprocally complementary. This complementarity is important. Every language helps to integrate the other, saying what the other does not say, still does not say, or merely points to. The harmonic conspiracy of languages, the harmony in their ways of intending, gives rise to a unity that in its becoming—which is the very becoming of language—is not a closed totality, but an open unity whose opening *interdicts* every totalitarian closure and preclusion, every Babelic totalitarianism. In a similar way, Humboldt emphasizes that knowledge of the world comes about only through the set of views that each language discloses, yet it does not exhaust itself in such views, in such a way that every new view, that is, every new language, enriches their shared perspective. In turn the translation, made possible through affinity, intervenes in this concordance of languages. Not in the sense that it can institute it, but in the sense that it can "represent it" because it realizes it in its embryonic and intensive form.[193] This is the true goal of translation. It is not a matter of substituting one sign for another, of transporting the contents from one language into another, but rather of discovering this affinity by making present and so making active, the possible concordance of languages. But more than making present or presenting an affinity that does not exist, or could never be present, in this presentation, translation calls to it, evokes and invokes it, and by alluding to this hidden affinity, it announces it and anticipates it messianically.

Such a hidden affinity of languages, such a harmony, has another name for Benjamin: *pure language* (*reine Sprache*). The pure language is a messianic language, the language that will proclaim itself at the end of time, at the end of history, and at the end of the history of languages, translation has a role in anticipating the pure language, because it is translation that switches itself on to the eternal survival of works and to the infinite rebirth of languages, because it is translation that tests and puts to the test that history as a "holy growth of language."[194] In the transition from one language to another, a transition in which both languages are transposed to a higher and purer realm, there emerges the extent to which what is hidden from them and in them is far removed from revelation, that is, their affinity, which converges in the pure language. But there also emerges the extent to which what is hidden from them and in them can be made present in the awareness of such a distance. Such coming to presence, which exists only in and through distance, is the result of an anticipation. It is here that translation, while announcing the messianic language, proclaims its own messianic nature together with the messianic nature of language.

If languages not only change thanks to translation, but rather find their affinity in the estrangement that separates them, their encounter assumes an importance that goes far beyond the languages themselves. Commenting on or translating Benjamin, Derrida speaks of a "marriage" and a "wedding" between the translation and the original, or of the promise of marriage between the two languages.[195] Dialogue is a word that Benjamin does not use, and yet it characterizes well his way of describing the encounter between languages and the transformation that follows from such an encounter. The translation, at least in the horizontality of its movement, appears as a dialogue between languages. Because of its *trans-* and *inter*, translation *inter*dicts every monological solipsism by establishing itself from the very beginning between the two languages. Whether it is a bad translation or an almost imperceptible substitution, translation will always leave a trace of the strange. No matter how faint this trace, it nonetheless speaks of the strangeness of another language and of the speaker who speaks in that other language. The experience of translation, a disquieting experience, is above all the experience of strangeness. When it comes to this strangeness, which is here unavoidable, Benjamin writes that there is no solution that is anything but "temporary and provisional."[196] The experience of translation is the experience of the strangeness of the other that marks the *proper* limit; it is the experience of one's own limit, of the incomplete and the imperfect. Babel is destined to infinite repetition because there is no end to that drama, because there is no translation that resolves everything. A translation is always and only different from another translation, but never better. In respect to the trace of the foreign, of the strange that remains in one's own language, the attempts to erase the trace, to ban and proscribe the strange, have been repeated successively throughout the centuries. Their aim is to preserve one's own language, the ownership of the language.[197] Yet translation, which is inevitable in the post-Babelic diaspora, allows for incursions and raids by other languages, by foreign languages, at the boundaries and beyond the boundaries of one's own language. Until the moment when one's own language will no longer be seen as *the* language, or as language *tout court*, it will be one language among others, and this is the first salvific effect of translation. After the attempts to estrange the stranger, one moves to the appropriation of the stranger, assimilated and incorporated into the body of one's own language. It is another way of erasing the trace, so as to preserve the ownership of the mother tongue. When translation begins to be perceived as a bridge between diverse languages, as an opening to another language in order to receive what it can offer us, the estrangement of one's own is then considered as the possibility of elevating the genius of one's own language to the genius of a foreign language, of rendering it more cultured and removing its provinciality. This is what the Romantics wanted and what Heidegger wanted to avoid. The appropriation of one's own is, in the recognition of the stranger, a new and more self-conscious affirmation of one's own and the superiority of one's own. The mother tongue needs to return monologically to itself and to its own origin, but it does not need a dialogue with other languages. The estrangement of one's own, however, remains concentrated solely on itself. Yet, the question about what will happen to the stranger is still to be asked. What is more—and this is what matters here—one's own and the stranger continue to confront each other at the border between languages, or along what one believes to be the border between the languages. And it is here, at the border, that the indefatigable and undefeatable translation continues to do its job, by opening up paths and passages with its *trans-*, by forcing open frontiers, and by removing lines of demarcation. In order to carry out God's command, translation, in this subversive action that is a prelude to liberation, confuses where it can and how it can what remains of the Tower, and leaves traces of the stranger in its own language, and leaves traces of itself in the stranger. Although it avoids the situation where one language asserts itself by translating all languages into itself, against every linguistic imperialism, it multiplies everywhere the *Schibboleth* of all the languages. In their intangibility, in their strange lack of semantic meaningfulness, and therefore in their untranslatability, these languages are as many challenges posed by translation, so that the violence of uniformity will not prevail, so that the absolute impossibility of translation becomes a necessity, and that starting from that untranslatability one still translates. This translation will not take place from one language to another, but between one language and the other, in the dialogue that is opened up in this *trans-*, where each language discovers itself as strange, strange enough to recognize its affinities with the other and foreign language, and to dispose itself toward translating it and being translated by it, to transform it and to be transformed by it, all in the name of such an affinity.[198]

A successful translation is, like every successful dialogue, one that brings about a transformation. The transformation is here also an eruption of the saying in the said—as Levinas understands it[199]—of which there remains a trace. This trace is in every language the trace of the other language, namely, the trace of the idiomatic difference that, while allowing the singular individuality of every language to come forth, in the way it has been modified in dialogue, refers already to the secret of their further and broader unity. The more apparent and numerous are the traces of idiomatic difference—the difference between the fragmented idioms of that very Tower—and the more powerfully each announces and pronounces itself as *Schibboleth*, proof of belonging and identity, but also the word of the path and the passage, the more do the marks and signs indicate the difference and claim together the participation in unity, the more does Babel stand out in the text.

The translator seems thus to move closer to the poet. Speaking is a translating and the creativity of the one here touches on the creativity of the other. But, according to Benjamin, between the two there is an "absolutely distinctive feature"[200] that cannot be passed over in silence. The poet finds himself within the forest of language where, by translating himself, he translates nature, and alleviates nature's "deep sadness" for being mute[201]; his intention is "naive, primary, intuitive," it is turned toward the origin. The translator, who finds himself not within, but facing this forest, by translating himself translates the other language, the word of the other to whom he will give voice; his intention is "derivative, ultimate, ideal," that is, it is turned toward the end of time, toward the dialogue between languages, toward the understanding that is yet to come.[202]

But there are figures that by moving closer to the poet or the translator are both one and the other. They are translator-poets, or poet-translators. In both cases their trade is a messianic one because in the dialogical opening that they disclose in their own language they allow the entrance of other languages, through which the promised language is announced. One could put forward many names, but one will suffice: Paul Celan, poet-translator, translator-poet, who by writing in the language of the other and of the *Shoah*, has inscribed, incised, and inflicted Babel into the body of each one of his poems.

7. "PURE LANGUAGE" AND MESSIANIC SILENCE

If the poet is turned toward the origin, the translator is turned toward the end. But, in this case, end means the messianic end of history. The entirety of the translator's work, "the integration of many languages into one true language," into the "pure language," strives to anticipate the times, to leave the door open for the yet to come, for the messianic advent. The work of the translator contributes to redemption, anticipates the reign of the yet to come, in which languages will reach "reconciliation and fulfillment."[203] For Benjamin, *translating is redeeming*.

The messianic value of translating, which refers to the Jewish tradition and to the way Judaism understands redemption, is also indicated by Rosenzweig, albeit differently, and initially in a less decisive manner, but ultimately in a more certain way. The two paths toward the redemption of languages, that of Benjamin and Rosenzweig, must be covered in parallel, because one sheds light on the other, helping us to understand, beyond the singularity of the path, the peculiarity of the goal. However, for both the point of departure is the same: Babel and the diaspora of languages. From here, and therefore from the diversity of languages, the unity is not projected toward the origin and the recovery of the origin, toward a lost Edenic unity to be restored. In the wake of Jewish hermeneutics, and of the positive meaning that it attributes to fragmentation, dispersal, and incompleteness, the unity is sought in the future rather than in the past.[204]

In an illuminating passage from the *Star of Redemption*, Rosenzweig summarizes his understanding of language, the "seal" of the humanity of mankind, in a penetrating way. This "morning gift from the creator" is the common good in which everyone participates in their own particular way.[205] One can say that language is common to everyone and particular to each one of us. After Babel, language is fragmented into historical languages and scattered in individual speech. Thus, language "unites and divides at the same time."[206] It unites because everyone participates in that common good, it divides because each one of us speaks under the sign of one's own singularity and in a historical language. That it unites and divides means that, if it permits understanding, it simultaneously *inter*dicts it. And thus understanding is always also not-understanding. Language, in its reality, "includes everything, beginning, middle, end."[207] This is because in revealing the present-day center, it is the "visible mark" of the beginning of creation, while it is dominated, in every single language, in the speech of every single individual, and in every one of his words, by the ideal of that "perfect understanding" that will be present in redemption.[208] The language of perfect understanding will be the language of humanity that is not yet, but that will nevertheless be there at the end.

The end is, in Rosenzweig's view, the completion of redemption after messianic times. In this end everything immerses itself again in its beginning. Thus redemption is the completion of all the promises and all the prophecies, it is *Vollendung*, more specifically, it is a *volle Endung*, a full completion, a full ending.[209] If the beginning is marked by sin, by fall and ruination, which has condemned man to the worst punishment that could be imagined, to incomprehensibility, to the impossibility of understanding the lip of the other, the end, and the completion of the end, in the re-immersion in that beginning, will be the reparation of that sin, that fall, that ruination. But it will not be the reparation of the Tower, nor even less a re-edification of it. The reparation will have a completely different sense and direction. The reparation will be translation. "Nothing shows so clearly that the world is unredeemed as the diversity of languages."[210] Between diverse languages there is only "the stammering word" as mediator.[211] But redemption is handed over and entrusted to this stammering word that translates, and by translating repairs. If in the unredeemed world the wound of incomprehension remains open, that is, of the lips that do not perceive, do not read, and do not understand each other, then the promise of perfect understanding will be kept in the redeemed world: "I will then give to the people a pure language because they all invoke the name of the Lord" (*Zephaniah* 3, 9). The language of perfect understanding will proclaim redemption.

For Rosenzweig, no less than for Benjamin, translating is redeeming to the degree that redeeming is above all repairing, according to one of the meanings in the *Kabbalah*. But what does repairing mean in the case of translation? And how could translation be a *repairing*? In one passage, which is not easy to interpret because of the different layers that constitute it, Benjamin speaks of translation by comparing it to the piecing together of a broken vase. It is the famous metaphor of the amphora, or "ammetaphor," as Derrida calls it.[212] By carefully reading it one can see how the movement of translation comes to be woven into the metaphorical fabric of the Lurianic *Kabbalah*. The act of translating appears as the act of *tiqqun*, the messianic reparation and recomposition. Benjamin writes:

> Fragments of a vase that are to be glued together must match one another in the smallest details, although they need not be like one another. Similarly, a translation, instead of imitating the meaning of the original, must lovingly and in detail incorporate the original's way of intending, thus making both the original and the translation recognizable as fragments of a greater language, just as fragments are part of a vase.[213]

It is difficult not to interpret these fragments as the *kelipot* of which the *Kabbalah* speaks in the doctrine of the "breaking of the vases." Scholem already, in the essay "Walter Benjamin and His Angel," perceives in Benjamin's philosophy of history the presence of *tiqqun*.[214] But the same can also be said for his philosophy of language which, however profane and secular, emerges against the background of the mystical, and in particular Jewish mysticism, known indirectly through Scholem himself, but also through Hamann, the great scholar and lover of the Kabbalah.[215]

The doctrine of the "breaking of the vases" belongs to the Kabbalistic narrative of creation.[216] Taking place through to the retraction of God, who by withdrawing gave rise to the world, the process of creation unfolded in the primordial space through an emanation. But in this emanation the force of divine Light, a synonym of His *Shekhinah*, of His Presence, was so strong that the vases, brought forth from His wisdom in order to receive it, shattered because they were unable to contain it. Hence, they let the Light flow all over each part of its creation. There is no corner of the world, no matter how deprived, no matter how remote, which does not contain a divine spark in exile that waits to be liberated and redeemed from its imprisonment.[217] Redemption is therefore the liberation of the scattered sparks, the reunification of God with His *Shekhinah*. Every *tiqqun*, every act of reparation, brings the end of the exile closer and anticipates redemption. To redeem means repairing in the sense of reunifying and unifying, in the same way that one repairs the fragments of a vase, by recomposing and reunifying them. But it must be emphasized, as Rosenzweig does, that the unification is already a redemption, that the unity "is as it becomes," that unity "is Becoming Unity."[218]

Every act of reparation, however humble it may be, is a messianic act. There are many trades, many types of work, and many tasks that have, perhaps secretly, a messianic value. But the task of the translator is the messianic task *par excellence*. This is because the dispersal of humanity took place through the scattering of language and speech that happened because mankind had "offended the purity of the Name"[219] by constructing Babel. Only the translator is capable of putting languages, and the speakers of those languages, into dialogue; and in this dialogue, in its becoming, which is the becoming of language, the translator allows the pure language, which waits to be redeemed, to emerge "from the harmony of all the modes of intention."[220] Benjamin summarizes the messianic task of the translator as follows: "It is the task of the translator to release in his own language that pure language which is exiled among alien tongues, to liberate the language imprisoned in a work in his re-creation of that work."[221] Translating therefore means redeeming, liberating the pure language which was in exile, confined and scattered among the many languages that, no matter how much they try to say the same thing, end up saying it in different ways. And in dialogue, the one says to the other what the other has not yet said, what the other wanted to say, or is about to say. And in this saying from one to the other, from this saying, emerges the infinity of what each language can say, that is, the infinity of the pure language. The "pure language"—which is reminiscent of Hamann's "language of Angels"[222]—is also called the "true language" by Benjamin. It is true because it says the infinity of everything sayable in every way that it could be said.

It would be a serious mistake to interpret this "pure language" or "true language" as a new universal language.[223] If this were the case, pure language would be the attempt to rebuild the Tower. Nothing could be further from Benjamin's mind, or from Rosenzweig's. Yet it would also be a mistake to think that the pure language is born from a dialogue among languages that would take place in a space between languages, in a sort of "interregnum" in which no one dominates.[224] There is no interregnum, just as there is no space between languages. If there were, there would be a region of the world without language, without idiom, and without speech, a space where one does not speak and where from on high one could judge which language is better, which translation is better. The pure language exists only in the heterological and dialogical opening of a language or a monolanguage, in the terrain of monolingualism.

Rosenzweig puts it clearly on two occasions, and in two different texts, when he affirms: There is only "One Language."[225] He takes up Humboldt's argument that in every language one can express everything, because every language potentially contains everything that has been actualized in other languages, and it would be enough to reawaken those tonalities that lay in waiting like a musical instrument not yet played.[226] Rosenzweig writes in a similar fashion: "There is no peculiarity of one language . . . that cannot be detected, at least in embryo, in every other language."[227] Here one finds the unity of languages in the possibility that each language can say everything that the other languages have already said, are saying, and will say. And this unity, for Humboldt, as well as for Rosenzweig and Benjamin, is the condition of understanding and translating. "It is possible to translate because in every language every other is potentially present."[228] Consequently, for Rosenzweig, this unity of languages, the One Language, present in all of them, says that one can and one must translate. Although it makes this possible, it also commands it. Translating is a "commandment," an instruction, and thus a task, a messianic task. In the dialogue between languages, transformation can happen and does happen because each language contains, in embryo, the possibilities of the others that are brought forth and actualized. But the renewal and the "breaking up of such an untilled linguistic earth" can happen only within each language, not between them. It is within each language, in its dialogical opening, where the messianic language seems to reemerge from exile. Thus, "there is an obligation to translate so that the day may come for that harmony of languages which can arise only in each individual language, not in the empty space 'between' them."[229]

But will that day ever come? Will that promised land of the reconciliation and accomplishment of languages ever be reached? And will the dialogue between languages, which thanks to its messianic value also unfolds vertically, ever reach a summit? Unsurprisingly, the responses that Benjamin and Rosenzweig offer diverge greatly on this issue. The kingdom yet to come of the messianic language is described in a very similar way. Not only would the messianic language be the true language, but the truth would be that very language in which letter and sense are no longer separated. In that language, in which what is intended is finally expressed through the ways of intending of all languages, in which it would no longer be possible to distinguish between the original and the translation, every intention, every communication, language itself, having achieved fulfillment, would be extinguished.[230] For Benjamin, this kingdom, predestined and denied, will never be touched, reached, and crossed by translation. And thus the promise of "pure lips" remains but a promise.

For Rosenzweig, on the contrary, if everything from the beginning comes from the Name, in the end everything will plunge back into the Name. The path to redemption, from creation through revelation, happens in the Name and for the Name. At the end of time, the "pure lips" will invoke the Name in order to herald the redemption, but only so that this Name can be kept silent, because the end is without Name, beyond all Names. Afterward, perfect understanding will illuminate the messianic silence. No longer can another name be counterposed to the One Name. And the One Name will be "all-one" (*all ein*).[231] And then the world will be silent. Redemption will also redeem God, because He will be redeemed from everything that He is not, so that He will be One and His Name will be One. In the great Sabbath of redemption, the ultimate silence, plunged into the divine Abyss of the One, will be silenced in us and there, redeemed by His Name, God himself will be silent.

NOTES

1. J. G. Hamann, "Aesthetica in Nuce," in *Sämtliche Werke* (Wien: Herder, 1950), vol. II, 199.

2. Franz Rosenzweig, "Scripture and Luther," in *Scripture and Translation*, eds. Martin Buber and Franz Rosenzweig (Bloomington: Indiana University Press, 1994), 47.

3. Walter Benjamin, "The Task of the Translator," in *Walter Benjamin: Selected Writings Volume I, 1913–1926*, eds. Marcus Bullock and Michael W. Jennings (Cambridge, MA: Harvard University Press, 2004), 261. Translation modified.

4. For a reconstruction and a discussion of Babel in Hebrew hermeneutics, see Donatella Di Cesare, "Das Rätsel von Babel. Sprache und Sprachen in der jüdischen Tradition," in *Philosophische Aktualität der jüdischen Tradition*, ed. Werner Stegmaier (Frankfurt am Main: Suhrkamp, 2000), 67–77.

5. My translation.

6. Jacques Derrida, "Des Tours de Babel," in *Difference in Translation*, ed. Joseph Graham (Ithaca: Cornell University Press, 1985), 166.

7. According to Zumthor, the Torah would judge negatively the diversity of languages, a difficult view to maintain. See Paul Zumthor, *Babel ou l'inachèvement*, La Couleur Des Idées (Paris: Editions du Seuil, 1997).

8. See Abraham Ibn Ezra, on *Genesis* 11, 3.

9. See Talmud *Sanhedrin* 109a.

10. On inventive artifice in the Torah and on the way in which technology is interpreted in the construction of Babel, there is an important chapter in the exegesis of the philosopher Jitzchaq Avravanel. See Donatella Di Cesare, *Das Rätsel von Babel*, 71–73.

11. The quantity of stone and pitch in the plain was very scarce and would not have been enough to construct an imposing city and a gigantic tower.

12. *Pirkej de Rabbi Eliéser*, 24.

13. Talmud *Sanhedrin* 109a.

14. See *Midrash Kohelet*, 28, 11, V, I.

15. Jacques Derrida, "Des Tours de Babel," 177.

16. See Jean-René Ladmiral, *Traduire: théorème pour la traduction* (Paris: Gallimard, Paris, 1994). See also the excellent philosophical reflections of John Sallis, *On Translation. Studies in Continental Thought.* (Bloomington: Indiana University Press, 2002).

17. Johann J. Breitinger, *Fortsetzung der Critischen Dichtkunst* [1740] (Stuttgart: Teubner Anastatic Reprints, 1966), 138.

18. Ibid., 139.

19. Ludwig Tieck, "Die altdeutschen Minnelieder," *Kritische Schriften. Zum erstenmale gesammelt und mit einer Vorrede herausgegeben von L. Tieck. Erster Band* (Leipzig, 1848), reprinted (Berlin-New York: de Gruyter, 1974), 187

20. August W. Schlegel, *Vorlesungen über schöne Literatur und Kunst-Vorlesungen über die romantische Poesie/3* in *Kritische Ausgabe der Vorlesungen*, 3 vols., eds. Ernst Behler and Frank Jolles (Paderborn: Schöningh, vol. I), 24.

21. Friedrich Schleiermacher, "On the Different Methods of Translation," in *German Romantic Criticism*, ed. A. Leslie Wilson (New York: The Continuum Publishing Company, 1982), 1. From here on the translation of this essay is modified.

22. Friedrich Schleiermacher, "On the Different Methods of Translation," in *German Romantic Criticism*, ed. A. Leslie Wilson (New York: The Continuum Publishing Company, 1982), 1.

23. See Eugenio Coseriu, *Structure lexicale et enseignement du vocabulaire*, in *Actes du premier colloque internationale de linguistique appliquée*, Nancy 1966, 175–217; 109–111. See also, *Kontrastive Linguistik und Übersetzung: ihr Verhältnis zueinander*, in *Kontrastive Linguistik und Übersetzungstheorie*, ed. Wolfgang Kühlwein, Gisela Thome, Wolfram Wilss (Munich: Fink, 1981), 183–199.

24. Friedrich Schleiermacher, "On the Different Methods of Translation," 2.

25. On understanding differently in philosophical hermeneutics, see Chapter VI, § 9.

26. Friedrich Schleiermacher, "On the Different Methods of Translation," 2.

27. Ibid., 4.

28. Ibid.

29. Ibid., 8.

30. Ibid.

31. Ibid.

32. Ibid., 9.

33. Ibid., 10.

34. Ibid.

35. Ibid., 15. Translation modified

36. Ibid.

37. Ibid., 16.

38. Ibid.

39. Ibid., 29.

40. Wilhelm von Humboldt, "From the Introduction to His Translation of Agamemnon," in *Theories of Translation*, ed. Rainer Schulte and John Biguenet (Chicago: University of Chicago Press, 1992), 58.

41. Ibid., 55.

42. Ibid.

43. Ibid.

44. Ibid., 56.

45. See Ibid., 56–57.

46. Ibid., 58. Translation modified

47. Ibid. See also Friedrich Schleiermacher, "On the Different Methods of Translation" 7.

48. Ibid. See Wilhelm von Humboldt, "From the Introduction to His Translation of Agamemnon," in *Theories of Translation*, eds. Rainer Schulte and John Biguenet (Chicago: University of Chicago Press, 1992), 56.

49. Ibid., 59.

50. See A.W. Schlegel, *Zur Philologie/2* in *Kritische Friedrich Schlegel-Ausgabe*, vol. 24, eds. Ernst Behler, Jean-Jacques Anstett, and Hans Eichner (Paderborn: Schöningh, 1981), vol. XVI, n. 43, 360.

51. Wilhelm von Humboldt, *On Language: The Diversity of Human Language-Structure and Its Influence on the Mental Development of Mankind*, ed. Charles Taylor, trans. Peter Heath, Texts in German Philosophy (Cambridge: Cambridge University Press, 1988), 146.

52. Ibid., 152.

53. Ibid., 63.

54. See Antoine Berman, *The Experience of the Foreign: Culture and Translation in Romantic Germany* (Albany: State University of New York Press, 1992).

55. August W. Schlegel, *Vorlesungen über schöne Literatur und Kunst-Vorlesungen über die romantische Poesie/3*, cit. p. 24.

56. Johann G. Hamann, "Aesthetica in Nuce," 199. My emphasis.

57. On this See Chapter IV.

58. Hans-Georg Gadamer, *Truth and Method*, trans. Joel Weinsheimer and Donald G. Marshall (New York: Crossroad, 1989), 166.

59. Friedrich Schleiermacher, *Hermeneutics: The Handwritten Manuscripts*, trans. James Duke and Jack Forstman (Missoula: Scholars Press, 1977), 64.

60. Hans-Georg Gadamer, 296–297. On this, see chapter VI §9 of this book.

61. Martin Heidegger, *What Is Called Thinking?* trans. F. D. Wieck and J. Glenn Gray (New York: Harper & Row, Publishers, 1968), 183.

62. See Hans-Georg Gadamer, *Truth and Method*, 384.

63. See Ibid.

64. See Ibid., 384.

65. Ibid.

66. Ibid.

67. Ibid. Here the Italian translation by Vattimo leaves out the word "spirit."

68. Hans-Georg Gadamer, "Language and Understanding," in *The Gadamer Reader: A Bouquet of the Later Writings*, ed. Richard Palmer (Evanston: Northwestern University Press, 2006), 106.

69. Hans-Georg Gadamer, *Truth and Method*, 381. Translation modified.

70. Ibid., 384.

71. Ibid.

72. Ibid., 385.

73. Ibid.

74. Ibid., 385–386.

75. Ibid., 386.

76. Ibid.

77. But this "decision" is rather far from Gadamer's hermeneutics that emerges later. See Chapter VI § 14.

78. Hans-Georg Gadamer, *Truth and Method*, 386.

79. Ibid., 387.

80. Ibid.

81. Ibid., 388.

82. Hans-Georg Gadamer, "Die Vielfalt der Sprachen und das Verstehen der Welt," *Gesammelte Werke: Ästhetik und Poetik I* (Tübingen: Mohr (Siebeck) UTB, 1999), 348.

83. Heidegger, *What Is Called Thinking?* 174.

84. Martin Heidegger, *Hölderlin's Hymn "the Ister,"* trans. Will McNeill and Julia Davis (Bloomington: Indiana University Press, 1996), 62. Heidegger touches on this again later on page 65: "Every translation is interpretation. And all interpreting is translating."

85. Ibid.

86. Martin Heidegger, *Parmenides*, trans. André Schuwer and Richard Rojcewicz (Indianapolis: Indiana University Press, 1992), 12.

87. Ibid.

88. Martin Heidegger, *Hölderlin's Hymn "the Ister,"* 63.

89. Ibid.

90. Martin Heidegger, *On the Way to Language*, trans. Peter D. Hertz (New York: Harper and Row Publishers, 1982).

91. Martin Heidegger, *What Is Called Thinking?* 175.

92. Martin Heidegger, "On the Question of Being," in *Pathmarks*, ed. William McNeill (Cambridge: Cambridge University Press, 1998).

93. Martin Heidegger, *Hölderlin's Hymn "the Ister,"* 63.

94. Ibid., 62.

95. The romantics would not agree with this way of viewing the dictionary, nor would, much later, Paul Celan, who worked with dictionaries like a craftsman.

96. See Martin Heidegger, *Hölderlin's Hymn "the Ister,"* 62.

97. Martin Heidegger, *Heraklit*, Gesamtausgabe, vol. 55 (Frankfurt: Klostermann, 1979), 44. My translation.

98. Martin Heidegger, "Anaximander's Saying," in *Off the Beaten Track*, eds. Julian Young and Kenneth Haynes (Cambridge: Cambridge University Press, 2002), 243.

99. Martin Heidegger, *Heraklit*, 44. My translation.

100. Martin Heidegger, "Anaximander's Saying," 245.

101. Martin Heidegger, *Heraklit*, 45. My translation.

102. Martin Heidegger, "Anaximander's Saying," 248.

103. See Martin Heidegger, *The Principle of Reason*, trans. Reginald Lilly (Indianapolis: Indiana University Press, 1991).

104. See Jacques Derrida, Theology of Translation," in *Eyes of the University: Right to Philosophy 2*, trans. Jan Plug (Stanford: Stanford University Press, 2004), 65.

105. Martin Heidegger, *What Is Called Thinking?*, 185.

106. Ibid., 175.

107. Ibid., 176.

108. Ibid., 186.

109. On this point, see Gino Giometti, *Martin Heidegger. Filosofia della traduzione* (Macerata: Quodlibet, 1995).

110. See, for example, the translation that Heidegger proposes of the "saying" of Anaximander that as such is already a distancing from that which the saying "says." Martin Heidegger, *Basic Concepts*, trans. Gary Aylesworth (Indianapolis: Indiana University Press, 1993), 81.

111. Martin Heidegger, "The Origin of the Work of Art," in *Off the Beaten Track*, eds. Julian Young and Kenneth Haynes (Cambridge: Cambridge University Press, 2002), 5.

112. Martin Heidegger, *Being and Time*, trans. John Macquarrie and Edward Robinson (San Francisco: Harper and Row, 1962), §35. On the issue of the progressive withdrawal of Being through translation, see Martin Heidegger, *Contributions to Philosophy*, trans. Parvis Emad and Kenneth Maly (Indianapolis: Indiana University Press, 1999), 139–140.

113. Martin Heidegger, *Heraklit*, 69.

114. Ibid. See also Ludger Heidbrink, "Das Eigene im Fremden: Martin Heideggers Begriff der Übersetzung" in *Übersetzung und Dekonstruktion*, ed. Alfred Hirsch (Frankfurt: Suhrkamp, 1997), 361–362.

115. Martin Heidegger, *Hölderlin's Hymn "the Ister,"* 62.

116. Martin Heidegger, *Nietzsche*, trans. David Farrell Krell (San Francisco: Harper and Row, 1991).

117. Martin Heidegger, *Heraklit*, 69.

118. Martin Heidegger, *Hölderlin's Hymn "the Ister,"* 65.

119. Ibid., 66.

120. Ibid.

121. Ibid., 49.

122. With regard to this, see Chapter IV §§ 2, 4 of this book.

123. *See Jacques Derrida, "Theology of Translation," in* Eyes of the University: Right to Philosophy 2, *trans. Jan Plug (Stanford: Stanford University Press, 2004), 64.*

124. See Chapter IV, §6 on this point and on the critique of Scholem.

125. Their reflection is parallel even though neither one knew the other.

126. See "Preface" (originally published as an "Afterword" in the original 1927 edition) in Franz Rosenzweig, *Ninety-Two Poems and Hymns of Yehuda Halevy*, trans. Eva Jospe Thomas Kovach and Gilya Gerda Schmidt (Albany: State University of New York Press, 2000), xlvii.

127. Franz Rosenzweig, "Scripture and Luther," 47.

128. Ibid.,

129. On this see Chapter IV § 5.

130. Franz Rosenzweig, "Scripture and Luther," 47.

131. Ibid.

132. Franz Rosenzweig, *The Star of Redemption*, trans. William W. Hallo (Chicago: Holt, Reinhart and Winston, 1971), 141.

133. Ibid., 142.

134. Ibid., 145.

135. Ibid., 146. On logic and grammar and the importance of the latter in Rosenzweig's work, see Donatella Di Cesare, "Die Grammatik der Zukunft. Ich, Du, Wir in Rosenzweigs Sprachdenken" in *Trumah* (*Zeitschrift der Hochschule für jüdische Studien Heidelberg*), II, 2001, 61–70.

136. Franz Rosenzweig, "The New Thinking" in *Philosophical and Theological Writings*, ed. and trans. P. Franks and M. Morgan (Indianapolis, Ind.: Hackett Publishers, 2001), 127.

137. But on all of the implications of this *dia-* See Chapter VII § 12.

138. Franz Rosenzweig, "Scripture and Luther," 47–48.

139. Ibid., 48.

140. See Ibid., 47.

141. Friedrich Schleiermacher, "On the Different Methods of Translation," 9.

142. Franz Rosenzweig, "Scripture and Luther," 48.

143. Ibid.

144. Ibid.

145. Ibid., 50.

146. Franz Rosenzweig, *Ninety-Two Poems and Hymns of Yehuda Halevy*, xliii.

147. Franz Rosenzweig, "The Unity of the Bible," in *Scripture and Translation*, eds. Martin Buber and Franz Rosenzweig (Bloomington: Indiana University Press, 1994), 25.

148. *Zohar* II, 161a.

149. *Zohar* II, 161a.

150. On this point, see Hans-Christoph Askani, *Das Problem der Übersetzung dargestellt an Franz Rosenzweig* (Tübingen: Mohr, 1997).

151. Franz Rosenzweig, "Scripture and Luther," 67.

152. Franz Rosenzweig, *Ninety-Two Poems and Hymns of Yehuda Halevy*, xlvi.

153. Ibid.

154. Ibid., xlvii.

155. See ibid. See also, Franz Rosenzweig, "The Unity of the Bible," 24–25. For Rosenzweig, etymology becomes an unavoidable criterion of translation. See also Rosenzweig, "Scripture and Luther," 68.

156. Franz Rosenzweig, *Ninety-Two Poems and Hymns of Yehuda Halevy*, liv.

157. Here see §6.

158. Franz Rosenzweig, *Ninety-Two Poems and Hymns of Yehuda Halevy*, xlv. My emphasis.

159. Ibid.

160. Ibid.

161. Ibid.

162. Ibid. See Walter Benjamin, "The Task of the Translator," 262.

163. Franz Rosenzweig, *Ninety-Two Poems and Hymns of Yehuda Halevy*.

164. Walter Benjamin, "The Task of the Translator," 263.

165. Ibid., 253.

166. Ibid., 254.

167. Jacques Derrida, "Des Tours de Babel," 184.

168. Walter Benjamin, "The Task of the Translator," 254.

169. See Jacques Derrida, "Des Tours de Babel," 185.

170. Walter Benjamin, "The Task of the Translator," 254.

171. See Ibid., 255.

172. On this, see Chapter VII § 9.

173. Walter Benjamin, "The Task of the Translator," 256.

174. Ibid.

175. See Jacques Derrida, "Des Tours de Babel," 188.

176. See Walter Benjamin, "The Task of the Translator," 254.

177. See ibid., 258.

178. Walter Benjamin, "On Language as Such and on the Language of Man," in *Walter Benjamin: Selected Writings Volume I, 1913–1926*, eds. Marcus Bullock and Michael W. Jennings (Cambridge, MA: Harvard University Press, 2004), 64.

179. See ibid., 71.

180. See ibid., 66.

181. See Walter Benjamin, "The Task of the Translator," 257.

182. Ibid., 260. Regarding the concept of "name," see in particular Benjamin, "On Language as Such and on the Language of Man," 65–66. One must note that Benjamin, in line with the Hebrew tradition, develops what might be called a "philosophy of the name" in his writing.

183. See Walter Benjamin, "The Task of the Translator," 261.

184. On this "ever yet," see Chapter VII § 5.

185. Walter Benjamin, "The Task of the Translator," 261. Translation modified.

186. See Jacques Derrida, "Des Tours de Babel," 190.

187. Walter Benjamin, "The Task of the Translator," 256. Translation modified.

188. See Ibid.

189. Ibid. Translation modified.

190. Ibid., 254.

191. Ibid.

192. Ibid.

193. Walter Benjamin, "The Task of the Translator," 255.

194. Ibid., 257.

195. Jacques Derrida, "Des Tours de Babel," 194.

196. Walter Benjamin, "The Task of the Translator," 257.

197. On this, see Chapter IV § 5.

198. From this point on I will use the word *Schibboleth* in the German transliteration of the Hebrew in order to refer to Derrida, namely, to his essay on Celan. See Jacques Derrida, "Schibboleth: For Paul Celan" in *Sovereignties in Question: The Poetics of Paul Celan*, eds. Thomas Dutoit and Outi Pasenen (New York: Fordham UP, 2005). *Schibboleth* is a word of command that the Galatians used to intercept and stop, along the Jordan River, the Ephraimites who were killed because they did not know how to pronounce it, saying *sibbolet* instead of *shibbolet*. See *Judges* 12, 4. *Schibboleth* is therefore a watershed word, and for Celan the symbol of alliance and solidarity. See Chapter VII, §15 of this book. For Derrida, the paradoxical nature of *Schibboleth* rests in the fact that the difference of the signifier, in itself not semantic, is nevertheless the condition for meaning and even the mark of belonging

to a linguistic community: "what enters and incises language . . . is that there is a partaking of the *Schibboleth*, a partaking at once open and closed." Jacques Derrida, "Schibboleth: For Paul Celan," 33.

199. Emmanuel Levinas, *Otherwise Than Being, or Beyond Essence*, trans. Alphonso Lingis (Pittsburgh, PA: Duquesne University Press, 1981), 5–7.

200. Walter Benjamin, "The Task of the Translator," 258.

201. Walter Benjamin, "On Language as Such and on the Language of Man," 72.

202. Walter Benjamin, "The Task of the Translator," 259.

203. Ibid., 257.

204. It is a mistake, often repeated, to believe that Jewish hermeneutics aspires to regain the lost language of paradise.

205. Franz Rosenzweig, *The Star of Redemption*, 110.

206. Ibid.

207. Ibid.

208. Ibid.

209. Ibid., 242.

210. Ibid., 295.

211. Ibid.

212. See Jacques Derrida, "Des Tours de Babel," 191.

213. Walter Benjamin, "The Task of the Translator," 260. Translation modified.

214. See Gershom Scholem "Walter Benjamin and His Angel" in *On Walter Benjamin: Critical Essays and Recollections*, ed. Gary Smith (Cambridge: MIT Press, 1988).

215. On the importance of Hamann in the reflection of Benjamin, see Winfried Menninghaus, *Walter Benjamins Theorie der Sprachmagie*, Suhrkamp, Frankfurt, 1980.

216. See Gershom G. Scholem, *Major Trends in Jewish Mysticism* (New York: Schocken Books, 1995).

217. On the exile of God and of His *Shekhinah*, see Chapter IV § 1.

218. Franz Rosenzweig, *The Star of Redemption*, 411.

219. Walter Benjamin, "On Language as Such and on the Language of Man," 71. On the significance of Babel for Benjamin and Rosenzweig, see George Steiner, *After Babel: Aspects of Language and Translation*, 3rd ed. (New York: Oxford University Press, 1998).

220. Walter Benjamin, "The Task of the Translator," 260.

221. Ibid., 261.

222. For an interpretation of the "language of angels" in Hamann, see Xavier Tilliette, "Hamann und die Engelsprache" in *Johann Georg Hamann*, ed. Bernhard Gajek (Frankfurt: Suhrkamp, 1979), 66–77.

223. This was done, for example, by Dimitrios Markis, *Quine und das Problem der Übersetzung* (Freiburg/München: Alber, 1979), 138.

224. The mistake is attributed to Waldenfels, but Hirsch also repeats it. See Bernhard Waldenfels, *Ordnung in Zwielicht* (Frankfurt: Suhrkamp, 1987), 206; A. Hirsch, *Der Dialog der Sprachen. Studien zum Sprach-und Übersetzungsdenken Walter Benjamins und Jacques Derridas* (München: Fink, 1995), 290.

225. Franz Rosenzweig, "Scripture and Luther," 67. Rosenzweig, *Ninety-Two Poems and Hymns of Yehuda Halevy*, xlv–xlvi.

226. See Chapter § 3.
227. Franz Rosenzweig, *Ninety-Two Poems and Hymns of Yehuda Halevy*, xlvi.
228. Ibid.
229. Ibid.
230. Walter Benjamin, "The Task of the Translator," 261.
231. Franz Rosenzweig, *The Star of Redemption*, 384.

FOUR

EXILED IN LANGUAGE

I have only one language and it is not mine; . . . [it] is the language of
the other.

—Jacques Derrida[1]

And Yukel said:
The country I live in is not the one my forbears gave their language.
I do not much like its landscapes.
And yet my language is the one I have acquired and perfected here.
My exile is anticipated in the exile of God.
My exile has led me, syllable by syllable, to God, the most exiled of words.
And in Him I had a glimpse of the unity of Babel.
God will speak to us in the language we happen to speak.

—Edmond Jabès[2]

1. "EXILE" IN THE JEWISH TRADITION

"Know that your descendents will be foreigners in a land not their own . . ."
(*Genesis* 15, 13). Exile, *galuth*, is part of the Jewish people; it marks their
history from its inception, and it constitutes its ineluctable destiny. From
the very beginning, Israel is in exile, from the very beginning, it has the
wandering of the diaspora before itself, the exodus toward the Promised
Land. Waiting and migrating are in its past, in its present, and in its future.

Yet in the Midrashic tradition, and above all in the Talmudic one,
exile, despite its ineluctability, has a reparative power both for the individual
and for the community.[3] In the *Haggadah*, its meaning is that of a blessing,
because in the side streets of exile the Jewish people can find a new way
to God.[4] In the literature, starting from the destruction of the Temple,

together with the fear that exile marks the end of Israel, the hope of return nonetheless grows stronger. Exile is a condition of passage. This transitory and temporary condition does not mean, however, that God abandons and forgets. "Would a mother forget her own son?" (Isaiah 49, 15) In the Berakhot treatise of the Talmud it is God Himself who weeps over the exile of his own children.[5]

But the exile is already in God. And the Kabbalah insists on this. The creation of the world is preceded by the tzim-tzum, by the retraction and concentration of God who, withdrawing and retreating, grants a site to the world. God withdraws into Himself, He divides Himself into Himself and differentiates Himself from Himself in order to leave room for the other to Himself. God goes into exile. Creation is thus a divine exile. This difference of God within God Himself precedes every other split, separation, and dispersion. Exile is the creation, but exile is also the revelation. God splits and separates, allowing the sparks of His Shekhinah, His Presence, to scatter themselves everywhere in the world. God is therefore the absence of God, the exile in exile. Exiled from Himself, God goes into exile. His Shekhinah wanders with His people, suffers with them, follows them in the misery of the foreign land, and accompanies them in their wanderings. This is what happens in every exile—says the Zohar, the Book of Splendor—in those of the past as well as in this present exile.[6] If God lives in exile with Israel, in its turn, Israel, in its diaspora, makes itself the dwelling place for the God in exile. And in the dispersion and desperation of the diaspora, the Shekhinah remains the unbroken bond with God, the thread of hope for the return, the open passage toward the Promised Land.

Separated from His Shekhinah, God Himself is full of nostalgia and longs for reunion.[7] Because He shares the exile of His people, God Himself "makes Himself in need of redemption."[8] Thus, by fulfilling the Law, each one must free the divine sparks scattered in the foreign places of the galuth, must collect and raise the Shekhinah from the dust of exile in order to reunite it with God. This is the tiqqun: the reparation, the messianic reunification. Redeeming is unifying God, where unity is as it becomes; it is this becoming unity. The return from exile is this unity. And if the exile is marked by the proscription of the name of God, "the most exiled of words,"[9] the exile comes to an end with the Name and in the Name of God. "My people will know my Name, and will understand on that day that I said: 'Here I am'" (Isaiah 52, 4).

2. "HOW MUCH HOME DOES ONE MAN NEED?"

Exile is first of all an exile from the land. With regard to being deprived of the land, of the native land, of Heimat, the testimony of Jean Améry, the French pseudonym chosen to conceal the German name Hans Meyer, takes on significance.[10] A Jewish exile of the Third Reich, Améry bears witness to a "limit-situation," namely, Auschwitz.[11] That being at the limit, at the boundary, despite everything—and against every illusion—does not change even in the *aftermath*, when the limits and the boundaries seem easily traversed. It is the situation of exile without return, of the definitive loss of *Heimat*, of homeland. That the homeland is Germany, makes the exile more conflictual, but also more perspicuous.

In such a context, Améry obsessively asks himself the question: "How much home does one man need?"[12] Put to himself in a "very specific" situation, in a limit situation, the question offers a starting point for a general reflection that, starting from the one who was banished and forced into exile, touches the human condition in modernity. Even if man's need for a *Heimat* is not quantifiable, the answer that Améry gives is firm and, in its firmness, conservative. It is an answer that clings to the land: "Man has much need for *Heimat*."[13] Expressed in very clear terms by one who has been expropriated from the right to a homeland, the need becomes more precise and appears inversely proportional to that which remains of the homeland, be it either a surrogate for the homeland, or the portable homeland of a Book, or even just a promise: "Next year in Jerusalem." In short, "man has so much more need for *Heimat*, as less of it he can carry with himself."[14] One needs to have a *Heimat* in order not to need it, in order to be able to give up and move on. Hence, the predictable outcome of the rigidly moralistic reflection of Améry is "it is not good to have no home."[15]

For the one who had to give it up, as much as for the one who wanted to give it up, the loss is a definitive loss. The one who has lost the *Heimat* remains *heimatlos*, homeless. Améry intends the homeland in the most traditional way as "the country of childhood and youth," "the place of origin," and because it is *originary*, it is also *unique*: "a 'new home' does not exist."[16] Therefore, it means "earth," *Boden* in the double sense of "ground" and "foundation" in which one can firmly sink one's roots. *Heimat* is thus "*security*" and outlines that semantic field centered on faith, fidelity, and trust, where there is no impending danger, where one does not have to fear the strange, and where dispersion is avoided. In this settled concept of homeland, the concept of the native land strays into that of nation, *Heimat* into *Vaterland*. Améry willingly makes them correlative and indeed one becomes the condition for the other: One who has no part in an autonomous state organism, has no homeland. And where the *Vaterland* extends itself beyond the nation state, in order to become an "empire," it can no longer be experienced as *Heimat*.[17] Hence, in respect to the mondialization of the world, which one could already foresee, Améry condemns the choice of modern man who trades the *Heimat* for the world.[18]

One needs to ask, is it choice or destiny? Already in *Being and Time* Heidegger translates *Heimatslosigkeit*, homelessness, as Dasein's "*not-being-*

at-home."[19] After the war, in the famous *Letter on "Humanism"* from 1946, homelessness is thought starting from the history of Being as the destiny of modern man that, in the ex-sistence of its Da-sein, lives in nearness to Being yet without being able to experience it and take it on as its dwelling.[20] "Exiled from the truth of Being" man circles around himself.[21] Exile becomes clear in light of the homelessness brought about by the destiny of Being in metaphysics. Homelessness, the absence of homeland, therefore results from the experience of the forgetting of Being. "Homelessness becomes a worldwide destiny."[22] And the *Heimat*, the homeland, thought from the perspective of the history of the world, is the nearness to Being that appears simultaneously as the nearness to the origin.[23] The "homecoming" is here a return to the origin.

If homelessness is therefore a choice for Améry, for Heidegger it is a destiny from which it is impossible to escape. But for both the question of *Bodenständigkeit*, of the possibility of contemporary man being rooted firmly in the land, still makes sense. And hence Heidegger asks himself: "Does that silent man's dwelling between earth and heaven still exist?"[24] If the old ground is lost, will there be a new one, a new foundation in which man can root himself?[25] In the future, will the work of man continue to flower from his own land of origin? The future is accepted only inasmuch as it is led back to the origin. Thus, exile assumes all the negativity of a detaching and distancing from the homeland, an expatriation, endured insofar as it is temporary, in light of the unique and unrepeatable origin, which is the real goal, the end, and the ending.

But is exile really a "Nowhere City,"[26] a homeland turned upside down? Exile can be nothing other for Améry, the German Jew who denies that Jewish belonging that he is forced to recognize when Nazism decrees his not-belonging to the non-Jews, his being not non-Jewish. As a man of negation, able to measure and dominate extreme nihilism in a disillusioned way, Améry remains in a neutral neither/nor, in which his not-belonging has deprived him of a *Heimat*, of Germany, by confiscating his past and his origin, whereas the not-not-belonging, Judaism, promises him nothing else than a future of wandering. Thus, Améry does not take the step from his limit situation to the human condition of modernity, he does not see prefigured in his particular Jewish exile the universal diaspora of humanity, in what will become the age of mondialization. But above all he does not grasp, in the *-los* of *heimatlos*, in the *-less* of *homelessness*, all the positive potentialities that the privative suffix contains.

3. EXILE FROM THE LAND, EXILE FROM THE LANGUAGE

When one is expatriated from the land, only the homeland of language remains. Or at least it should remain. This is the conviction to which exiles cling, and which, in different forms, returns in diaries, autobiographical memoires, interviews, newspaper articles, and philosophical essays. What remains? What of the exile remains in exile? The mother tongue remains.

Cut off forever from the root of the land, the identity of the exile still finds a safe and well-protected place in the womb of the mother tongue. Who would ever be able to expatriate the exile from there? Who would ever be able to expropriate the mother tongue from the exile? And how would one do that? The land is one thing, language is another. This place seems the safest, the most familiar, the most intimate (*heimlich*) of places. There is the exile's true dwelling in the time of wandering. If he no longer has a *Heimat*, a homeland, at least he has a *Heim*, a refuge and shelter.

As Hannah Arendt states with certainty in 1964: "What remains? The mother tongue remains."[27] And, already in 1958, in an even more cautious and articulated way, Paul Celan confesses: "Reachable, close and not lost amid many losses, only one thing remained: language. Indeed language, in spite of everything, remained secure against loss."[28] *Unverloren*, not lost, means the possibility that it could be lost, and at the same time the fear and perhaps also the effort not to lose it; it means that the language does not remain in and of itself necessary. Jean Améry was forced to notice with an almost incredulous sadness: "And we lost our language."[29]

The various testimonies that one could present here, all drawn from events of exile, as great as they are singular, would give rise to a complex taxonomy that extends from German-speaking Jews (Adorno, Arendt, Benjamin, Rosenzweig, Scholem) to non-German Jews who spoke German (Kafka, Canetti, Celan), and finally to non-German Jews who had a close relation with the German language (Levinas). This focus on the German language is not motivated with the intention of understanding the history and structure of the "German-Jewish psyche" more deeply[30]; nor even less does it want to exclude the presence of analogous phenomena on the other shore of Judaism, that is to say, not only among the Ashkenazi Jews, but also among the Sephardic. Derrida's testimony is enough.[31] Rather, the choice of the German language is determined by motivations within the discourse on linguistic exile. The relation between the German language and the German and non-German Jewish speakers, already strained before Auschwitz, traumatically interrupts after it. *Auschwitz* is the name of the fracture, the abyss, the hole that cannot be covered up, the definitive wound that follows the loss, also and above all of language.[32] The tension, already present in every relation between the language and the individual, reaches its extreme limit here, and makes emerge, with unprecedented clarity, the irreducible strangeness that always separates the speaker from "her/his" language, and takes on a value that demands, far beyond the singular case, reflection in contemporary debate. The Jewish exile, inasmuch as it is not just a territorial exile, but also a linguistic exile, prefigures that exile in the mother tongue that is the human condition, both originary and destinal at the same time.

4. ON THE MOTHER TONGUE

The mother tongue, in a specific and singular sense, in opposition to the general sense of "language," is the object of observation and reflection already prior to and outside of philosophical discourse. First named metaphorically through the organs of articulation (Hebrew *safah*, *lashon*, Greek, *glôssa*, Latin, *lingua*, French, *langue*, Italian, *lingua*, German, *Zunge*, English, tongue, etc.), the mother tongue refers to the way one comports oneself with language, that is, the *way of speaking* of a group whose members reciprocally understand each other. All those who do not follow such a way of behaving, often and not by chance rendered through verbal or adverbial forms (e.g., *hellenízein*, *hellenikôs*), are also excluded from understanding. From the beginning, the border between one language and the other, tacitly or not, is marked by the line of *understanding*. That this line is felt as an unbridgeable abyss is testified to by the myth of the Tower of Babel, which for centuries and millennia has continued to haunt the memory of peoples (*Genesis* 11, 1–9).[33] This uneasiness is always kept, however, at the border between one language and another. *We* understand one another, it is *the others* who *do not* understand. If they do not understand when we speak, it is because they are not even able to speak. The other peoples are rather defined through their *nonlanguage*. For the Greeks, almost unsurpassed models of ethnocentrism, the others are *bárbaroi*, "stutterers."[34] But almost everywhere throughout ancient history equally eloquent examples are not lacking. For the Russians the German language is *nemetzkij*, that is, "dumb." Making one's own language *the* language *par excellence*, *the one language*, in comparison with which the others are simply nonlanguages, is a first way of ridding oneself of the problem constituted by mankind's many ways of speaking.

On the other hand, the diversity of languages cannot help but later catch the eye, in times of the homo-hegemony of one language, for example Latin. Yet the abyss appears to be still bridgeable: It suffices that the diversity is passed off as a diversity of sounds, admittedly annoying, but certainly not harmful or even less so frightening. Everyone thinks in the same way, but they express themselves differently. This is the most common, albeit still unaware of itself, conception which is widespread in the modern age. Philosophical reflection intervenes at first only in order to confirm it further—it would be enough to refer to Descartes and his appeal to universal reason.

But in the seventeenth century the diversity of languages becomes, already with Leibniz, a philosophical question destined to be widely discussed throughout the eighteenth and nineteenth centuries, to the point of assuming an unexpected centrality in Humboldt. What changes is the way of understanding language, no longer as an instrument for expressing thought, but rather as the "organ" and "criterion" of reason.[35] If language manifests itself in many diverse languages, each language will articulate thought differently. The diversity of languages is not only and not so much a diversity of sounds, but also a "diversity of worldviews."[36] The abyss of incomprehension, which seems to irrupt once again, is, however, less frightening if it is true that "everyone has to carry in oneself the key to understand each language."[37] The uneasiness remains, however, always at the border between one language and another. And the problem is that of *trans-lating* from one's own language to the foreign language and vice versa.

The *Einzelsprache*, around which a nation is constituted, the national language, forms and shapes the thoughts and feelings of all the speakers from the very start. The "features" of a language prescribe a "direction" to the speaker's way of thinking.[38] The concern with uncovering the nature of a language, which is the "matrix," the *Gebärmutter*, of reason, pushes Hamann to draw on the metaphor of the feminine and the maternal. However, there has been talk of the "mother tongue," *Muttersprache*, for some time. And what is usually meant by this is the language absorbed together with the milk, the language matrix that, almost in the same way as the mother, brings the child into the world, because, by imprinting even its most delicate feelings, it disposes and traces its orientation.[39] One's access to things is thus mediated not so much by language, but more concretely by the mother tongue, and the mother therefore becomes a mediator of the world that, in that historical language, has been articulated in the course of generations, but which for the child will be simply *its* world. This does not mean, however, that the mother tongue determines one's way of thinking and feeling. Aware of the risks that such a determination would imply, the Romantics emphasize the freedom of the individual who, as Schleiermacher underlines, is always able to "construct language."[40] With regard to this, one repeatedly speaks of the "violence" of the individual over the "power" of language.[41] It is not surprising that, by giving space to the individual freedom in language, linguistic diversity is brought back to the diversity of individual speaking. It is starting from here that the question of understanding is posed in all of its grave significance. Not-understanding no longer concerns others only; even *we* can *not understand ourselves*. The uneasiness of the incomprehension crosses the border and insinuates itself into the same language. Between a foreign language and one's own, Humboldt, with regard to understanding, speaks only of "a more and a less."[42]

Yet, the concern of indicating the matrix of thought in language ends up instituting the *tópos* of the mother tongue, unique and irreplaceable, intimate and originary, which can neither be translated nor betrayed. It is impossible to leave the world of the mother tongue unless one passes into that of the foreign language, a passage that is doomed to failure because one always ends up carrying one's own language into the other language.[43] The mother tongue, which accompanies us from birth to death, therefore appears as a second skin or garment, a portable dwelling that moves around with us. In any case, it seems to be the most inalienable place.

After the "turn," Heidegger accentuates the intimacy of language. Language becomes the "house of Being."[44] But then "language speaks" (*die Sprache spricht*) and the speaker is the questioner in nearness to that dwelling.[45] In such a context, the *Muttersprache*, the mother tongue, takes on an incomparable value: "a language is language as mother tongue"— Heidegger writes in his 1960 essay *Sprache und Heimat*.[46] Together with the mother tongue, and beyond it, the *Mundart*, literally "mouth" and "manner," is revalued, and hence that peculiar manner of moving and positioning one's mouth, or rather the dialect, referring back to the Greek διαλεγειν, to that peculiar and chosen conversing, which is even more originary than the mother tongue. If language is the mother tongue, the mother tongue is in turn dialect. Dialect is the originary essence of language. Dialect is the secret source of every evolved language, it is everything that the spirit of an authentic language hides within itself.[47] *Mundart* is not only the *Sprache der Mutter*, the language of the mother, but even prior to this it is the *Mutter der Sprache*, the mother of language. It is therefore in the *Mundart* that the *Heimat*, the homeland, sinks its roots.[48]

Even if a language, even one that takes on worldly dimensions, remains forever and originarily a dialect, contemporary man, being far from the poetic word, seems destined to lose the language, namely, the dialect that is assigned to him, and to become *sprachlos*, "without language." Yet *sprachlos*, without language, means *heimatlos*, without a homeland, if it is only in language that homeland is preserved.[49] For Heidegger, homeland is once again and more than ever the origin that only gives itself in the originary word, which is at once the poetic word *and* the word of dialect.

Language appears increasingly as the dwelling of man, but in the sense of his wearisome sheltering that nonetheless reveals itself to be overly suffocating and closed. Hence, Gadamer asks: "But who is ever 'at home' in a language?"[50] Suddenly that intimately familiar place appears disturbingly foreign. The *Sprachheimat*, the fleeting and ephemeral homeland that language offers, is hard earned starting from the most essential foreignness and absence of homeland that defines the finitude of the human Being in language even prior to the world.[51]

The idea of possession and ownership, which has characterized the relation with the mother tongue—in the double sense: The language belongs to the speaker and the speaker belongs to the language—starts to be called into question. Can one still speak of a language in terms of *possession* and *ownership*?

5. IN THE FIRMAMENT OF ROSENZWEIG: THE HOLY LANGUAGE AND THE LANGUAGE OF THE GUEST

Things are, however, different for the Jewish people. Just as the ownership of the land is forbidden, so too the ownership of the language is interdicted. But once again the meaningful parallelism between *land* and *language*, between *Muttererde* and *Muttersprache*, shows itself here. The story of the "eternal people" does not begin, like the history of others, with "the narration of its autochthony."[52] Abraham, father of Israel, "has emigrated"[53]; his history begins with the divine command to leave the land of his birth in order to go to the one that God will show him. And subsequently the Jewish people—as Rosenzweig writes—are "a people in exile."[54] Thus, exile is their root, their certainty, and their dwelling, insofar as they can dwell in no land, unlike others who, by putting down roots, make it their own homeland. The land that is *their own* is only the holy land whose property, however, rests with God alone: "the land is Mine" (*Genesis* 23, 4; *Leviticus* 25, 23). From the beginning, they are already expropriated from the only land where they could be at home; they are already deprived of their being with themselves. From the beginning, they are expatriated from the homeland that will remain the land of their inexhaustible nostalgia. Exiled forever, the Jewish people will not be authentically by themselves, if not in that space and time of the nostalgia that always separates them from the Promised Land. But nowhere will they be able to feel at home; even in the land that has been pointed out as *theirs*, but at the same time has been denied to them as *their own*, they are destined to be only foreigners and guests. And so they will always be foreigners in themselves and for themselves, those who came from elsewhere, those who are never from here, those who cannot speak, if not but equivocally, in the name of the others.

Actually, language is also forbidden to them. Together with the land, language is the mark of belonging to the community. A people who have lost the land keep the language, no matter under which sky they settle. If the land is, in its exteriority, separable, then the language, which is much more proximate and contiguous, due to the intimacy that ties it to the life of a people, is inseparable from them. Yet, it is not because of this that it is less transient: Because it is tied to the life of a people, it shares with it even death. Like the land, also the language is thus "time" and not "eternity."[55] Of this time, once again, the "eternal people" are deprived.

Because the land they inhabit is not their own, so too the language they speak is not their own. The eternal people "have lost their own language."[56] Hence, they do not have a language of their own; their language is always the language of the other, the language of the host. It is the language of the people who host them and, thus, it is a foreign language. Even when they do not claim the "right of hospitality" and live in "closed settlements," they speak in a foreign land, a foreign language, borrowed from the people with whom they ultimately lived and from whom, when emigrating, they took their leave. Rosenzweig puts forth the most well-known examples, namely, Hebrew-Spanish and Yiddish.[57] But even where there is no trace of schizophrenia between a language and a land, even where they speak the language of the host, the Jewish people will nevertheless not be at home in that language and the peculiarities of its way of speaking, its lexicon and grammar, will impede their possible full identification with that language.[58] Just as they pass from land to land without ever being able to recognize their own homeland, so too they pass from language to language without ever mistaking it for their own dwelling. According to a famous Midrash: "There is no people and no language that has not been reached by the exiles and by the proscribed of Israel."[59] And the passage, the exodus, is infinite.

"Since time immemorial" their language, the holy language, is no longer their own; they no longer speak it on a daily basis.[60] Replaced by other languages, starting from the Aramaic of the Babylonian exile, Hebrew has ceased serving the everyday and, from being the living language of a people, it has transformed itself into a holy and sacred (*heilig*) language. "Holy," Rosenzweig observes, but "not dead."[61] Bound to the service of God, this language is removed from mortality and rendered eternal. Its life is a "cannot, will not, and may not, die."[62] The holiness of the eternal language is analogous to the holiness of the Promised Land. Both, while they escape ownership in the here and now, in the here and now also bear witness to non-ownership, to the foreignness of the other lands and of other languages.

In locking up the highest, most intimate and spontaneous moment of its feeling within its *grille*, the moment in which one speaks with God in prayer, the holy language deprives the Jew of the freedom and spontaneity that consists in nothing other than being able to say everything that one thinks and feels, and knowing that one can do it. In fact, it is only in the holy language that Jews can pray. Thus, even the most authentic and own-most word, because it is the freest and the most spontaneous, the most heartfelt, the word addressed to God, is shown as *theirs*, but is denied to them as *their own*. Even more than the holy land, the holy language is that "root which uproots and grounds the wandering."[63] Always already exiled from the word of the holy language, the Jewish people will migrate into the words of foreign languages, moved by an inexhaustible nostalgia for the promised word. They will never be able to be authentically by themselves, fully at home, in a foreign world of a foreign language. It is the holy language itself that, after having proscribed, expropriated, and expatriated them, forbids them from being fully at home. The Jewish people can only pray in the holy language, but precisely because of this they will always feel as if they are "in a foreign land,"[64] in the language in which they can only speak. The holy language will bear witness to their "real linguistic homeland" (*seine eigentliche Sprachheimat*), which is never there, but always *elsewhere*: in the realm of the eternal language inaccessible to everyday speech.[65]

Inaccessibility does not, however, mean effective separation. On the contrary, the daily language maintains a connection with the holy language already by means of the "mute signs of writing" which, differently from what usually happens, remain alive in their daily use and refer, in their expressivity, to the holy language.[66] And so "the Jew feels that his daily language is still familiar in its holy language."[67] This language is therefore not dead, and even less so abstractly severed from other languages; despite its holiness, "it is never rigidified in a simulacrum."[68] Rather, there are innumerable ways that connect it with everyday languages. And by leaving traces, memories, citations, and translations along these paths, it can transform them and transfigure them in a powerful way.[69] There is no text, there is no sentence, there is no word, and there is not even a letter that does not carry in itself a trace of the holy language. This trace, while reviving it, and by reviving it, reveals the eternal life of the holy language in other languages, and also shows its fissure, opening, and wound that cuts it originally from within. Nothing more, in a language, seems to be able to designate directly, and everything seems destined to the exile of deferral. The exile is therefore in every word and thus, in every word, the nostalgia for the holy language will be aroused. *No word is ever originary, rather, every word is always translated.* And, as such, it loses every semblance of natural, intimate maternity. If this happens, it is because the holy language affects the other languages to the point of making them reveal their *Unheimlichkeit*, their disturbing foreignness. The holy language prevents the feeling of safety and homeliness in any language and forbids all trust and faith in "the power of the word"[70]— the Jewish trait that in no way contrasts with the tradition of the people of the Book and the primary value attributed to the word.

The eternal language is therefore a living language; it is the only living language because it exiles from the mortal languages and from the idolatrous faith in their power. It is, rather, the word of exile. If the eternal language were not continually breaking into them, one could even believe that these lands are our lands, that these languages are our mother tongues.

6. IF GERMAN IS THE LANGUAGE OF THE ORIGIN

The radicality with which Rosenzweig insists on the expropriation of languages in the history of the Jewish people does not preclude him from an ethics of language through which a corresponding position is outlined: that of the guest who, welcomed and shown hospitality, can in turn welcome, offer hospitality, and love without reserve the language of his country, of Germany. This love without reserve, and "without demands," concretizes itself, as is well known, in the German translation of the Torah that Rosenzweig undertook together with Martin Buber, who subsequently completed it by himself. In his eulogy, held in Jerusalem in 1961 on the occasion of the work's publication, Scholem speaks, not without irony, about a *Gastgeschenk*, a "gift" in gratitude for the received hospitality, but actually a "tombstone" of the supposed Jewish–German relation. "When you prepared yourself for this undertaking—Scholem says—there was still a German-Jewish community in which your work would have had to produce a living effect, by stimulating a return to the original. . . . To whom will this translation be devoted now? Where will it act? The Jews for whom you have done it, no longer exist. The children of those who escaped this horror will no longer read German."[71]

The question of the German language, which was already complicated before Auschwitz, explodes in its wake, leading to the most diverse positions, which go from the intentional rejection to the more or less conscious denial, from the tireless and obstinate search for the lost language, or almost lost, to the complete and unlimited identification. Paradigmatic—and certainly far from the balance of Rosenzweig—is Adorno's attitude, who addressed the question in a 1965 radio transmission, subsequently published under the title *Auf die Frage: Was ist Deutsch?*[72] The context is that of his ill-endured exile that was lived under the negative terms of constraint. Adorno maintains without hesitation: "Not for a moment during the emigration did I give up hope of coming back."[73] His reasons are many: the need for that which is "familiar," the feeling of being able to do something good at home, but above all the estrangement with respect to America. Hence, the decision to return to Germany, not obvious and, moreover, not shared at that time by other exiles, for example, Arendt. Even though this could appear as determined by the demands of nostalgia, there is nevertheless an "objective" argument that legitimates the decision for Adorno. And it is *the language*.[74] The problem was not so much English, and the difficulty getting by in English, but rather German. By completely identifying with German, Adorno recognizes himself in the sounds that evoke in him his childhood.[75] But completely unexpected comes his praise of German and its "elective affinities with philosophy," which would make it a language suitable like no other for speculation and would render the great works, the *Phenomenology of Spirit* and the *Science of Logic*, almost untranslatable, as well as the single concepts. Even if he found a homeland again in the German language, and primarily a philosophical homeland, Adorno nonetheless sets himself the task of maintaining an "untiring vigilance" in order to escape the mystifications that this language could favor, and in order to avoid believing that the "metaphysical excess" (*metaphysischer Überschuss*) of the German language guarantees in itself the truth of the metaphysics which is inherent in it, or of metaphysics in general.[76] He claims to have written *The Jargon of Authenticity* also for this purpose.[77] Just because he considers language to be constitutive of thought, in the wake of the German tradition and of Humboldt, he aims at a razor-sharp style that is born, according to Nietzsche's suggestion, from a critical vision of the all-too-celebrated "depth" of the German language.[78] It is in this vigilance that Derrida, after having criticized it, sees the possibility of a readjustment in Adorno's position.[79] It is a position that could be "exemplary" in today's Europe by pointing the way toward cultivating the poetic nature of the idiom, of saving linguistic difference, and therefore resisting the international hegemony of a language, without nevertheless giving in to the "revivalrevival of identities" and to "the old ideology—pro-sovereignty, separatist."[80]

For Levinas, instead, there is no metaphysical privilege granted to a language, whether it is Greek, German, or French. Every language can be a language of philosophy. Everything can and must be "expressed" in Greek, the language of the West's philosophical tradition; "but perhaps it is not the place of the first meaning of beings, the place where meaning begins."[81] If "the essence of language is friendship and hospitality" then every language is capable of welcoming the meaning that arrives from elsewhere.[82] Levinas refers to French, which welcomed him and became his "familiar" language—an "acquired familiarity"—not then a mother tongue, but familiar like Lithuanian, Russian, German, and Hebrew. This is another way of saying that no language, not even the mother tongue, and even less so the mother tongue, is the originary and irreplaceable site of meaning. This is another way of breaking with the idolatrous sacralization of the root, of the motherland as the mother tongue, to which Levinas opposes the sacredness of the Law.

7. "WHAT REMAINS? THE MOTHER TONGUE REMAINS": ON HANNAH ARENDT

Was bleibt? Es bleibt die Muttersprache is the title of a famous interview given by Hannah Arendt to Günter Gaus and broadcast on German television on October 28, 1964.[83] Whoever listened that interview would have been surprised by the perfect German accent after decades of exile. If an accent indicates a wrestling with the language, here there is no wrestling, no conflict, no contrast; rather there is consonance, and in the end a full identification with the language.

In effect, Arendt shows an unshakeable attachment to her own mother tongue, to her own language, to the German language. What remains and what is irreparably lost of the Europe prior to Hitler? This is the question that is put to her. And her response leaves no margin for doubt and hesitation. "The Europe before Hitler? I cannot say I have nostalgia for that. What remains? The mother tongue remains."[84]

As Derrida points out, when critically discussing the interview, Hannah Arendt's response, and also the way in which it is articulated, appears to be "disarming," "naïve," and "conceited."[85] *Immer*, "always," this response obsessively gives rhythm to this answer, affirms the indestructible bond and attests to her absolute familiarity with the language.[86] Arendt "always" refused to lose the mother tongue, "always" kept a certain detachment from other languages, in this case from French and from English, she was "always" aware of having preserved the German language "even in the most bitter times"— "always."[87] It is as if this "always" marks the rhythm of the language: Not only is the mother tongue always there, it is the always there, it is the always already there, and the always still there; but, there is not and can never be an experience of the "always"—and of the "same"—if not there where the language is. The experience of the "always" and the fidelity to the other, as well as to oneself, would thus pass through the language, through the faith in the mother tongue. Derrida accepts this experience, which bases itself on the faith, fidelity, and unlimited trust in the mother tongue, but only in order to take it up in its paradigmatic significance. The paradigm is that which, just like in Adorno, repeats itself in many German intellectuals, be they Jewish or not. In thinking and feeling the mother tongue as the unique and sacred place of the origin, Arendt proves to be deeply Heideggerian. Thus, there is no dwelling and habitation outside of this place. " 'Removed' or not, this language remains the final essence of the soil, the foundation of meaning, the unalienable property that one carries with oneself."[88] The exile itself is appeased, attenuated, and put into perspective by it.

Arendt *always* continued to dwell peacefully and rather stubbornly in her own mother tongue, the German language, even "in the most bitter times," that is, even during Nazism, even when one could no longer close one's eyes and cover one's ears in front of the sudden hostility and strangeness of the language of the mother, which had become the language of death. To the insistent question: "even in the most bitter times?," Arendt adds another comment, apparently superfluous, to the "always" repeated with absolute conviction and held to be in itself already sufficient and exhaustive. "Always. I told myself: What can be done? It is not the German language that is gone mad! And then, there is no alternative to the mother tongue."[89]

Derrida tries to say what Arendt does not say, to save from erasure what is decidedly denied, to throw open the abyss that is disclosed in these two sentences, under these two sentences, which were inspired by an exasperated common sense. It is precisely this common sense that, where it would claim to have certainties, spreads doubt instead. Common sense demands that a language cannot go insane. It demands that the mother tongue is singular, unique, and irreplaceable. It demands that the ghost of this uniqueness excludes all possible insanity.

But, why could not a language go insane? Arendt seems to exclude this very possibility. It would be unreasonable and delusional, it would be insane to believe that a language could go insane. Certainly, one cannot cure a language, subject it to analysis, or hand it over to a psychiatric institution.[90] Hence, it is not the language, it is not the German language, which has gone insane. If anything, it is the speakers who have gone insane, the subjects of the language, the people, namely the Germans, or certain Germans, the Nazis. After having made themselves the masters of everything, they were unable to master the language. Older than them, the language will continue to live, spoken by Germans who are no longer Nazis or, as Derrida suggests, by "non-Germans."[91]

After the Nazi insanity, the language still remains—the neutral and exterior residue of radical evil (the residue of reparative possibility?), and thus embraceable as the "*residue* of belonging" that one does not want to reject.[92] But did this residue really *always* remain neutral and exterior, through all time, through all exile? Furthermore, is the language really only this neutral and exterior means? Is it really only a tool that, in its aseptic and exterior neutrality, can be simply and peacefully preserved, taken up again, and reused after every insanity, after the greatest insanity? It is this instrumental and reductive conception of language that leads Arendt to convince herself that the language, the mother tongue, has remained untouched by the insanity.

But precisely if one thinks of language in the Heideggerian sense as dwelling, where, despite everything, one sojourns and inhabits, it becomes difficult to believe that language, the German language, did not have a hand in that insanity. And therefore, starting from Heidegger, but in order to set out in a completely different direction, Derrida turns Arendt's sentence upside down. It is really the German language that has gone insane. As the very site of the insanity, the mother tongue permitted this insanity. The language was necessary in order to make the speakers of the language go insane, perverse, diabolical, authors and bearers of radical evil. So, Derrida notes, "a non-speaking being, a being without a 'mother' tongue, cannot become 'mad,' perverse or evil, murderer, criminal or diabolical."[93] The insanity articulates itself linguistically, it occurs with and within language, with and within the mother tongue. It is in this most intimate site of our dwelling, in the mother tongue, that the insanity explodes. But it explodes in close connection and in dialogue with the language that, on the one hand, welcomes insanity in itself and preserves its trace, and on the other, gives it back and even promotes it through those meanings that pass themselves off as common but that, however, are already twisted, distorted, alien, and insane. For the one who speaks an insane language, all the conditions to become insane are present, unless one is protected from that insanity through unavoidable hostility and foreignness. Améry bears witness to this: "For us the basic content of every German word modified itself and finally, whether we wanted it or not, our mother tongue became just as hostile as the one who spoke it. . . . The words were laden with a concrete reality, which was called the threat of death."[94] *The German language was an accomplice to Nazism.* It was more than an accomplice and one would understand little of Nazism if one separates and excludes the language. The guilt of the German language is guilt in the most profound sense. The rigid regulation through which the Shoah was hidden in the language, already in the Wannsee protocols, where it is spoken of as "moving toward the East," testifies to this.[95] The difficulty involved in naming the extermination is a reflection of this.

But there is something more to say, something that concerns not only the limit situation of the German language, but also every mother tongue, or rather every "mother." Why could the mother not go insane or why could she never have been insane? Why could one's mother never go insane? This is what Hannah Arendt did not seem to have been able to see or have wanted to see. But it is precisely the uniqueness of the mother—and of the mother tongue—that constitutes the insanity of the relation to the mother, even prior to the mother's insanity. The insanity rests in the absolute uniqueness of which the mother, or maternity, is the example *par excellence*. As unique (and one cannot forget here the natural trait of this uniqueness), the mother is irreplaceable. This means that the mother, in this unique and irreplaceable relation, while permitting the self to be close to itself, to be at home, simultaneously threatens the self in its intimacy.

Therefore, it is the mother who, as an irreplaceable unicum, as the place of the mother tongue, makes insanity possible, and precisely because she is this always open possibility, she is insanity itself. What makes one insane is the absolute uniqueness, the experience of the absolute uniqueness, that can be replaced only because it is irreplaceable, translated only because it is untranslatable.[96]

But the relation with the mother is, from the start, the language. That which remains of the mother is the mother tongue. Even in the absence of the mother, the residual place, the excess of insanity, is the mother tongue. Here one continues to listen and speak with the unique and irreplaceable mother. In the likeness of this mother, the mother tongue appears altogether unique and irreplaceable. But are there really—as Arendt holds—"no alternatives" to the mother tongue? If this were the case, one would need to postulate absolute untranslatability. And the limit between one language and the other, between the mother tongue and foreign languages, would instead be the edge of an abyss. Even so, we translate, we traverse that limit, and bring ourselves out of it. We translate the untranslatable. Imperfectly, but we translate it nonetheless.

Because it passes through the mother, the relation with the mother tongue is the most intimate, but also the most alienated, and is therefore perhaps the most paradigmatic within language. As the first and final condition of appropriation and belonging, the mother tongue is always and at the same time the experience of expropriation. When the mother tongue—which has gone insane—rises up in all its hostility and strangeness, the experience is that of an "irreducible *ex-appropriation*."[97] Always already the "language of the other," my one language reveals itself here to be the most proper and inalienable place that, while granted to me, is already alienated and expropriated from me. And even this extreme dwelling, this residual homeland, seems *forever* lost.

8. MY LANGUAGE WHICH IS OF THE OTHER: DERRIDA AND MONOLINGUALISM

Je n'ai qu'une langue, ce n'est pas la mienne—"I have only one language and it is not mine."[98] It is with this apparent logical contradiction, which is also a pragmatic contradiction, or better a performative one, that Derrida opens his essay on monolingualism. The contradiction is even deepened by being stated in French, in the language of which, while stating possession, one denies it—and in such a way the specter of the liar is conjured up again. But how is it possible not to have but one language without having it? How is it possible to simultaneously affirm that you are monolingual, to speak *only one* language, while nevertheless speaking a language that *is not one's own?*

And yet this contradiction indicates the place in which every speaker inhabits language, the place of his dwelling in the language that inhabits him. In order to speak of everyone's monolingualism, Derrida begins by speaking of his own. And he does so by putting himself in a place that is neither outside nor inside, a site that is at the edge, *"au bord du français,"* on the riverbank, along its elusive shoreline.[99] This non-place, reached after a crossing, across the sea and across the mother, the symbolically infinite space of the *mer*,[100] is the margin where, with a sort of autobiographical *anamnesis*, the Franco-Algerian Jew questions himself about his mother tongue, about his one language that is not his own. *Neither inside nor outside*: this enables him to avoid the two antithetical perspectives, which are antithetical insofar as they are unilateral, within which the mother tongue has been seen. From the external perspective, according to the instrumental conception that after all determines it, the mother tongue is seen as an object of possession on the part of the speaker. From the internal perspective, the one gained with great difficulty between the nineteenth and twentieth centuries, it is the speaker who is spoken and perhaps even possessed by the language. Hence, *neither outside nor inside* indicates that perspective at the margin from which one should interrogate oneself about the filiation of the language and the affiliation with the language.

Monolingualism is thus the speaking of that one language—which is not one's own, never has been, and never will be. But even prior to ownership, monolingualism is already not absolute. Once again a contradiction, or better an antinomy, indicates the place where the speaker lives: *I never speak but one language and I never speak only one language*. This is because *the* language is an abstraction that is always concretely blended with other languages, just as monolingualism is blended with bilingualism and pluralingualism.[101] This antinomy is the *nómos*, the very law of translation; it is, better still, the law *as* translation.

In my monolingualism, which is blended with bilingualism and plu-ralingualism, I speak the only language that, however, is not mine, is not my own. But can one say "my own" about a language? Can one possess a language on one's own just as one owns a good? And can one really be possessed by the language? Who possesses the language? And who is the one who the language possesses? And furthermore, when it comes to language, can one really speak of *ownership* and *possession*? These are the questions that guide, in deconstructive writings, Derrida's encounter with monolingualism.

The language that I have, or better—and this makes a difference—the language that I speak, is never mine, my own, but is always *the language of the other*. To say "of the other," "others"—does not mean to say "foreign."[102]

The language of the other is at the same time *mine*, it is indeed the only language I have. The question is primarily a question of belonging—or of not belonging—or better still, of allocation. It is an allocation *by birth*.[103] No one chooses to be born into a language. To speak with Heidegger, one is "thrown" into a language. Just as one does not choose one's own mother, so too one does not choose one's own mother tongue. In its singularity it is a universal destiny that allocates me to one language. Although it allocates me to one language, it also forbids my appropriation of it. That which must become, that which becomes my language, is always already the language of the other, starting with the other of the mother. My mother tongue, that interior and intimate place to which I am destined from birth, always already reveals itself as external and strange. It reveals itself as *unheimlich*. It is in this disconcerting intimacy that I will be able to say *I*, that I will be permitted to identify myself.

Behind the question of allocation there is ushered in the question of identity and identification. To identify oneself means to identify oneself with the other. But even before that, it means to identify oneself with the language in the language. Before and outside that strangely familiar place, properly improper, there will be no thinking *I* nor thinkable *I*. The mother tongue is me before me, since outside of it I would not be myself. It is my dwelling. I inhabit it and it inhabits me. For me, it is that in which I breathe—not a natural element but, much more, the absolute place, my absolute place. It is undeniable, because I cannot deny it without attesting to its omnipresence in me. Thus, always and everywhere, it precedes me. How could I not identify myself with it? Through and through it traverses the place of my suffering, my passions, my desires, and my thoughts; it gives voice to my prayers, to my hopes. However, at the margin, on the riverbank, or on the shore, I cannot avoid asking myself, how I could scream, rejoice, love, and pray in another language, or how I could do it without a language.

The identifying modality that grants me the ability to say *I* is language. My I, the *I*, *io*, *ich*, *je*, *yo*, is not independent of it. The mother tongue constitutes me, dictates my identity, prescribes my ipseity which is the power of an "I can" more originary than the "I" in a chain where the "*-pse*" of *ipse* is not separable from the power, the mastery, or the sovereignty of the *hospes*—the semantic chain that refers both to hospitality *and* hostility.[104]

This chain refers to the hospitality and to the hostility of the other and of the other's language at once, insofar as the language that I speak always comes *from the other*, returns to the other, and remains with the other. It is a completely asymmetrical and paradoxical situation in which my own identification, the identification of the other and me with the other, takes place. It is the situation of an *auto-heteronomy*. The monolingualism of the other is the language that comes from the other, language as law of the other, and the law of the other that sovereignly affirms itself as language. It is Language as Law and Law as Language. On the one hand, this Language Law is *autonomous* for me, because I must speak it and understand it as if I were giving it to myself; on the other hand, just as with every law, it remains necessarily *heteronomous*. The language of the mother—as we have seen—is the insanity of the law that dwells in the familiar space of this *auto-heteronomy*.[105]

And yet, without this language I cannot say I. Ipseity, since it occurs in language, and passes through the hospitality and hostility of the other, will never be pure. Hence, while appropriating my own identity, I am being already ex-appropriated—*dis-owned*—of it. Yet ex-appropriated from what? In reality, this ex-appropriation does not expropriate and does not alienate me from any property, any ipseity, from any self that could ever precede it or follow it. This ex-appropriation without ownership, this alienation without alienation, this inalienable alienation—the listening to oneself speaking in order to mean—seems essential to what is one's own and to the ownership of language.

9. LANGUAGE FORBIDS OWNERSHIP

It is peculiar of language not to permit ownership. In a language I have nothing, I possess nothing, I have nothing of my own. This excludes the absolute, exclusive ownership of language. Ownership, the possession of language—even of the mother tongue—reveals itself as impossible. It is language itself that escapes possession and proscribes possessive adjectives: mine, yours, ours, and so on. *Language forbids and prohibits ownership.*

But this means that even the *other*, the other who hosts me in the language, seemingly possessor, master, and sovereign of the language, has nothing of his own. Even less so the language that he says to be *his own*, insofar as there is no *natural* property in the language. This holds for me, but also for the other. And if the other wants to claim the language as his own good, *natural*, ingrained, inborn (here lies the dangers of naturalisms!), he will have to affirm and endorse this appropriation by passing through that *un-natural* process of the historical-political (phantasmatical) construction that is language.[106] With the violence of a cultural usurpation (always and essentially colonial) he will be able to pretend to have appropriated it and will be able to impose it as "his own." But it is language that will denounce itself as not being a natural good, because language escapes appropriation and remains inappropriable.

Yet even prior to any emancipation, liberation, and revolution, language forbids ownership and, by pointing to appropriation, uncovers the path to reappropriation—the one and the other are therefore never absolute. However, it does not act by neutralizing; on the contrary, by recognizing the historical phenomena of appropriation as such, it allows them to be repoliticized. Thus the monolingualism imposed by the other, which secretly or not tends toward the hegemony of the homogenous, toward the colonizing homo-hegemony (more insidious and more effective than many other imperialistic undertakings), the hegemony of the language of the master, of capital, of machinery, will always be stopped at the frontier of the language that is *the other's*—not because of the ownership, but only because of the provenance, because it originates, *it comes from the other*. Taken at its word, language opens up to an ethics, a politics, a right yet to be written by prescribing the right and the limits of the new right of ipseity, of ownership and of hospitality.

But if there is no such thing as lost ownership, because language is always disturbingly foreign, if nothing remains, not even that residue of the homeland of the mother tongue, if there is no dwelling place to which one can return, then there will not even be a return. Homelessness does not spare language. Living in language then will be instead a wandering through the desert. And the condition of the speakers in language will be that of emigrants, refugees, the stateless, destined to settle nowhere, shoved from border to border, from limit to limit. And perhaps one could put it thusly: in language there are only exiles; there are no owners.

Behind every exile that, starting from this shore or from this common origin, remains singular, there hides the universal and originary alienation in language, the *exile of every speaker in language*.

10. THE EXILE OF LANGUAGE

Deprived of its own language, but also of every other language, the speaker is "thrown" into absolute translation, without a language of departure and without a language of arrival (i.e., translation from a language that still does not exist to a language that will never exist). Because there is no point of departure (i.e., no lost originary language), there is not even a point of arrival, a language of arrival, a language that arrives in the end and at the end. Instead, it will be a language of the future, which comes from the other, but only as a *pro-mise*.[107]

Therefore, one is dealing here with an itinerant language, which follows a well-worn and repeatable itinerary that is hence retraceable, reproducible, and subject to reinvention. It crosses the desert by searching for traces of the other and by leaving traces for the other, always on the way of exodus. There is no departure and there is no return; there is only a long and difficult crossing. *Speaking* is *crossing* the silence of the desert. It is migrating from word to word, from exile to exile. And thus it is translating, translating itself into the word of the other. Without the other and its traces, without that itinerary, without that worn track, the desert would be the nothingness of the night.

The experience of speaking and the encounter with the word, which always comes from the other, is therefore the experience of the strange.[108] Yet, where one does not experience the trace of foreignness and alterity in the word, one neither feels the exile and the nostalgia for the home. Simply put, one dwells elsewhere thinking of being at home. Or, perhaps, one does not dwell and does not inhabit, because dwelling and inhabiting are possible only starting from that difference that characterizes exile and nostalgia. The seemingly less foreign word, the one that obstructs the reference to the other, which conceals the other and the elsewhere of its provenance, which hides the fissure that severs it originally, the word that claims to be proper and originary, which denies its exile, is the most exiled of words.

Language is in exile. Is there an exile of language? Can language be expatriated, while one believed that it was the homeland—*Sprache als Heimat*, as Heidegger said[109]—intimate and authentic, insuppressible and inalienable, even in times of exile? And to where would language be banished and exiled?

One can say that language is in exile where the light is blinding and where it seems to make everything clear, limpid, evident, without a shadow of doubt, without a shadow and unshaded (but when the tents are up, the shadow of the desert is beneficial) and where to opaque words one responds with transparent words, words reduced to signs. In this zone of mere signification, language is in exile. Here the itinerant language no longer encounters a well-worn itinerary or track. The way of exodus is closed off and there are only "blind alleys." "TO SPEAK with blind alleys" (*Mit den Sackgassen sprechen*)—this, for Celan, is the exile of language.[110] And it is, in the exile from the land and in the exile from the language, the most painful mockery, when language falls short—and with language also the other.[111] How can one "speak with blind alleys"? What kind of dialogue would it be? Even to words that have become closed and empty signs, dead ends, blind alleys that lead nowhere, one can speak of their and from their *Gegenüber*, from what stands in front of them, that other that they claimed to have banished and erased, and that nevertheless faces them. One can speak of this proscribed sense and, starting from this proscription, one can speak in the name of its "expatriate sense" (*von seiner expatriierten Bedeutung*).[112] Therefore, by digging up from the sand the erased traces of signification separated from its signifier, of semantics expatriated along with its history, which is the history of exile and exiles ("names and seeds"[113]), the most exiled of the speakers, the poet, can still take up the word and speak. But speaking is here a "stuttering," namely reproducing, following the stutterings of others, the world in which the poet is only a "guest."[114] And language, or what remains of language exiled from itself, becomes "bread," stale and hard, almost petrified, "to chew this bread, with writing-teeth."[115]

What then is the word torn from the sign and returned to its destiny of exile, that in itself bears the exile and leads to the exile? What then is the wandering word? It is the word that has in itself the fissure and the opening from which springs forth, which keeps the trace of difference, which, in differing, provokes the nostalgia for the other and the elsewhere to which it refers. It can be, primarily and simply, the word of one's own language, which, in its ineffable foreignness, once again says that language is not one's own, that it is of *the other*.

But perhaps the wandering word has to be sought outside of the well-worn itinerary, off the well-beaten track that needs to be sidetracked, if the monological tendency of monolingualism, which would make it *one and homogeneous*, is not to prevail. The wandering word is at the margin and at the edge of the track, and leaves side traces. These are significant traces that, by carrying all their semantic power within themselves, point to the most extreme and foreign place of language, where language reaches out and offers itself in all its uprooting foreignness and makes itself the word of exile.

The word that manifests itself as a mortal word of mortal language is a wandering word. Such a word quotes and translates the eternal language, and by showing itself as *translated* word reveals that the homeland that it offers, in comparison with that other homeland, is only temporary and transient. The metaphorical word is a wandering word, which in its apparent impropriety casts doubts on what wants to pass itself off as its own, which lets emerge the difference alongside the identity, and by differing, flowing, making fluid, is never the last word, but always the penultimate, *meta-phora*, *translatio*, transposition, *translation*, the word of passage that in the "language grille" opens up a passage and a crossing.[116] The word of the *Schibboleth* is a wandering word, it is at a crossing between languages, it is the keyword needed to cross the forbidden border, to shatter the barrier of language. The desert word of writing is wandering *par excellence*.

This is the crossing, the translating, and self-translating of poetry that is needed in order to return into the light. In such a sense, and only in such a sense, poetry is return and reparation, because it translates signs into names and redeems in signs the "names, steeped in every exile."[117]

NOTES

1. Jacques Derrida, *Monolingualism of the Other; or, the Prosthesis of Origin*, trans. Patrick Mensah (Stanford, CA: Stanford University Press, 1998), 25.

2. Edmond Jabès, *The Book of Questions*, trans. Rosmarie Waldrop, II vols., vol. I (Hanover: University Press of New England, 1991), 254.

3. See Talmud *Sanhedrin* 37b.

4. See *Midrash Pesikta rabbati* 136 a. See also Talmud *Pesahim* 87 b.

5. See Talmud *Berakhot* 3 a; *Midrash Eikha rabbati, petita* 2.

6. See *Zohar* II, 216 b.

7. See *Zohar* I, 84–85, 132 a; III, 69 a.

8. Franz Rosenzweig, *The Star of Redemption*, trans. William W. Hallo (Chicago: Holt, Reinhart and Winston, 1971), 410.

9. Edmond Jabès, *The Book of Questions*, 254.

10. Jean Améry, *At the Mind's Limits*, trans. Sidney Rosenfeld and Stella P. Rosenfeld (Bloomington: Indiana University Press, 1980), 43.

11. See Ibid., 1.

12. Ibid., 41.

13. Ibid., 60.

14. Ibid., 44.

15. Ibid., 61.

16. Ibid., 48.

17. See Ibid., 52–55.

18. See Ibid., 56.

19. See Martin Heidegger, *Being and Time*, trans. John Macquarrie and Edward Robinson (San Francisco: Harper and Row, 1962), 233.

20. See Martin Heidegger, "Letter on "Humanism,"" in *Pathmarks*, ed. William McNeill (Cambridge: Cambridge University Press, 1998), 256.

21. Ibid., 260. Translation modified.

22. Ibid., 258.

23. See ibid., 257.

24. Martin Heidegger, "Memorial Address," in *Discourse on Thinking*, trans. John M. Anderson and E. Hans Freund (New York: Harper and Row, 1966), 48. See also Martin Heidegger, "Building Dwelling Thinking," in *Poetry, Language, Thought* (New York: Harper and Row Publishers, 1971). Translation modified.

25. Martin Heidegger, "Memorial Address," 48–49, 53.

26. Emil M. Cioran, "The Advantages of Exile," in *The Temptation to Exist* (Chicago: Quadrangle Books, 1968), 77.

27. Hannah Arendt, ""What Remains? The Language Remains." A Conversation with Günter Gaus," in *Essays in Understanding*, ed. Jerome Kohn (New York: Schocken Books, 1994), 12. Translation modified.

28. Paul Celan, "Speech on the Occasion of Receiving the Literature Prize of the Free Hanseatic City of Bremen," in *Collected Prose* (Riverdale-on-Hudson, NY: The Sheep Meadow Press, 1986), 34. Translation modified.

29. Jean Améry, 42. On the language of the lager, opposed to and victorious over the mother tongue, see Aharon Appelfeld, '*Al kol hapesha'im (ebr.) Für alle Sünden* (München: Dtv, 2000), 182–188.

30. However that would be completely legitimate. On the "German-Jewish psyche," see Jacques Derrida, "Interpretations at War: Kant, the Jew, the German," in *New Literary History* 22 (1991): 39–95. With "psyche" or "soul" Derrida

intends both the psychic place of a "pulsional phantasmatical" that constituted the exemplary couple, as singular as it is impossible, of these two peoples, and that which in French—but also in Italian—one calls psyche, a "device of specular reflection."

31. Jacques Derrida, *Monolingualism of the Other*, 12–18, 44–73. But it is also worth remembering here the once more absolutely unique case of Elias Canetti and his two mother tongues: Jewish-Spanish, the first language, the one of his first infancy, and German, the second language, the "belated mother tongue, implanted in true pain," that of his "second birth." Elias Canetti, *The Tongue Set Free* (London: Granta Books, 1999), 70.

32. Hannah Arendt, "What Remains? The Language Remains." A Conversation with Günter Gaus," 14–15.

33. See Donatella Di Cesare, "Das Rätsel von Babel. Sprache und Sprachen in der jüdischen Tradition" in *Philosophische Aktualität der jüdischen Tradition*, ed. Werner Stegmaier (Frankfurt am Main: Suhrkamp, 2000), 62–77. See also Chapter III §1.

34. See Plato, *Cratylus*, 406a, 409e–410a. See on this Albrecht Dihle, *Die Griechen und die Fremden* (München: Beck, 1994); Wolfgang Detel, "Griechen und Barbaren. Zu den Anfängen des abendländischen Rassismus," in *Deutsche Zeitschrift für Philosophie*, XLIII, 1995, 1019–1043.

35. See Johann G. Hamann, *Metakritik über den Purismus der Vernunft*, in *Sämtliche Werke*, ed. Josef Nadler (Wien: Herder, 1953), vol. III, 286; J.G. Herder, *Verstand und Erfahrung. Eine Metakritik zur Kritik der Reinen Vernunft*, in id. *Sämtliche Werke*, ed. B Suphan (Berlin: Weidmann, 1877) vol. XXI, 20, 317; Wilhelm von Humboldt, *On Language: The Diversity of Human Language-Structure and Its Influence on the Mental Development of Mankind*, ed. Charles Taylor, trans. Peter Heath, *Texts in German Philosophy* (Cambridge: Cambridge University Press, 1988).

36. Wilhelm von Humboldt,"Über das vergleichende Sprachstudium" in *Gesammelte Schriften*, ed. Albert Leitzmann (Berlin: Behr, 1903–1936) vol. IV, 1905, 1–35, 27.

37. Wilhelm von Humboldt, *On Language: The Diversity of Human Language-Structure and Its Influence on the Mental Development of Mankind*, ed. Charles Taylor, trans. Peter Heath, Texts in German Philosophy (Cambridge: Cambridge University Press, 1988), 218.

38. Johann. G. Hamann, *Versuch über eine akademische Frage*, in *Sämtliche Werke*, vol. II, 122–123.

39. See A.W. Schlegel, *Vorlesungen über schöne Literatur und Kunst. Erster Teil: Die Kunstlehre*, in *Kritische Ausgabe der Vorlesungen*, ed. Ernst Behler (Paderborn: Schöningh 1989) vol I, 181–472; See also *Volesungen über philosophischen Kunstlehre*, in *Kritische Ausgabe der Vorlesungen*, 1–177, 21.

40. Friedrich Schleiermacher, *Hermeneutics: The Handwritten Manuscripts*, ed. Heinz Kimmerle, trans. James Duke and Jack Forstman (Missoula: Scholars Press, 1977), 59.

41. Wilhelm von Humboldt, *On Language: The Diversity of Human Language-Structure and Its Influence on the Mental Development of Mankind*, 63.

42. Wilhelm von Humboldt, *Über die Verschiedenen des menschlichen Sprachbaues*, in *Gesammelte Schriften*, vol. VI, 1907, 111–303, 183.

43. Wilhelm von Humboldt, On Language: The Diversity of Human Language-Structure and Its Influence on the Mental Development of Mankind, 60.

44. Martin Heidegger, "What Are Poets For?" in Poetry Language Thought, ed. Albert Hofstadter (New York: Harper and Row Publishers, 1971). Heidegger, "Letter on "Humanism" in Pathmarks; Martin Martin Heidegger, On the Way to Language, trans. Peter D. Hertz (New York: Harper and Row Publishers, 1982).

45. Martin Heidegger, On the Way to Language. On the language of neuter, Celan questions himself in the famous Gespräch im Gebirg. See Paul Celan, "Conversation in the Mountains," in Selected Poems and Prose of Paul Celan (New York: W.W. Norton, 2001), 398. On this theme, see Chapter VII §6.

46. Martin Heidegger, "Sprache und Heimat" in Aus der Erfahrung des Denkens 1910–1976, Gesamtausgabe 13, (Frankfurt am Main: Klostermann, 1983), 156.

47. See Martin Heidegger, "Hebel—Der Hausfreund" in Aus der Erfahrung des Denkens, 134–135.

48. See ibid., 134.

49. See Martin Heidegger, "Sprache und Heimat" in Aus der Erfahrung des Denkens, 156.

50. Hans-Georg Gadamer, "On the Truth of the Word," Symposium 2, no. 6 (2002): 132.

51. On the difference between Heidegger and Gadamer here, see Chapter I, §3. However, for Gadamer the mother tongue always remains an instance of the main reference of the speaker. For example, see Hans-Georg Gadamer, "Die Vielfalt der Sprachen und das Verstehen der Welt," Gesammelte Werke: Ästhetik und Poetik I (Tübingen: Mohr (Siebeck) UTB, 1999), 341.

52. Franz Rosenzweig, The Star of Redemption, trans. William W. Hallo (Chicago: Holt, Reinhart and Winston, 1971), 300.

53. Ibid. See also, Franz Rosenzweig, "Geist und Epochen der judischen Geschichte," Kleinere Schriften (Berlin: Schocken, 1937). 1937.

54. Franz Rosenzweig, The Star of Redemption, trans. William W. Hallo (Chicago: Holt, Reinhart and Winston, 1971), 300.

55. Ibid., 301.

56. Ibid.

57. See ibid.

58. One thinks of the particularity of the Jewish-Italian languages.

59. Midrash Shir ha-Shirim, ed. Lazar Grünhut (Jerusalem: Gross, 1897), 47 b.

60. Franz Rosenzweig, The Star of Redemption, trans. William W. Hallo (Chicago: Holt, Reinhart and Winston, 1971), 301.

61. Franz Rosenzweig, "Geist und Epochen der judischen Geschichte," Kleinere Schriften (Berlin: Schocken, 1937).

62. Franz Rosenzweig, "Classical and Modern Hebrew. Review of a Translation Into The Hebrew of Spinoza's Ethics," in Franz Rosenzweig: His Life and Thought, ed. Nahum N. Glatzer (New York Schocken, 1961), 267.

63. Massimo Cacciari, Icone della Legge (Milano: Adelphi, 2002), 45.

64. Franz Rosenzweig, *The Star of Redemption*, trans. William W. Hallo (Chicago: Holt, Reinhart and Winston, 1971), 302.

65. Ibid. Translation modified.

66. Ibid. Rosenzweig evidently refers to the use, which was still widespread then, of Hebrew letters, even in the writing of Yiddish.

67. Ibid.

68. Franz Rosenzweig, "Classical and Modern Hebrew. Review of a Translation Into The Hebrew of Spinoza's *Ethics*," in *Franz Rosenzweig: His Life and Thought*, ed. Nahum N. Glatzer (New York Schocken, 1961), 266.

69. Ibid.

70. Franz Rosenzweig, *The Star of Redemption*, trans. William W. Hallo (Chicago: Holt, Reinhart and Winston, 1971), 302.

71. Gershom Scholem, "An einem denkwürdigen Tage" in *Judaica* (Frankfurt: Suhrkamp, 1968), 214–215.

72. Theodor W. Adorno, "On the Question: What Is German?," in *New German Critique*, no. 36 (1985).

73. Ibid., 125.

74. Ibid., 129.

75. Ibid., 126.

76. Ibid., 130.

77. Theodor W. Adorno, *Jargon of Authenticity*, trans. Knut Tarnowski and Frederic Will (Evanston: Northwestern University Press, 1973).

78. Theodor W. Adorno, "On the Question: What Is German?," 131.

79. Jacques Derrida, "Fichus: Frankfurt Address" in *Paper Machine*, trans. Rachel Bowlby (California: Stanford University Press, 2005), Adorno's position, however, is criticized by Derrida in *Monolingualism of the Other*, 85.

80. Jacques Derrida, "Fichus: Frankfurt Address" in *Paper Machine*, trans. Rachel Bowlby (California: Stanford University Press, 2005), 170.

81. Emmanuel Levinas, *Ethics and Infinity: Conversations with Philippe Nemo*, trans. R. A. Cohen. (Pittsburgh: Duquesne University Press, 1985), 24–25.

82. Emmanuel Lévinas, *Totality and Infinity—An Essay on Exteriority*, trans. Alphonso Lingis. (Pittsburgh, PA: Duquesne University Press, 1969), 305. See Jacques Derrida, *Sur parole. Instantanés philosophiques* (La tour d'Aigues: editions de l'aube, 1999), 65.

83. The interview, recorded for the series *Zur Person* on German station Two, was also awarded the Adolf Grimme prize and thus published later in the volume *Gespräche mit Hannah Arendt*, ed. Adelbert Reif (München: Piper, 1976).

84. Hannah Arendt, "What Remains? The Language Remains." A Conversation with Günter Gaus," 12.

85. Jacques Derrida, *Monolingualism of the Other; or, the Prosthesis of Origin*, 85.

86. In the course of the interview, recalling the first strong impressions during her return to Germany, Arendt again speaks of the German language and again in terms of affection and devotion: "Above all the experience of hearing people speaking German on the streets. For me, that was an indescribable joy." Hannah Arendt, "What Remains? The Language Remains." A Conversation with Günter Gaus," 15.

87. Ibid., 12.

88. Jacques Derrida, *Monolingualism of the Other; or, the Prosthesis of Origin*,

89. Hannah Arendt, "'What Remains? The Language Remains.' A Conversation with Günter Gaus," 13.

90. See Jacques Derrida, *Monolingualism of the Other; or, the Prosthesis of Origin*, 86.

91. Ibid.

92. Jacques Derrida, *Of Hospitality: Anne Dufourmantelle Invites Jacques Derrida to Respond*, trans. Rachel Bowlby (Stanford, CA: Stanford University Press, 2000), 89.

93. Jacques Derrida, *Monolingualism of the Other; or, the Prosthesis of Origin*, 87.

94. Jean Améry, *At the Mind's Limits*, 53.

95. On the jargon of the lagers, and on the language in the universe of the concentration camp, another important issue within the question of the German language's guilt, see Chapter VII § 9.

96. See Jacques Derrida, *Monolingualism of the Other; or, the Prosthesis of Origin*, 68.

97. Jacques Derrida, *Of Hospitality: Anne Dufourmantelle Invites Jacques Derrida to Respond*, 89.

98. Jacques Derrida, *Monolingualism of the Other; or, the Prosthesis of Origin*, 1.

99. Ibid., 2.

100. See ibid., 43.

101. See Abdelkebir Khatibi, *Du bilinguisme* (Paris: Denoël, 1985), 10.

102. Jacques Derrida, *Monolingualism of the Other; or, the Prosthesis of Origin*, 5.

103. This does not exclude that there can be a belonging to language *unto death*.

104. See Jacques Derrida, *Monolingualism of the Other; or, the Prosthesis of Origin*, 14. Derrida refers to Émile Benveniste, "L'hospitalité," in *Le vocabulaire des institutions indo-européennes* (Paris: Minuit, 1969), vol I, 87ff.

105. See Jacques Derrida, *Monolingualism of the Other; or, the Prosthesis of Origin*, 39.

106. See ibid., 23.

107. On this issue, see Chapter VII § 13.

108. See Hans-Georg Gadamer, *Hilde Domin, Dichterin der Rückkehr*, in id., *Gesammelte Werke 9: Ästhetik und Poetik II*, (Tübingen: Mohr (Siebeck) UTB, 1999), 323–328.

109. See here § 4.

110. Paul Celan, "To Speak" in *Snow Part*, trans. Ian Fairley (New York: The Sheep Meadow Press, 2007), 51.

111. This is moreover the "exile of the word" in the absolute silence of Auschwitz, as Neher understands it. See André Neher, *The Exile of the Word, from the Silence of the Bible to the Silence of Auschwitz* (Philadelphia: Jewish Publication Society of America, 1981).

112. Paul Celan, "To Speak" in *Snow Part*, trans. Ian Fairley (New York: The Sheep Meadow Press, 2007), 51.

113. Paul Celan, "And with the Book from Tarussa," in *Speech-Grille and Selected Poems* (New York: E.P. Dutton and Co, 1971), 207–209.

114. Paul Celan, "World to be stuttered after," in *Selected Poems and Prose of Paul Celan* (New York: W.W. Norton, 2001), 337.

115. Paul Celan, "To Speak" in *Snow Part*, trans. Ian Fairley (New York: The Sheep Meadow Press, 2007), 51.

116. See Chapter VII § 6.

117. Paul Celan, "Crowned Out," in *Selected Poems and Prose of Paul Celan* (New York: W.W. Norton, 2001), 191.

FIVE

THE DIALOGUE OF POETRY

Where there is no longer authentic dialogue,
Poetry no longer exists.

—Martin Buber[1]

1. PAUL CELAN AS A WITNESS TO HERMENEUTIC DIALOGUE

For hermeneutics, is there a place where one can live with the other as
the other of the other? Is there a place that will be dialogical *par excellence*,
where one becomes the other of the other? This place does exist, and it is
poetry. The affirmation sounds paradoxical. How can the model of dialogical
understanding, in which Gadamer locates the originary phenomenon of
language, accord with the singularity and uniqueness of the poetic text?
What could possibly link *dialogue* and *poetry*? Or will it be poetry perhaps
that reveals itself to be the infinite dialogue to which hermeneutics aspires?

Wer bin Ich und wer bist Du? (*Who am I and who are You?*)—this is
the title of the book that Gadamer dedicated to Paul Celan's collection
of poems *Atemkristall* (*Breathcrystal*), the first part of his 1967 *Atemwende*
(*Breathturn*).[2] Other essays were added to this book later on—a book that
Heidegger held in even higher esteem than *Truth and Method*—essays that
document the significance of Celan for Gadamer.[3]

From the beginning, Gadamer's hermeneutics is modeled on the
listening of poets such as Jean Paul and Hölderlin, Stefan George and Rainer
Maria Rilke. Yet the encounter with Celan takes on particular importance.
Gadamer mentions him along with Wittgenstein and Derrida as the most
significant names he encounters after the publication of *Truth and Method*.[4]
But he also mentions Celan in another context, namely, when he emphasizes
how the philosophical language of Hegel and the poetic language of Celan,
in their polarity, have enabled him to see the relation between philosophy

and poetry.[5] This theme is dealt with in the essay "Philosophy and Poetry,"[6] where the proximity of philosophy and poetry is to be found at a remove from everyday language. Such a proximity, in turn, divides itself in the two extremes of the word that sublates itself, and the word that stands firm in itself.

It is true that Gadamer's book on Celan has been widely criticized. And it is also true that the criticisms are, for the most part, justified. Gadamer does not place Celan within the Jewish tradition and, aside from sporadic allusions, he does not recognize Celan for what he is and who he wants to be, that is, the poet of the *Shoah*. Yet it is also true that Gadamer refrains from chaining Celan to this role and elects him as the witness to the hermeneutic dialogue, taking up the question of Celan's poetry: "Who am I and who are you?"

2. THE EVERYDAY WORD AND THE POETIC WORD

In order to understand the question "Who am I and who are you?," it is first of all necessary to return to the poetic word from which the question arises. Speaking is, for Gadamer, "the most deeply self-forgetful action," because when one speaks, one is so deeply "within the word" that one is not turned toward the word but, rather, to what one wants to say by the word.[7] This is the way of being of all linguistic behavior. Anyone can experience the forgetfulness of language when, all of a sudden, speech breaks down and one turns toward the word rather than to what one is saying; with this breakdown of speech, which recovers almost as a stuttering, the search for the "right word" begins.[8]

In everyday language the word does not stand for itself, rather, it does not "stand," but passes over into what is said, it disappears by evoking it. In poetic language, on the contrary, the word "stands in itself" (*steht in sich selbst*).[9] It does not pass over and does not withdraw itself in front of what it says, but remains unique, irreplaceable, and autonomous and, in its indissoluble intertwining of sound and meaning, articulates itself perfectly and completely. "The poetic word is thus a statement in that it bears witness to itself and does not admit anything that might verify it."[10] By means of an etymological trope, Gadamer has thus often emphasized the aspect of dictation (*Diktat*) in poetry (*Dichtung*).[11] The poetic word "fulfills itself" and, as such, it must to be taken "at its word."[12] Hence, the difficulty that the translation of poetry entails. Poetry is in fact language "in a preeminent sense."[13] Gadamer recalls an example offered by Valéry in order to clarify this: Whereas everyday language is like pocket change, poetic language is like gold coins whose face value is equal to melt value.[14] It does not merely refer to something else beyond and detached from itself; on the contrary, while deflecting attention from itself, it simultaneously points to itself. "In a similar way, the language of poetry is not a mere pointer that refers to something else, but, like the gold coin, is what it represents."[15]

3. POETIZING AND INTERPRETING

This is even more valid for the word of lyric poetry that Gadamer, along with Hegel,[16] privileges with respect to other artistic forms.[17] Both the extreme and paradigmatic case is represented by contemporary hermetic poetry, and in particular by the poetry of Celan. This poetry, knowingly situating itself at the margins of silence, is nonetheless a word that does not fall silent; rather, deriving from a sober, attentive, reflexive concentration on language, albeit between contrasts and dissonances, it maintains a semantic polyvalence thanks to a strong condensation of meaning. There is a "message" enclosed within the ciphered writing of this poetry. Celan himself speaks of a "message in a bottle," taking this example from the Russian poet Osip Mandelstam.[18] "A poem, as a manifestation of language and thus essentially dialogue, can be a message in a bottle, sent out in the—not always greatly hopeful—belief that somewhere and sometime it could wash up on land, on heartland perhaps."[19] Such a message is a message that is deciphered as if one were dealing with signs that have become almost illegible.

Deciphering, reading, and listening articulate the hermeneutic labor that gives voice to the sense enclosed within the written word. And it is by performing it faithfully, that is, by reading it word for word, syllable by syllable—if reading is allowing the text to speak, and is therefore already interpreting[20]—that one brings the message to its destination.

The proximity between poetizing and interpreting (*Dichten und Deuten*)[21] emerges here in Gadamer, and it also emerges in its specificity with regard to the proximity of poetizing and thinking (*Dichten and Denken*) in Heidegger. For hermeneutics, interpreting means putting oneself at the service of the poetic text. Interpretation does not introduce a sense foreign to the text, but puts in relief that which the text itself indicates. One can say that the interpretation of a poem is successful only as it fades completely into a new experience of the poem itself.[22]

Insofar as interpreting (*Deuten*) is brought back by Gadamer to its originary meaning of "indicating something" (*auf etwas deuten*), which is closely tied to "interpreting something" (*etwas deuten*), interpreting means to interpret an indicating (*ein Deuten deuten*), where this indicating is, in turn, an interpreting. Particularly eloquent in this sense is the poetic word, which, like a sign, points beyond itself; in its fullness, the poetic word is already the interpreting word. Thus, poetizing is always already present in interpreting; and, vice versa, an interpreting is always already present in poetizing.

Poetizing and interpreting are thus co-originary. It is hence the ambiguous fullness of language, where, unsurprisingly, both poetizing and interpreting come into themselves, which constitutes the link between the one and the other. Therefore, the interpreting word, interwoven with the poetic word, and thus in the same way as this poetic word, does not replace what it indicates, but merely points beyond itself, to what is other than itself. Both the one and the other consist precisely in this pointing beyond. "Neither the poet nor the interpreter possesses any special legitimation as such. Whenever we find ourselves in the presence of real poetry, it always transcends both poet and interpreter. Both of them pursue a meaning that points toward an open realm."[23]

4. "YOUR IRREFUTABLE WITNESS"

The poetizing of Celan is an interpreting because it is a poetry of poetry, a reflection on poetry that is at work in the poetry itself. The poet is a wayfarer who attempts to find a way within conventional language to open a crossing toward the "true word," which is beyond every syllable and every word. The poet is an angler who tries to fish it out "in rivers north of the future."[24] The poet is a pilgrim who, by gasping for air in the falling snow, finally achieves the "breath crystal"[25] (Atemkristall) that springs from that obstructed breath (Atem) of the one who finds himself short of breath and on the verge of that unsayable absurdity that he nonetheless wants to say.[26] Breathing turns itself around: The poetic word originates in this hushed instant between inhaling and exhaling, which condenses in the "breath crystal." For Celan, poetry is this "breathturn" (Atemwende).[27] Gadamer interprets it as the "silent, whisper-like transition and alternation of inhaling and exhaling, whereby the 'breath-crystal' of the poem emerges in pure form like a single snow-flake."[28] In this pure form, the word appears condensed and concentrated. It is the silent event of poetry that can be only perceived with an "inner ear."[29] But precisely because poetry is brought back to its originality, to the word of poetry, which is "ensilenced,"[30] it condenses itself and stands firmly in the breathing, in the vital breath, which we all share.

From its uniqueness, the poetic word elevates itself to universality. It is not Meingedicht, that is, a mendacious "poetry of mine," mendacious poetry—Celan was here thinking of Meineid, "perjury"—which in its inauthenticity bears false witness. It is not my poetry—and here it is impossible not to think of Mein Gedicht—which one can articulate as they please, and therefore is articulated in a hundred different languages, is "versi-colored," that is, closed in the particular subjectivity and thus monological, mine as much as a nullity (i.e., of nobody, a *Genicht*, a "non-verse," a *noetry*, a nothing of poetry). Poetry is rather *dein unumstößliches Zeugnis*, "your irrefutable witness."[31] And *your* witness is such because it comes from "the radiant wind of your voice," from the language of "you" that launches, or relaunches, the word, from that originary dialogical place of language that, despite its uniqueness, is universal because it is the place where language manifests itself. In its surging forth from the language of the you, poetry, which can testify universally, appears yet again as dialogue.

This allows Gadamer, who nonetheless safeguards the principle of fore-understanding, to claim an understanding void of particular information, that is, void of everything that directly concerns the poet. "No reader can understand without specialties, and yet every reader understands only when the specialty of the occasion is sublated by the universality of occasionality."[32] The interpretative difficulty of Celan's poetry indeed shows why the reader must necessarily recall his or her own experiences. Here the dialogue is set in motion. And this means understanding—or even not understanding—a poem. In the case of Celan and his poetry, understanding, as elsewhere and more than elsewhere, does not indicate a procedure but rather "the attitude of a person who wants to understand someone else."[33]

5. YOUR I AND MY THOU: THE UNIVERSALITY OF POETRY

This universality appears a lot more clearly within the dialogue opened up by poetry.[34] *Gedicht und Gespräch* (*Poem and Conversation*) is the title of a collection of essays in poetic hermeneutics that Gadamer published in 1990. In this collection, poetry is considered the place where the fundamental question issues forth: "Who am I and who are you?" The simplest response to this question would be that the "I" is that of the poet and the "you" is that of the reader.

But this is not so for Gadamer. The "I," although often understood as the poetic I, is nevertheless the "I-form" in which the I of the poet is understood, but also the I of each individual, that is, the I that speaks and addresses the word to the you.[35] The "you," in turn, is the "you-form" that listens to the word of the I, is the "privileged partner" of the poetic message, is the you of the I, which is turned toward God, to a lover, or to the you of one's own soul.[36] Even in the closest intimacy, the detachment between the I and the you becomes increasingly evident. Thus, the question "Who am I and who are you?" takes on a new significance.

First of all "I" and "you" are not distinct and defined once and for all. "I" and "you" are correlated because the one defines itself only in relation to the other and even takes the place of the other. Hence, the meaning of the statement: Because perhaps my I can take the place of your "I" and your you can take the place of my "you." "Take the place of" means taking on the form of the I or the you by recognizing and, in fact, identifying itself in it. The two poles of the I and the you remain open and this opening is the invitation to enter into a dialogue that the poem address to the reader. The invitation is confirmed in the possibility offered to the reader of taking up, from its perspective, both the role of the I as well as the you.

The I and the you of the dialogue opened up by poetry are in fact *absolutes*. The you is the You of the absolute interlocutor and the I is the absolute I of the poet. The I and You in their absoluteness translate the humanity of the I and you into a universal language. Thus, the poet gives voice to the destiny of everyone, to human destiny. As a reader, I can neither distinguish nor separate myself from the poet as speaker.[37] "These allow the reader to be the I that the poet is, because the poet is the I that we all are."[38]

Because the poetic word is a question, an interrogation, so too is it a "word of response," here, as in every dialogical word, there echoes that which is not expressly said, and there resounds the not yet said.[39] Therefore, the poetic word is always a word within the horizon of the unsaid, indeed within the horizon of the not-sayable and the unsayable.[40] This in no way puts into question the binding character of poetry that, in its irreplaceable uniqueness, "stands firmly in itself."[41]

The poetic word, as a "word of response," is that "right word" that, frantically sought after, offers shelter and dwelling to the you exiled in language.[42] And in the response of the you, to whom the word of the poet is addressed, the poet in turn finds a dwelling place "as his own listeners and readers."[43] For Celan, the paths of poetry open "a kind of homecoming."[44] For Gadamer, poetry, insofar as it discloses the opening of dialogue, is an invitation to make a home for oneself.[45] In our experience of fleeting temporal beings, the poetic word, in contrast to the everyday word, that simply passes, holds the fleeting of time in its *Da*, in its "there," so that it *stands*.[46] This means that in the poetic word *there is* (*ist da*) the proximity itself in which one can dwell, that is, "the poetic word that by being there bears witness to our own being."[47]

6. THE FLOW OF DIALOGUE AND THE CRYSTAL OF POETRY

Here the difference between poetry and dialogue should be seen. The poetic word, insofar as it withholds itself, lingers in itself, does not pass, nor does it take part in a process. On the contrary, dialogue appears as a process. Between these two modalities, in which something is given to be understood, there is an internal tension—as Gadamer notes—that goes beyond their already stressed affinity.[48]

All of our being stretches and unfolds between these two poles. If the prodigy of language is in the "maturation of meaning," such maturation nevertheless is realized differently in the flow of dialogue and in the crystal of poetry. It is as if from the same element, namely language, that two forms were produced: on the one hand, one that is fleeting and fluid, and on the other, one that is solid and crystalline.[49]

Precisely because it condenses in a crystalline form that stands firmly in itself, the word of poetry, in its fixity and repeatability, is "text" more than any other word. Instead, one cannot speak of a "text" in respect to the dialogue, made of absolutely unrepeatable questions and answers because dialogue occurs in a process that is ill-suited to be recorded and brought back to writing. Just like with poetry, here too there is no previous text about which one seeks understanding. On the contrary, it *pre-scribes* by dictating the text to which one will be asked to listen. Here however Gadamer recognizes a priority of writing over orality because all living speech is a more or less successful attempt to make the text of poetic dictation speak. Poetry and dialogue reveal themselves as opposing extremes. "Poetry acquires existence as 'literature' while dialogue lives on behalf of the instant."[50]

Nevertheless, there is maturation of meaning in both. And in both, "sense" indicates a "sense of orientation."[51] Both poetry and dialogue are forms of this orientation toward sense. Poetry reconciles and harmonizes everybody around its sense—no less than dialogue that, between diverging questions and answers, seeks out a sense that communalizes them. But, as with dialogue, so too in poetry there is no pregiven sense that should be brought to light; rather, there is only the indication of a sense that, as such, can never be definitively acquired. "Infinite poetry, infinite dialogue . . ."— it is almost a motto of the *Frühromantik*.

But poetry and dialogue are infinite, although yet again in a different manner. Poetry is infinite in the expressive word (*Aussage*) whose meaning, entrusted to the interpretation of the you, is vertically inexhaustible; dialogue is infinite in the word (*Wort*) that demands and solicits the possible response words (*Antworte*) in the horizontal *infinity* of the *Miteinandersprechen*, the speaking with one another.[52]

7. THE "SOUL'S REFRAIN"

As with every other speaker, more than every other speaker, the poet addresses the other. *Hörstdu*, "Hear!"—according to the suggestion of one of Celan's poems[53]—is that absolute vocative in which one must perhaps seek out the essence of poetry in its movement toward the you. But the I of the poet, addressing the you, asks nothing precise—it wants only to be heard. The poet does not ask, with his own word, for the counter-word of the other, in a dialectical process from which a shared word will emerge because that word belongs no more to the poet than it does to others. It is already—before, but at the same time beyond every dialectical process[54]— the word of both, which is already communal and communalizing, because it is poetic and therefore universal. Poetry is "the soul's refrain," indeed it is the refrain in which the I and the you, by coming to accord, discover that they are "the same soul."[55] But the soul's refrain is not a simple accordance on the basis of a sung text or a previously known melody. Rather, it is from the outset a going in unison (*Mitgehen*) with all of the song to which poetry appeals and that really reaches its fulfillment only in this song. Gadamer has in mind here a festive song that everyone sings together.[56]

Thus, poetry reveals itself to be originarily and constitutively dialogical. Buber had already observed that, precisely because poetry is always a word addressed to a you, "where there no longer is authentic dialogue, there would no longer be poetry."[57] And on the trail of Buber, even Celan writes: "Poetry wants to reach an Other, needs this Other, needs to be face to face [*Gegenüber*]. It seeks it out and turns to it."[58] And so one can rightly speak of a *dialogue of poetry*.

Indeed, poetry is the open place of infinite dialogue which hermeneutics seeks. To the question "Who am I and who are you?" poetry responds by keeping the question open.[59] It shows that this question does not allow for definitive answers and, on the contrary, as a question, already constitutes its own response. "How else can one define 'the other' in general?"[60] "Who am I and who are you?" is the question raised by the dialogue of poetry in which, following the greatest aspirations of hermeneutics, one can attempt to be *the other of the other*.

NOTES

1. Martin Buber, "Das Wort, das gesprochen wird," in *Wort un Wirklichkeit. Sechste folge des Jahrbuches Gestalt und Gedanke* (München: Oldenbourg, 1960), 17.

2. See Hans-Georg Gadamer, *Gadamer on Celan: "Who am I and Who are You?" and Other Essays*, trans. Richard Heinemann and Bruce Krajewski (Albany: State University of New York Press, 1997).

3. See Hans-Georg Gadamer, "Are the Poets Falling Silent?" and "Under the Shadow of Nihilism" in *Hans-Georg Gadamer on Education, Poetry, and History* (Albany: State University of New York Press, 1992), 73–82, 111–124; "Was muß der Leser wissen?" in *Gedicht und Gespräch* (Frankfurt: Insel, 1990), 115–122; see also "Meaning and Concealment in Paul Celan" and "A Phenomenological and Semantic Approach to Celan?" in *Gadamer On Celan*, 167–178, 179–188.

4. See Hans-Georg Gadamer, "Hermeneutics Tracking the Trace," in *The Gadamer Reader: A Bouquet of the Later Writings*, ed. Richard Palmer (Evanston: Northwestern University Press, 2006).

5. "Reflections on My Philosophical Journey" in *The Philosophy of Hans-Georg Gadamer*, Library of Living Philosophers, ed. Lewis E. Hahn (LaSalle, Ill: Open Court Press, 1997), 3–63.

6. See Hans-Georg Gadamer, "Philosophy and Poetry," in *The Relevance of the Beautiful and Other Essays*, ed. Robert Bernasconi (Cambridge: Cambridge University Press, 1986). Hans-Georg Gadamer, *Hegel's Dialectic*, trans. P. Christopher Smith (New Haven: Yale University Press, 1976), 96.

7. Hans-Georg Gadamer, "Language and Understanding," in *The Gadamer Reader: A Bouquet of the Later Writings*, ed. Richard Palmer (Evanston: Northwestern University Press, 2006). See more on this Chapter VI §7.

8. See Chapter I § 8.

9. Hans-Georg Gadamer, "On the Contribution of Poetry to the Search for Truth," in *The Relevance of the Beautiful and Other Essays*, ed. Robert Bernasconi (Cambridge: Cambridge University Press, 1986), 107. Translation modified. Hans-Georg Gadamer, "Zur Poetik und Hermeneutik: Lyrik als Paradigma der Moderne," *Gesammelte Werke 8: Ästhetik und Poetik I* (Tübingen: Mohr (Siebeck) UTB, 1999), 60.

10. Hans-Georg Gadamer, "On the Contribution of Poetry to the Search for Truth," 110.

11. Ibid. Hans-Georg Gadamer, "Philosophy and Literature," *Man and World: International Philosophical Review* 18 (1985). Hans Georg Gadamer, "Letter to Dallmayr," in *Dialogue and Deconstruction: The Gadamer-Derrida Encounter*, eds. Diane P. Michelfelder and Richard E. Palmer (Albany: State University of New York Press, 1989). On this point, see also Chapter VI, §15.

12. Hans-Georg Gadamer, "On the Contribution of Poetry to the Search for Truth" 107; Hans-Georg Gadamer, "Philosophy and Poetry," 139.

13. Hans-Georg Gadamer, "On the Contribution of Poetry to the Search for Truth," 106.

14. See Hans-Georg Gadamer, "Composition and Interpretation," in *The Relevance of the Beautiful and Other Essays*, ed. Robert Bernasconi (Cambridge: Cambridge University Press, 1986), 67; Gadamer, "Philosophy and Poetry," 132; Hans-Georg Gadamer, *Gedicht und Gespräch* (Frankfurt: Insel, 1990), 123.

15. Hans-Georg Gadamer, "Philosophy and Poetry," 133.

16. See G. W. F. Hegel, *Aesthetics: Lectures on Fine Art*, trans. T.M. Knox, II vols., vol. II (Oxford: Oxford Univeristy Press, 1975), 100–111, 111–128.

17. See Hans-Georg Gadamer, "Zur Poetik und Hermeneutik: Lyrik als Paradigma der Moderne," 58–69.

18. Mandelstam writes: "a seafarer throws into the ocean waves a sealed bottle, containing his name and an account of his fate. Many years later, wandering along the dunes, I find it in the sand, read the message, learn the date of the event and the last will of one now lost. I had the right to do so. I did not open someone else's mail. The message sealed in the bottle was addressed to the one who would find it. I found it. That means I really am its secret addressee." Osip Mandelstam, "On the Interlocutor" in *Selected Essays*, 234–235.

19. Paul Celan, "Speech on the Occasion of Receiving the Literature Prize of the Free Hanseatic City of Bremen," in *Selected Poems and Prose of Paul Celan* (New York: W.W. Norton, 2001), 396.

20. See Hans-Georg Gadamer, "The Eminent Text and Its Truth," in *The Horizon of Literature*, ed. Paul Hernadi (Lincoln: University of Nebraska Press, 1982), 337–347. Hans-Georg Gadamer, "Lesen ist wie Übersetzen," *Gesammelte Werke 8: Ästhetik und Poetik I* (Tübingen: Mohr (Siebeck) UTB, 1999), 279–285. See also "A Phenomenological and Semantic Approach to Celan?," 180.

21. See Hans-Georg Gadamer, "Composition and Interpretation," 66–73.

22. Hans-Georg Gadamer, *Gadamer on Celan: "Who am I and Who are You?" and Other Essays*, 165.

23. Hans-Georg Gadamer, "Composition and Interpretation," 72.

24. Paul Celan, "In Rivers," in *Selected Poems and Prose of Paul Celan* (New York: W.W. Norton, 2001), 227.

25. Paul Celan, "Eroded," in *Breathturn* (Los Angeles: Sun and Moon, 1995), 95.

26. Paul Celan, "The Meridian," in *Selected Poems and Prose of Paul Celan* (New York: W.W. Norton, 2001). See Chapter 7 §2.

27. See Ibid., 407.

28. Hans-Georg Gadamer, *Gadamer on Celan: "Who am I and Who are You?" and Other Essays*, 162.

29. Hans-Georg Gadamer, "Text and Interpretation," in *Dialogue and Deconstruction: The Gadamer-Derrida Encounter*, ed. Diane P. Michelfelder and Richard E. Palmer (Albany: State University of New York Press, 1989), 43.

30. Paul Celan, "Argumentum e Silentio," in *Selected Poems and Prose of Paul Celan* (New York: W.W. Norton, 2001), 78.

31. Hans-Georg Gadamer, *Gadamer on Celan: "Who am I and Who are You?" and Other Essays*, 123–126, 36–38. See Paul Celan, *Breathturn*, trans. Pierre Joris (Los Angeles: Sun and Moon, 1995).

32. Ibid., 134.

33. Ibid., 161. On this particular theme, see also Chapter VI.

34. On dialogue, see in particular Chapter VII, § 8.

35. See Hans-Georg Gadamer, *Gedicht und Gespräch*, 161.

36. See Hans-Georg Gadamer, *Gadamer on Celan: "Who am I and Who are You?" and Other Essays*, 134; Hans-Georg Gadamer, *Gedicht und Gespräch*, 102, 30.

37. See Hans-Georg Gadamer, *Gedicht und Gespräch*, 101.

38. Ibid., 130.

39. See Hans-Georg Gadamer, *Gadamer on Celan: "Who am I and Who are You?" and Other Essays*, 130.

40. See Hans-Georg Gadamer, *Gedicht und Gespräch*, 178.

41. "Poetry, whether it is epic, lyrical, or dramatic, has its proper eminence that we are in no position to question; in fact, it rather places us in question." Hans-Georg Gadamer, "Europa und die Oikoumene," in *Gesammelte Werke 10* (Tübingen: Mohr (Siebeck) UTB, 1999), 283.

42. See Hans-Georg Gadamer, *Gedicht und Gespräch*, 151–159; Hans-Georg Gadamer, "Heimat und Sprache," *Gesammelte Werke: Ästhetik und Poetik I* (Tübingen: Mohr (Siebeck) UTB, 1999), 366–372. On the issue of exile in language, see Chapter IV.

43. Hans-Georg Gadamer, *Gadamer on Celan: "Who am I and Who are You?" and Other Essays*, 129.

44. Paul Celan, "The Meridian," 412. On the impossibility of return in Celan, see Chapter VII.

45. Hans-Georg Gadamer, "Zu Poetik und Hermeneutik: Lyrik als Paradigma der Moderne," 66.

46. See also Chapter I §10.

47. Hans-Georg Gadamer, "On the Contribution of Poetry to the Search for Truth," 115.

48. See Hans-Georg Gadamer, *Gedicht und Gespräch*, 165–185.

49. See Ibid., 168.

50. Ibid., 171.

51. Ibid., 173.

52. See Hans-Georg Gadamer, "On the Truth of the Word," *Symposium* 2, no. 6 (2002): 115.

53. Paul Celan, "Ein Krieger" in *An den Toren, Gesammelte Werke*, eds. Beda Allemann and Stefan Reichert, with the collaboration of Rolf Bücher (Frankfurt: Suhrkamp, 1986) vol. III, 16.

54. Dialectic, if there is such a thing, is that of the I that passes to the you, and of the you that passes to the I in the open question "Who am I and who are you?"

55. Hans-Georg Gadamer, *Gedicht und Gespräch*, 57, 169, 80. Gadamer's reference here is to Stefan George's *Jahr der Seele*.

56. See Ibid., 169.

57. Martin Buber, "Das Wort, das gesprochen wird," 17.

58. Paul Celan, "The Meridian," 409. Translation modified.

59. See Hans-Georg Gadamer, *Gadamer on Celan: "Who am I and Who are You?" and Other Essays*, 70.

60. Hans-Georg Gadamer, "The Diversity of Europe: Inheritance and Future" in *Hans-Georg Gadamer on Education, Poetry, and History*, 233.

SIX

UNDERSTANDING

Between Hermeneutics and Deconstruction

Nobody means by a word precisely and exactly what another does, and the difference, be it ever so small, vibrates, like a ripple in water, throughout the entire language. Thus all understanding is always at the same time not-understanding, all assent in thought and feeling is at the same time a dissent.

—Wilhelm von Humboldt[1]

1. PARIS 1981: AN "IMPROBABLE DEBATE"

The first encounter between Gadamer and Derrida took place between April 25 and 27, 1981, during a conference organized by the Goethe Institute in Paris. The aim was that of a public debate. Participants and witnesses of the event, however, are almost unanimous in considering it a dialogue between the deaf. The proceedings, later published in France, Germany, and Italy, seem to confirm this fact.[2] The key phrase to define this debate is the one used by the French editor Philippe Forget, who referred to it as an "improbable debate,"[3]

And yet the debate was an epoch-making one. The American edition, entitled *Dialogue and Deconstruction. The Gadamer–Derrida Encounter*, which followed in 1989, added new contributions from philosophers in both camps, who, if, on the one hand, still called it as an "improbable debate," on the other, attempted to extend the virtual exchange between the two philosophers.[4]

In the years after their Parisian encounter, Gadamer welcomed the challenge put forward by Derrida and sought to clarify his own position in various essays. It is worth mentioning here the following essays: "Destruktion and Deconstruction" (1985), "Hermeneutics and Logocentrism" (1987), "Letter to Dallmayr" (1988), and "Hermeneutics Tracking the Trace" (1994).[5] In this way, Gadamer shows how seriously he took that debate and, above all, how he valued and appreciated the French philosopher. It is not by chance he will point to Derrida as one of the most important figures he got to know after the publication of *Truth and Method*. Gadamer writes:

> Back in the 1960s, when I had finished up my own project in philosophical hermeneutics and offered it to the public, I paused to take a look at the world around me. At that time, two important things struck me, in addition to the works of the later Wittgenstein. The first of these was that I met the poet Paul Celan, in whose late works I began to immerse myself. The other was the fact that Derrida's essay, *"Ousia et Grammè,"* published in the *Festschrift for Beaufret*, came into my hands, followed later by the several important books that Derrida published in 1967 which I immediately began to study.[6]

In turn, Derrida engaged Gadamer's hermeneutics only on occasion and almost only in order to underscore their respective differences.[7]

The two philosophers met again in Heidelberg, at the beginning of February 1988, in order to discuss the theme "Heidegger and Politics;"[8] and on Capri, from February 28 to March 1, 1994, on the occasion of a conference dedicated to the theme of "Religion."[9] These encounters, however, were of little relevance to the debate between hermeneutics and deconstruction.

But on February 15, 2003, Jacques Derrida, the great provocateur of French thought, the "marrano" of philosophy, and the anarchist of deconstruction, returned to Heidelberg, a year after Gadamer's passing, to honor the founder of philosophical hermeneutics and the most famous and influential German philosopher of recent decades. This was more than just a commemoration. Derrida's talk had a meaningful and programmatic title: "Rams: The Uninterrupted Dialogue Between Two Infinites, the Poem."[10] *Dialogue, Gespräch*, is an unfamiliar word in the French philosopher's lexicon, as if it came from a foreign language, but even more so, as if it came from the language of an other. Derrida, who had always avoided using the word dialogue, now welcomed and showed hospitality to it as the word of the other, of the friend who is no longer. The word became a testimony of admiration and affection. But it also heralded a new and unforeseen interpretation. Was that "improbable debate," in Derrida's memory, a "dialogue"? Moreover, was it "uninterrupted"? Was it uninterrupted even though it began with that strange interruption in Paris, or precisely thanks to that interruption or caesura? And what do the "two infinites" mean? And the "rams"? And what does the "poem" point to in the distance?

2. HERMENEUTICS AND DECONSTRUCTION: WHICH DIFFERENCE?

The question concerning the difference between hermeneutics and deconstruction, which exploded in contemporary debate, is a legitimate question since they are philosophies that have grown from common soil.[11] Both have pursued the way opened up by Heidegger's philosophical turn. Both refer to another philosopher whose presence, in both thinkers, is still little discussed, namely Hegel. Both, albeit via different paths, go back to Greek philosophy and continually confront it—a trait that is not at all obvious in the contemporary landscape. The historico-philosophical proximity, and therefore also the philosophico-theoretical proximity, is reflected in the themes they share. It is enough to think of the importance of art, and above all of literature and poetry.

The proximity is such that doubts have been raised as to the possibility of singling out two different positions behind the names "hermeneutics" and "deconstruction."[12] Is one perhaps confronted with two labels for the same philosophical item? If this were the case, the comparison would make little sense—and one cannot exclude that it appears this way from an external perspective, for example, from the perspective of analytic philosophy. But the question is far more complex. The two main currents in contemporary European philosophy, although so close that they could be considered as two aspects of the same project, represent divergent philosophical options and therefore require their divergence to be shown and their difference, and the import of their difference, to be evaluated. The protagonists themselves, pointing to this difference, or merely letting it be glimpsed, outlining nonetheless their own position in relation to the other's, have in this way confirmed the legitimacy and, at the same time, the need for this comparison. But neither of the two has delved into confrontation. Indeed, the dialogue was interrupted from the start. Nevertheless, despite the interruption and the unclarified difference, or maybe just because of it, this dialogue has animated contemporary philosophy. The question, raised within the American context in the 1980s, remains relevant today: How hermeneutic is deconstruction, and how deconstructive is hermeneutics?[13]

One of the reasons why the confrontation between hermeneutics and deconstruction continues today can be seen in the *question of understanding*. Among the various threads of the "improbable debate," unraveled by Forget, it is the question of understanding that offers the guiding thread to reconstruct it in what is perhaps its more interesting aspects. This also makes it possible to avoid the broader question of the relation between hermeneutics *and* deconstruction. It is possible, however, that understanding sheds light on that very "and," which is interpreted in the most diverse, and at times opposed, ways.

The question of understanding initially finds an extreme, and in many ways misleading, formulation. From Gadamer's introductory lecture, Derrida extrapolated the words: "good will to understand," which in fact recur only once.[14] These are the very words that give the debate its starting point. Derrida attacks Gadamer, accusing hermeneutics of being a "metaphysics of the will."[15] The accusation is also repeated by others and always on the basis of those single words. And yet no one explains the role that this "good" would play in philosophical hermeneutics. No one explains, which is even worse, how understanding grounds itself in good will. And, in effect, hermeneutics has never derived understanding from good will. The one who accuses hermeneutics of this fails to do justice to its way of discussing the question of understanding, and instead merely takes a slogan as its starting point and does not shift from there.[16] Hence, the accusation seems to be used as a pretext. In its simplicity, the accusation can be easily synthesized: for hermeneutics, or, one should say, even for hermeneutics, understanding is an appropriation of the other. Deconstruction places itself on the opposite side. But despite all the difficulties that Gadamer could still have with the language of metaphysics, in *Truth and Method* he puts it clearly: "*when one understands in general, one understands differently.*"[17] This is, moreover, the position that Gadamer also makes explicit in the later essays and. in particular, in his dialogue with the poetry of Celan.[18]

Nevertheless, it is not important whether the accusation crumbles or not. It is important that, through this accusation, the debate has been deflected, also and especially from the questions posed by Derrida, the most philosophically pertinent of which is not that of "good will," but rather that of "interruption." Derrida's memorial lecture confirms this. If one stops at the first question, one ends up losing sight of the difference between hermeneutics and deconstruction, which lies not in the good will to understand, but in understanding itself, in the manner of understanding it from the *unity* of the *uninterrupted dialogue* or from the *difference* of *interruption*. More than in the discussion of other themes, such as the proverbial opposition between dialogue and writing, it is in tackling the question of understanding that one can illuminate the distance, but also the proximity, between the two philosophies. Thus, it is precisely in understanding that the *unity* from which hermeneutics moves and the *difference* from which deconstruction moves are clearly outlined.

3. DERRIDA AND HERMENEUTICS:
PLAIDOYER FOR INTERRUPTION

When Gadamer delivered his introductory lecture in Paris entitled *Le défi herméneutique* (*The Hermeneutic Challenge*), later published under the title *Text and Interpretation*, he had in mind also Derrida's deconstruction of texts. Undoubtedly, he also aimed at it. Focused on the question of understanding, which is here immediately related to hermeneutics and its claim to universality, Gadamer's essay briefly goes through the stages of philosophical hermeneutics up to the revival of Greek dialectic that leads to recognizing in dialogue, particularly in its Socratic form, the originary phenomenon of language and thus the locus *par excellence* of hermeneutics. Ever since the linguistic turn in the twentieth century and the role taken by language, the inescapable interworld that discloses the access to the world, the question of the universality of hermeneutics has been put to the test on the basis of the concepts of "text" and "interpretation." Both terms have achieved universal extension. Nevertheless, hermeneutics favors one over the other: If interpretation is "to bestow sense," the text constitutes itself in relation to interpretation by presenting itself as "that which has to be understood." Yet, faced with the multiplicity of possible interpretations, the text is what stands and subsists (*dasteht*) in its givenness.[19] This givenness, however, is not fixed. And for hermeneutics the text is not a "final product," but rather always only the "intermediate product"[20] of the communicative event, insofar as "everything that is fixed in writing refers back to what was originally said."[21] The text is destined to be read, and thus heard and understood—and this corresponds in German to the same word *gehört*. The interpreter's listening to the text is therefore a sort of written dialogue that ultimately refers to the living dialogue, to the authentic and originary dialogue in which it is possible to let the text "speak" again by establishing its "meaningful identity,"[22] Not even the "eminent texts" of literature, which are almost "written in the soul," are an exception; if they are "on the way to writing," they have been first and foremost on the way to reading. More than others, they need to be read and listened to, although only with the "inner ear"; they need one to dialogue intimately with them. Even in such a case, the text exists only insofar as we, by interpreting it, return to it. But the difference and eminence with respect to other texts consists in this: It is not necessary to let them speak, because eminent texts speak for themselves. This means that the literary text, and in particular the poetic text, does not fade away like every other text, but rather *stands*, and in this standing acquires a "full *self-presence*."[23] Thus, the literary text, by not referring back to an originary linguistic act, *pre-scribes* every linguistic act and every repetition, assuming however that there is no word that can fulfill the prescription of a poetic text.

Even in the nonirrelevant affinities, the concept of "text" seems to mark the watershed that separates hermeneutics from French philosophy in general, and from deconstruction in particular. Gadamer is aware of this and he says it explicitly.[24] Yet, this does not prevent him from affirming the primacy of speech over writing, it does not prevent him from speaking of a "task of understanding," which must be fulfilled "without interruption," "by integrating" the "right meaning" in view of an "adequate understanding" that is realizable only where one can replicate, clarify, and defend its own *lógos*, namely, in dialogue. It is as if Derrida's reflections as a whole are to be either attacked directly or completely overlooked. To this one must add the undeniable and frequent stylistic lapses into the "language of metaphysics"— the proof of which is already present in the above quotations—which are too numerous to list here.[25] All of this would have sounded to Derrida's ear like an unpleasant provocation. The highpoint is the passage that causes the debate to explode:

> In the written dialogue one appeals to the same fundamental con-
> dition which is also valid for the oral exchange: in both cases *the
> good will to understand one another* is present. Thus, whenever one
> tries to understand one another, *good will* is present.[26]

Hence, it is not surprising that the day after Derrida replied with a talk formulated in three brief, and equally provocative, questions that attempted to strike, beyond the theses defended by Gadamer in his lecture, at herme-neutics as a whole. The three questions converge on one aim, as the title of Derrida's talk suggests: *Good Will to Power*.[27] Behind hermeneutics's effort to understand the other, behind its "appeal to good will," behind its striving toward "consensus," a "will to power" lay hidden, which had to be unmasked.

And hence the first question that starts the debate is posited, the inaugural one on the "good will," The moment Gadamer resorts to the "good will to understand each other," Derrida catches him in the act. In this recourse to good will, Derrida sees the symptom, the sign, or rather the proof of an obsolete metaphysics, and he does it through a clamorous gesture that equates Gadamer's "good will" with Kant's notion of "good will." The will to understand, which precedes every concrete interaction between speakers, when looked at more closely, exhibits the features of an ethical axiom that lies rather at the beginning of ethics. This axiom brings good will into accord with Kantian "dignity," that is, with what in the human being is beyond any comparison and thus beyond any scale of values. In fact, for Kant there is nothing in the world that could be considered "good" without qualification except the "good will" that, by abstracting from the effects that it can bring about, is "good in itself."[28] This is, as Kant himself writes, the idea of the "absolute value" of the will.[29] But does not the "good will to understand," axiomatic and unconditioned like Kant's "good will," therefore appear to be that "willing subjectivity" that is prepared, according to Heidegger's accusation, to determine and dominate Being? And does not hermeneutics thereby fall back into the "metaphysics of will"? Furthermore, does not hermeneutics reveal that it still belongs to the epochs of metaphysics?

The "good will" seems to test hermeneutics severly there where, coming into contact with psychoanalysis, it claims to integrate it. In this respect, Derrida asks his second question—what would the "good will" be for psychoanalysis? Does it not constitute here a difficulty? And is psychoanalysis not a limit situation, nevertheless paradigmatic, of the withdrawing or the weakening of good will, and therefore of the failure from the start of that "living dialogue" that is the focal point of Gadamer's argumentation? Habermas had already pointed out a problematic boundary in psychoanalysis by raising serious doubts about the possibility of integrating it into a general hermeneutics.[30] In turn, Derrida raises the same doubts, but by pointing the finger at the expansion of the interpretative context proposed by Gadamer, which appears insufficient when faced with the demands of psychoanalytic discourse. The latter instead makes the context explode and requires, if anything, a "discontinuous re-structuring" or even a "rupture," thereby referring to an interpretation of the Nietzschean type.[31]

The third and final question revolves around the concept of "interruption," which is perhaps the more philosophically complex one, certainly the decisive question.[32] Here Derrida's target is what Gadamer calls Verstehen, "understanding the other," "understanding each other." Whether one starts out from understanding or misunderstanding, one must ask, however, if the condition for understanding, far from being the unlimited readiness to dialogue that hermeneutics solicits, far from being the continuity of the relation with the other, is not rather "the interruption," the rupture [rupture] of the relation, a certain rapport of interruption, the suspension of all mediation."[33]

This last question seems to delineate what appears to be a genuine alternative to hermeneutics. Rupture, interruption, the absence or the suspension of all mediation, non-mediation in the process of understanding, is not only accepted, but is welcomed favorably. It is this acknowledgment, the "agreement" in the dialogue of which Gadamer speaks when referring to an experience that should be familiar to everyone, which the inexorable suspicion of deconstruction targets. How does one know that one is really experiencing agreement? Incidentally, is this not a relapse into metaphysics, where metaphysics had always claimed to describe experience as such? So how does one know that one is coming to an agreement? But above all, how does one know that agreement would be preferable to disagreement, continuity to rupture, understanding to not-understanding? Is not this harmony perhaps an illusion, as disagreeable as it is risky, against which one should protect oneself? And rather than leading to harmony and agreement, should not dialogue, including dialogue as the reading of a text, preserve the difference of opinions and respect the other in its inappropriable alterity, the other which therefore escapes exhaustive and accomplished understanding? And finally, should not dialogue safeguard the disagreement, the interruption, and the not-understanding? It is this impossibility to understand which deconstruction wants to take up.

4. GADAMER AND DECONSTRUCTION: ". . . AT THE BEGINNING OF A DIALOGUE"

Gadamer responds to Derrida's three questions with an equally brief lecture entitled "Nevertheless: The Power of Good Will."[34] By means of the classical argument used against the skeptics, albeit revised from a phenomenological perspective, Gadamer first of all attempts to make the contradictory nature of his interlocutor's position emerge: "I am finding it difficult to understand these questions that have been addressed to me. But I will make an effort, as anybody would do who wants to understand another person or be understood by the other."[35] This effort, however, has nothing to do with the epochs of metaphysics. Nor even less can it be brought back to the Kantian concept of the "good will." The reply to the first question is actually relatively simple: It is not Kant, but Plato, who is the philosopher to whom Gadamer refers. The "good will" is nothing but a translation of what Plato, in the *Gorgias*, calls *euméneis élenchoi*. Gadamer here takes up the position that Socrates already assumed toward the sophist Gorgias, declaring himself to belong to those who "willingly let themselves be refuted when they say anything untrue and willingly refute when somebody else says anything untrue, and who anyway let themselves be refuted not less willingly as they love to confute."[36] This principle, which, as is well known, constitutes the principle *par excellence* of hermeneutics, is summed up effectively by Gadamer in a later work: "One must seek to understand the other, and that means that one has to believe that one could be in the wrong."[37] Yet this principle is not an ethical injunction, insofar as even "immoral beings try to understand one another."[38] Rather, it is a "pure ascertaining," as Gadamer observes.[39] To clarify its nature, one could say that it is a phenomenological ascertaining that permits the passage from "originary knowledge"—in the Husserlian sense—to the reflexive knowledge of the speaker, or one could also say, from *bekannt* to *erkannt* in Hegel. This principle is thus the result of a reflection that is born out of the daily *praxis* of speaking and understanding.

Yet how could Derrida not "agree" [*zustimmt*]?[40] Derrida's questions bear witness to this. And asking them would be a waste of time if he did not count on the effort on the part of his interlocutor to understand them. Derrida, but also Nietzsche, who is called into question by the French philosopher, here wrong themselves.[41] An important point, overlooked in the critical debate surrounding this encounter, is the question, raised by Gadamer, of *Zustimmung*, of agreement. Even prior to "consent," *Zustimmung* means "assent." The one who speaks, and speaks always and inevitably in a determinate historical language, gives his own assent to that which is "shared" [*Mitgeteiltes*] and can thus be "reciprocally communicated" [*Miteinandergeteiltes*], readying himself, even though unaware of it, to attune his own voice [*Stimme*] to the voice of the speakers of that language, already starting from the utterance of meaningful sounds. This is the phenomenon of "collocution."[42] In short, the one who speaks a language underwrites a sort of tacit pact with past, present, and future speakers of that language, articulating its own self in the meaningful sounds, and therefore in the words, of that language which, before being one's own, always already belongs to others.[43] One's speaking is thus a "mutual accord" [*Übereinkommen*].[44] To denote this tacit or implicit agreement, which precedes every explicit agreement, Plato speaks of *homología* and Aristotle of *synthéke*.[45] The passage from implicit agreement [*Einverständnis*] to that which is explicit in understanding [*Verstehen*] is extremely complex and destined to be always transformed into disagreement because of the individual difference at work in speaking.[46] On this Gadamer is certainly under no illusions. And already classical hermeneutics takes its start from the question of not-understanding and of misunderstanding. On the other hand, the apparent concordances, misunderstandings, and unsuccessful interpretations, originate already in the meanings of the words and, if they can be loosened from and dissolved in the sense of the sentences, they can also be rendered more acute, intense, and profound. Thus, for Gadamer, who in this respect "agrees" with Derrida, understanding does not take place without fractures, breaches, and interruptions [*ein bruchloses Verstehen*]. The *Bruch*, the *rupture*, the fracture and the interruption, constitute the understanding that, if it were deprived of it, would be taken for granted and obvious [*selbstverständlich*] and would not even constitute a problem.[47] The psychoanalytic dialogue, which in comparison to hermeneutic dialogue has its own special status for Gadamer, is a further and extreme witness of this *rupture* because it aims to understand not what the speaker wants to say, but, rather, what he does not want to say.[48]

Hence, the difference between the two philosophers does not lie in the *rupture* and the necessity of the *rupture*. Where then should it to be sought? Already in this short text, Gadamer gives invaluable hints. Interruption cannot be considered by hermeneutics as something fundamental and originary. Before interruption exists the tacit agreement that in language, or better, in speaking a language, is the *prelude* that opens the way to every successive play of agreement and disagreement. And the prelude of the language exists, because one has already spoken and dialogued, walking together long stretches of road disclosed by language. It is impossible to escape the prelude in which dialogue articulates itself. Thus, for hermeneutics, the interruption, the rupture, inscribes itself in the constellation of language. It is the difference that cleaves the unity. It is in the context of the latter that one must see *in nuce* all "solidarity among humans."[49] Here hermeneutics shows its proximity to ideology critique.[50] But its further distance from deconstruction emerges in the manner of taking up interruption and of carrying it on. Even where interruption is most marked, the fracture deeper, the conflict stronger, as in the work of art, and above all in the poetic text, as Heidegger had already seen, hermeneutics accepts the conflict, but does not reinforce it, as well as not deepening the fracture.[51] Rather, the *Bruch*, the interruption, marks for hermeneutics the start of engagement and dialogue and does not bring it to a conclusion. This fracture will never be mended and not-understanding will never be eliminated. Here hermeneutics and deconstruction converge. But even if it knows this, because it experiences it every time in the limits of the dialogue, hermeneutics disposes itself to what alone could lead it to a full understanding between two infinites, and, starting from interruption, is destined to an infinite dialogue.[52]

Moreover, this is the position that Gadamer also adopts in the encounter with Derrida. In an essay written a year after their encounter in Paris, Gadamer writes: "Whoever wants me to take deconstruction to heart and insists on difference, stands at the beginning of a dialogue, not at its end."[53]

5. ON THE LANGUAGE OF METAPHYSICS AND ON LANGUAGE IN GENERAL

The dialogue was interrupted here and many questions were held over. Derrida returns to this suspension in his memorial lecture, yet this does not keep him from pointing out, in the years following the Parisian encounter, the aspects of hermeneutics that need criticizing, namely its points of contact with the metaphysical tradition. The accusation, however, which is not altogether veiled, is also echoed in Derrida's final talk in Paris, which is entitled *Interpréter les signatures (Nietzsche/Heidegger): Deux questions.*[54] The polemic here is the interpretation that Heidegger gives of Nietzsche, who considers him to be the last metaphysician. When Nietzsche says that everything is "will to power," in making a general affirmation, he esoterically turns this doctrine, which is not a doctrine, against all metaphysical ontologies. Heidegger, instead, in his work on Nietzsche, takes this doctrine at face value and as a doctrine truly up-held by Nietzsche. Nevertheless, he underestimates how problematic the concept of "doctrine" is for Nietzsche, but also how problematic it is to speak in general terms. Once again, it is writing, and the name, or names, which deconstruct metaphysics. Thus Heidegger's attempt, which identifies the unity of a doctrine with the name *Nietzsche*, is metaphysical in its presuppositions. Instead, Nietzsche's writing is a fragmentary writing that disseminates itself in a plurality of signatures and names, is a plural writing which, in its endless masks, escapes from the power of the *lógos* by deforming it.[55] On the contrary, Heidegger's position, which questions Being and the *sense* of Being, by claiming to seize and hold it by means of *lógos*, is logocentric and, by default, so too is Gadamer's position.[56]

In the essays dedicated to his engagement with deconstruction, Gadamer takes up again the observations, the objections, and the questions posed in Paris and tries, by continuing to answer them, to clarify his own position. At the same time, he also attempts to single out both the points of contrast and affinity between hermeneutics and deconstruction. Even though the picture that Gadamer paints is fragmentary and dispersive, the brushstrokes excessively shaded and tenuous, there is one question that stands forth as a guiding thread. What does "metaphysics" mean? Or better, what does the "language of metaphysics" mean?

The answer allows Gadamer to distance himself not only from Derrida, but also from Heidegger, and ultimately from Nietzsche. It is a way, perhaps a detour, toward giving a more defined profile to hermeneutics. The distancing already concerns the keyword overcoming (*Überwindung*) or recovery (*Verwindung*) that guides Heidegger's conception of metaphysics. Gadamer's position does not "coincide" with Heidegger's.[57] And Gadamer's doubts are such that he reconsiders the critique of Greek ontology in terms of presence or "simple presence" (*Vorhandenheit*), of *présence*. Hence, Gadamer asks, "can the concept of metaphysics be applied to Plato at all?"[58] But the question of metaphysics deepens and appears more acute in Heidegger— in line with his linguistic turn; it becomes the question of "the language of metaphysics." Because one is fatally imprisoned in this language, one is also a prisoner of metaphysics and its tradition. Even before Heidegger and Derrida, the question already looms large in Nietzsche. From the start, Gadamer clearly distanced himself from this question. "There is no language of metaphysics. There is always only one's own language where conceptual formations of the metaphysical tradition live on in various metamorphoses and stratifications."[59] In fact, what would a "language of metaphysics" be? Gadamer's suspicion does not involve the constitutive role of language in thinking, and therefore also in the formation of philosophical concepts.

Rather, it is directed against the hypothesis that a philosophical language exists separated from the language of life. "I have not been able to follow Heidegger, or anybody else, when they speak of the 'language of metaphysics,' the 'right language of philosophy,' or the like. Language, for me, is always simply that which we speak with others and to others."[60] This does not mean that there is no consolidated tradition of metaphysical thought—and perhaps to this one can give the name "metaphysics"—which is however characterized simply by linguistic and conceptual fixity. Solidified in a sort of terminology, philosophical concepts impose themselves in their rigidity.[61] *Metaphysics is this rigidity*. But one cannot extend this rigidity to concepts as such. One can realize this by taking them back to the living language from which they have sprung and making them speak. Moreover, this is possible—Gadamer observes by recalling Wittgenstein—because linguistic use always forms itself in the life of language, and thinking in concepts always presents undefined contours.[62] In order to make them speak, it is necessary to free them from that rigidity. But what else can Heidegger's *Destruktion* and Derrida's deconstruction do? What is dismantled and deconstructed is the conceptuality of metaphysics. Thus, Gadamer indicates two ways, perhaps only one path, that in the wake of Heidegger's attempts to leave the language of metaphysics behind, could lead us out into the open: the way of hermeneutics, which returns from dialectic to dialogue, and the way of deconstruction that, starting from *écriture*, brings about the laceration of metaphysics.[63]

The position that Gadamer takes up in the face of metaphysics and the language of metaphysics also allows him to shed light on the question of the relation between language *and* metaphysics. Because the case of metaphysics is just a particular case, the position of hermeneutics in respect to language in general is thus clarified. Metaphysics is not inside of language, or, put otherwise, language is not the bearer of metaphysics, that is, it is not responsible for, or even guilty, of metaphysical thinking. Metaphysical is what one thinks in language, or better in a language; what is contained in a language is not metaphysical. This is the case insofar as what is contained and thought in a language can always be thought and re-thought differently in speaking. Language is at the same time a "limit" but also a "bridge."[64] If it were not so, we would be prisoners of language, imprisoned in a "Roman columbarium."[65] And Nietzsche would be right: Language would be a power that dominates the individual, even his speech, in a tragic opposition, with no way out. Language would be nothing other than this power. For hermeneutics, this is not the case. And this is not the case already in Humboldt and Schleiermacher. In language, they see the condition for the individual's freedom and in the relation between language and speaker, even in the tension that characterizes it, and rather because of this tension, they catch sight of a dialogue, even the model of a dialogue, which occurs each time and continues thanks to the individuality of speech and, thus, thanks to the difference of the not-understanding that remains beyond every understanding. The space that hermeneutics grants to individuality in language is vast, but not as vast as that which it grants to foreignness. And although it claims that between one's own language and the other's language only "a more and a less"[66] subsists, a difference only quantitative and not qualitative; although it interprets speech as a self-translating in the language that is always the language of the other, it is still tacitly pervaded by the idea that one's own language is one's own, and the foreign language foreign. It is deconstruction that radicalizes the question and brings out the foreignness at the core of one's own language. The trace of writing is the ultimate way to split language by means of difference.[67]

6. THE BEING-FOR-THE-OTHER OF LANGUAGE

If one opens one's mouth, if one writes a letter, or if one taps the keys on a computer, it is because one wants to be understood, unless one has something to hide, something that should be kept from foreign ears and eyes, something to dissimulate. The fact that one *wants* to be understood has no connection with the voluntarism of a metaphysics of the will. Rather it finds justification in language itself, because that which characterizes language is its *being-for-the-other*. When one speaks, one speaks *for* others; when one writes, one writes *for* others. "To speak means to speak to someone."[68] Language is not only the manifest form, but also the first and primary form in which the alterity of the self, its *being for the other*, comes to light with clarity. This is what Hegel emphasizes in the *Phenomenology of Spirit*. Language "is the *real existence* of the pure self as self; in speech, self-consciousness, *qua independent separate individuality*, comes as such into existence, so that it exists *for others*."[69]

This moving out of oneself is the process of *estrangement* that is at the root of speaking. In speaking, one goes out of oneself in the moment that one articulates one's own self in a language that belongs to others—in the *language of the others*. The language that I speak *as if* it were my language is always already the language of the other. The going out of oneself, which occurs in language and through language, is therefore a *translating* of one's own self into the other, into the foreigner, that is, in the foreignness of the language of others. But in this way, while I speak and translate myself into the other of the language of the other, the language of the other also becomes mine. And this translating takes place in the foreign language as in the mother tongue. On the other hand, already because of its *being-for-the-other*, the language is never really *only* mine, yours, his, hers, or ours. Language forbids ownership.[70] And it is always only *common*. Moving from this community, which—still following Hegel—is not an abstract community, but is rather, insofar as it is linguistic, a *concrete* community, it is possible to clarify not only the being-for-the-other of speaking, but also the being-for-the-other of understanding.

Speaking and understanding are reciprocally linked; one recalls the other. Understanding is no less *linguistic* than speaking. It always refers to language, or to a language, or better still, to speaking. Hermeneutics has always insisted on the fundamental *Sprachgebundenheit* of understanding, on the bond that ties understanding to the universal medium of language, thinking that it is therefore indispensable to ask the question of understanding from the question of language and from within it.[71] The fact that one speaks, both to the other and for the other, is the concrete condition of understanding. And, vice versa, the fact that one understands the other is the concrete condition of speaking. Just as understanding constantly points back to speaking, so too does speaking constantly point back to understanding, mainly because one cannot speak without having understood and without understanding what one is saying.

The reciprocity between speaking and understanding, however, requires an even more effective reciprocity between speaker and listener. There is here an interchangeability of roles. Everyone is ready to take on the role of the other. Every speaker is a potential listener, and every listener a potential speaker. However tacitly, this reciprocity is felt, recognized, and ultimately presupposed by every speaker. The one who speaks always presupposes the one who welcomes and understands one's speaking. From a phenomenological point of view, one can say with Merleau-Ponty: "When I speak or when I understand, I experience the presence of the other in myself or of myself in the other."[72] Language is always, and constitutively, *for the other*, even if the other does not understand what is said. In effect, one does not know, nor is it possible to know, if the other understands. But when one speaks, one presupposes the faculty of speaking and understanding in the other—one recognizes the *other* not only as a *you*, but also as a potential *I*. However, this tacit recognition *of the other I* in the *you* that the *I* has in front of itself when speaking, is the place where language fulfills itself each and every time. It is, according to Humboldt, the *Urtypus*, the "prototype of language."[73]

7. WANTING TO SAY AND WANTING TO UNDERSTAND

Wanting to understand refers to wanting to say, and in this reference, which is a reciprocal reference, it assumes a value that cannot be reduced to subjective "will." Gadamer's counter-argument in Paris could have had a misleading effect by displacing the discourse from the level of phenomenological description—"whoever opens his mouth wants to be understood . . ."— where it takes its start, to that of a reflexive intentionality with reference to the *euméneis élenchoi*.[74]

But in *wanting to understand*, as in *wanting to say*, there is no intentionality of a subject in such "wanting." This is because intentionality, in the sense of a deliberate reflection, is absent in language. The one who speaks, speaks in an irreflexive manner. It is the phenomenon of *Sprachvergessenheit*, of the forgetfulness of language. "Speaking is the most deeply self-forgetful action."[75] Irreflexivity characterizes the attitude of the speaker and distinguishes him, for example, from the reflexive and thus forced and artificial attitude of the linguist who reflects and meditates *on* language. "An even abyssal self-forgetfulness belongs to the essence of language."[76] Therefore, a phenomenology of the word, spoken and written, should consider this irreflexivity and indeed takes its start from the forgetfulness of language that permits every movement *in* language. In order for this movement to be easy, it must forget language; if it does not forget it, it is no longer easy and begins to trip up, just like a child learning its mother tongue or an adult learning a foreign language—but also like the poet who cannot find the "right word." These limit situations are powerful precisely because they point to an *intentionality* directed toward language that is absent in everyday speech. But this does not mean that in everyday speech there is no *intending*. The distinction, subtle but unavoidable, is clearly seen by Jaspers who opposes to the "absence of intentionality" of language that intending which is "the fundamental phenomenon of language."[77] To such an end, he refers to Husserl who, in the *Logical Investigations*, in order to characterize the linguistic expression in respect to the indicative sign, writes that the linguistic expression "is more than a mere phonetic complex. It means something, and in so far as it means something, it relates to what is objective."[78]

But the intending in everyday speech is the intending of the one who is so much within the word that he is no longer turned toward the word, but rather toward that which the word intends, that which the word means, and that which the word wants to say.[79] It is first of all the word that wants to say, the word that means. Only in a *meta*linguistic intercalating does one stop to ask: "What do you mean?" But it is precisely the pause—of the question and of the response: "I mean . . ."—that spells out the reflexive moment in the irreflexive flow of speaking that entrusts the intending to the speaking subject. This happens because the latter, in the everydayness of speech, gives itself over to the word and to what the word means. One can then ask—through an unexpected move, but perhaps not completely unpredictable—what is meant here by "giving oneself over"?

This can be clarified by the affinity between language and play, which is the point of convergence between Gadamer and Wittgenstein.[80] The one who plays gives himself over to the game—and does so seriously, separating from himself, and forgetting himself. This loss of self-possession is nonetheless lived as an elevation. The one who plays, subjecting himself to the game, recovers from his own subjectivity that he must now abandon. By giving oneself over to the game, one at the same time recovers from the Western malady of subjectivism. Thus, the "recovery" evokes here Heidegger's *Verwindung*. The game is then that movement that undermines from the ground up, unhinges, and puts at stake the metaphysics of subjectivity.

What holds for the game also holds for language, which, not by chance, has indicated within philosophy the way to recover from metaphysics. In the language game, all subjectivity and the transcendental intentionality of the speaker are dismissed. To speak and to understand, the movements of dialogue, are "structurally similar" to those of the game.[81] Gadamer finds this affinity in the *medial* character.[82] Already emergent in art, this character sheds light on the active and yet undergone process of the language game, medial indeed as the form of the middle voice in Greek that indicates an activity in which the subject is implicated in such a way as to stray into passivity. As the title of one of Gadamer's works suggests, *understanding is a game*—it is a medial game.[83] One who understands is at play: one gives oneself over to the game and is put into play by the game.

Here one can get a sense of the distance from a metaphysics of subjective will. It is the passage through the game and, in a sense closer to Wittgenstein than Heidegger, through the language game, that offers the possibility of recovering from metaphysics—or at least that promises such a possibility. More than "subjective will" (*Wille*) one should speak then of a "non will" (*Unwille*) of subjectivity, of a renunciation of subjective identity, of a sought after dissolution of the achieved ipseity that is no longer the subject of this willing. It is not such a subject, because it already gives itself over to the word that wants to say and to that which the word wants to say.

More than a *wanting to say*, that of the speaker is a *letting oneself be said* from what the word wants to say. But does not there occur here also a form of domination, even if it is that of the word? Are there not still evident traces of a metaphysics of the will in the wanting to say of the word? Could not this giving oneself over to the wanting to say of the word be a relapse into metaphysics? After all, in whose name, on whose behalf, and by whose will, does one speak? Should not one opt rather for the word that "does not want to say anything?"

In order to respond to these questions, it is worth following Derrida's critique of Husserl and his distinction between indication and expression. In contrast to indication, expression intends, or rather signifies. Derrida proposes to translate *bedeuten* with "wanting to say" (*"vouloir-dire"*), used indifferently for the speaking subject who, expressing himself, wants to say and for an expression that wants to say.[84] But the expression, the emergence of a sense that lies within, the hyper-metaphysical aspiration of Western metaphysics, finds its ground in the subject that animates it. The expression is a decisive, conscious, voluntary, and intentional exteriorization, only thanks to the intention of the subject. This intentionality, concerned with remaining "pure" in its intention, with keeping itself separated from the involuntary effectuality of the indication, is one and the same with the will that aims at saying-itself, which wants-to-say-itself while retaining its presence to itself.[85] Here is the *télos* of language: the wanting to say of the willing and intentional consciousness. But can this *télos* be achieved? Evidently not, since the "lived," the "within," of everyone, cannot be present to the other immediately and originarily, but only as mediately indicated by signs. "The relation to the other as nonpresence is therefore the impurity of expression."[86] This irreducible and definitive limit also signals intentional communication.

Therefore, the saying of this originary *"wanting to say,"* which is intentional and pure, does not reach its destination. It is at this point that, with Derrida, the question of an "other" saying arises. Yet this other saying cannot be that of the word that "does not want to say anything," because this word is a non-word or, better, it is not a word. The alternative, then, is no longer a wanting to say. It is rather accepting a saying in the way in which the word says, and lets oneself be said by the saying of the word, giving one's own wanting to say over to the wanting to say of the word. This also involves accepting its mistaken intention and destination, its wandering without origin and without return. Thus, the exit reveals itself as an exile. But it is only in this exile, in this infinite deferral of the word, that one can still say, that one can still want to say. One's own wanting to say, however, giving itself over to the wanting to say of the wandering word, gives itself over to the wanting to say of others, or better declines itself to the saying of others, conjugates itself with this saying of the other that can perhaps be the "other" saying.

The "wanting" of wanting to understand, because of the reciprocity that binds them, mirrors the "wanting" of wanting to say. In daily praxis, one hears in the "I want to say . . ." the echo of the "I want to understand . . .," the "I would really like to understand . . .," the "help me understand . . .," or the "you don't understand me . . .," Wanting to say and wanting to understand expose the speculative character of language, attest to the aversion of speakers to that limit of the said and the understood, and reveal the common will, one declined to the other, to overcome it every time, one for the other, one with the other.

Wanting to understand, then, does not mean that understanding is possible—absolutely and unconditionally. It means rather that understanding—in an irreflexive and unconscious manner—is thought to be possible and is presupposed as a condition by the speakers. If it were not for this condition, even in its finitude and individuality, one would not even be able to continue speaking, that is to understand and make oneself understood. Wanting to understand is the condition that has to be absolutely presupposed as the condition for speaking.

But this in no way implies that, at a certain point in this process, one achieves true understanding, one that is adequate and hence definitive. If this were so, understanding would have an end and would come to an end. It would end up with a truth that would transcend the process itself and the individuals who are the protagonists in it, a supra-individual truth that would put aside and eliminate individuality, possibly that of the other well before one's own. To understand would then consist in appropriating the alterity of the other—for love of the truth. In this case, Nietzsche would not be wrong.

8. *"COMPRENDRE C'EST ÉGALER"*? ON NIETZSCHE

In its traditional acceptation, "understanding" means making the other one's own—what is strange, foreign, foreigner. The movement of understanding has been the movement of appropriation *par excellence*. The logo-, ethno- and Eurocentric product of such appropriation, which took place under the banner of violence and forgetting, under the banner of the erasure of the trace of difference, is the "white mythology": the Western *lógos* that, by forgetting and concealing the metaphorical and mythological origin, the *mýthos* of its own idiom, passes itself off as universal Reason.[87]

As is well known, Nietzsche has narrated this "fable" in a deconstructive genealogy by overturning the relation between truth and error; truth is redescribed as a *"kind of error."*[88] The decisive step is that through which Nietzsche goes back from concept to metaphor in order to show that every concept has its origin in a metaphor. Moreover, only through the forgetting and cancellation of its metaphorical origin can it pass itself off as a concept. Hence, its incompleteness, imperfection, provisional character, that is, its becoming takes on the predicate of Platonic Being. This is possible because, whereas metaphor holds difference alongside identity, the concept eliminates difference, closes itself off in identity, and exhibits it as true. "Every concept arises from the equation of unequal things."[89] The famous example is that of the leaf. No leaf is perfectly *equal* with any other leaf. The concept of "leaf" is formed by forgetting the unequal, by letting individual differences fall away. With an ontological hypostatization, metaphysics makes the "leaf," beyond leaves, the model and the cause of leaves, which is called *leaf*.

What is valid for the truth of the concept is also valid for the truth of understanding. In both cases, it is, according to Nietzsche, a matter of illusions whose illusory character have been forgotten; in both cases it is a matter of rendering *equal* that which is *unequal*. It would therefore make sense to say "*comprendre c'est égaler*," understanding is a rendering equal by eliminating individual differences.[90] It is no wonder then that a striking individuality such as Nietzsche's feels there is "something offensive" about being understood.[91] Understanding is here an offense. But it is so because, according to a conceptual schema of understanding, it is an offense moved against the other in its ineffable individuality. If this is so, who would ever want to be understood? It is better to remain not-understood—all the more so because to the offense moved against individuality there is added the intent, which is not too hard to unmask, of becoming "*Herr*," of becoming masters.[92] What would appropriating (the other) be if not dominating (the other) under the banner of the one, absolute, irrefutable truth (i.e., one's own)? The offense is legitimated by power. The "will to understand," underhandedly insinuated as "good will," reveals itself as nothing other than "will to power."[93] Rather than being an end in itself, understanding becomes a means for power. To escape this will to power, by escaping understanding and by choosing to be misunderstood or not-understood, is in turn a defensive power play. One responds to power with power and rebuts power with power.

Therefore, it becomes legitimate to speak of the injustice of understanding, of wanting to understand, and above all of having to understand the other, insofar as understanding is indeed "*égaler*." If understanding is this appropriating understanding, which wants to affirm itself as true and appropriate, how would it be possible not to appear unjust? Would it therefore be just to not understand and, vice versa, to not be understood? For Nietzsche, if anything, it would be just *to misunderstand* and *to be misunderstood*.

Starting from the conceptualization of understanding, his words, according to which it is preferable to be "misunderstood" (*mißverstanden*) than "not understood" (*unverstanden*), take on significance.[94] Not understood and understood are the two sides of the same coin. In both cases, whether one claims to understand the other by making the other equal to oneself, or whether one lets the other be completely other than oneself, in its almost inorganic incomprehensibility, one feels the "coldness" that offends. Hence, the necessity of *misunderstanding* which, in respect to that indifferent coldness, enables the play of the different. Misunderstanding can shed light on the difficulty of understanding (*Verstehen*) that has always been taken for granted (*selbstverständlich*).

To the two-thousand-year-old paradigm of understanding *equally*, Nietzsche thus opposes that of understanding *differently*. It is the revenge of the individual, and of its individuality, against the all-engulfing egalitarianism of power. The revenge consists not only in taking the individual away from the concept, in which it would disappear through the process of making the unequal equal, but also and above all in placing the individual before the concept, in preferring the individual to it. Such a preference is given moreover in the understanding that is now finally an understanding differently, starting from the alterity of the individual. Even though the individual, however, is made commensurable and, in its turn, makes the other commensurable, it is supposed and presupposed in its incommensurability.

Understanding differently—or metaphorically—can occur on "good days" when one renounces interpretation in order to "grant his friends abundant play-space [Spielraum] for misunderstanding."[95] The "good days" are those when one's own, appropriating "will to power" fades, which for Nietzsche is expressed in the interpretation, without "the faith in being" taken over—since there are "only interpretations" and not "facts."[96] Understanding differently means here to understand without interpreting. Just because one gives up understanding the other, that is interpreting the other, then by making its "personal" individuality emerge in its inevitable difference, one understands it—and one is understood. In this way, one leaves free play (Spiel) to its own, other and different, understanding of itself and of the other. This play-space (Spielraum), which is not open to everyone, but in fact only to friends, is not offensive because it does not claim to say what the other is in a judgment. This would signify the reduction of the other to that which appears and to nothing other. The play would become serious and would no longer be play because the subject, who has had "good days" by playing down its own subjectivity, having considered the stakes, would get the upper hand. The aesthetic opacity of the person would fade away in the logical transparency of apophantic judgment. Yet "good days" are as rare as friends; bad days are much more frequent and with them there emerges the risk of egalitarian understanding or of not-understanding. Misunderstanding, that is, letting the other and the different understanding of the other be, is thus a limit case.[97]

The radicality with which Nietzsche defends individuality, even against interpretation, by proposing an understanding "without interpretation," collides however with the metaphysical idea of understanding that, although not tacit, always still functions through conceptual schemes.[98] In such a context, understanding (Verstehen) means conceiving (Begreifen), that is, leading the individual back to the universal concept, reducing it to universal identity. But the problem here is the universal. Nietzsche seems to stop at the opposition between the universal and the individual (i.e., at difference). This is not surprising if one reflects on Nietzsche's conception of language and on the antithesis, which is outlined in it, between the power of language and the creativity of the individual, an antithesis that assumes the features of an insoluble conflict—without mediations. Either the individual offers resistance to the universality of language, or succumbs to it and is overtaken, *aufgehoben*, taken out or eliminated.

But the linguistic universal is a universal that can never be elevated above the speaking of individuals and that, on the contrary, is realized only in this individual speech. It is not a supra-individual universal, but rather a universal that is always *interindividual* and therefore also *individual*, which occurs and can occur only in its being *inter-*, *between* individuals, that is, in their *dia*logue. It is language that therefore suggests a new way of understanding the "universal" that, by opening up a pathway beyond the metaphysical concept of the universal, reveals itself as an *interindividual universal*. Linguistic community, in the interindividual universality that distinguishes it, by clarifying the possibility of understanding also from the theoretical point of view, along with the possibility of misunderstanding and not-understanding, indicates also a new and different way of understanding, that is, of *understanding differently*.

9. UNDERSTANDING IS UNDERSTANDING DIFFERENTLY

The *question of understanding* constitutes the nucleus of hermeneutics and its history. Although it is understood and interpreted in the most various ways that show, together with its possibility of self-differentiating, its internal complexity, this question remains the point of orientation for diverse and diverging hermeneutic positions.[99] Philosophical hermeneutics is no exception. therefore, it continues to center on the nucleus of such a question that, thanks to the distance taken both from classical hermeneutics and from the existential analytic, is nonetheless posed in a new way. Classical hermeneutics starts from the *prius* of *not-understanding* and *misunderstanding* in order to direct itself toward understanding, and thus sees the hermeneutic task in the passage from the one to the other[100]; Heidegger's existential analytic overturns the premises by indicating the *prius* of *understanding* that, far from being a state of privation, is the originary phenomenon from which not-understanding and misunderstanding are produced as derivative phenomena.[101]

Philosophical hermeneutics, which inherits Heidegger's assumption, according to which understanding is always already given, is, from the outset, engaged in posing the question of understanding from the starting point of understanding. This has provoked, it should be said, many misunderstandings, the majority of which point the finger at the *furor* of understanding that would allegedly animate hermeneutics, and at its so-called conciliatory intent.[102] The wanting-to-understand has been interpreted as further proof of this. It is as if philosophical hermeneutics would claim that it can and must understand in a better way and, finally, that it can and must reconcile and harmonize. It is as if understanding (*Verstehen*) were obvious and taken for granted (*selbstverständlich*). But, if this were so, hermeneutics would have no motivations to exist. And if it exists, it is because it raises the philosophical question of understanding.

The place where understanding, in its immemoriality, is always already given, is for Gadamer that of self-understanding. In such a way, every understanding (*Verstehen*) is self-understanding (*Sichverstehen*).[103] More precisely put, every understanding refers back primarily to a self-understanding—the place where one always already understands. But the distinction at stake here is that between already understanding and not yet understanding. Thus, self-understanding does not actually mean understanding the *self*, because there is not an *autós* here that excludes a *héteron*.[104] On the contrary, already starting from the self-understanding, understanding can no longer separate the self from the other. Understanding is understanding the self and the other *at the same time*. Because the understanding of the self can articulate itself only through the understanding of the other. If it were not so, the self-understanding would fall away into the fixity of the auto-understanding from which it could not get out. Self-understanding, by revealing itself as the understanding of the already understood, while avoiding the insurmountable passage from not-understanding to understanding, necessarily welcomes the other *in itself* from the start. That which is already understood has the other, the strange, in itself no less than what is not yet understood. There is a more and a less, rather than an absolute break. For hermeneutics, difference is always a relative difference, that is, a difference that relates itself to the previous unity of understanding and that takes place starting from understanding. Different, that is, strange, means not-understandable.[105] Difference, brought out into the open, inscribes a "collision" that sets the process of understanding into motion. In this sense, understanding, in its unity, thanks to such a difference shows from the start its dynamism by unfolding itself circularly. This is the movement of the hermeneutic circle as it is delineated in the constellation of understanding: When it returns every time to the already understood, it must again take leave of it. For in the "interactive play" (*Ineinanderspiel*) between the understood and the one who understands, that which is understood, no less than the one who understands, modifies itself and turns out to be different in the very act of understanding.[106] Thus, taking leave distinguishes understanding. And the happening of understanding is a continual modifying and self-modifying, or better, differentiating and self-differentiating—though without end and thus endless. Hence, Gadamer's famous sentence: "It is enough to say that *when one understands in general, one understands differently* [*anders*]."[107]

Through the act of taking leave, which distinguishes understanding, a *suum esse conservare* does not belong to it. In modifying and differentiating itself, understanding is always other and always in an other; in itself it is understanding differently. Thus understanding, no less than speaking, is a continual going into exile, expatriation, and emigration. Therefore, even the self of the subject is destined to exile. That is to say, what modifies and differentiates itself is not only that which is understood and, as it is understood, it does not and cannot remain identical. Understanding does not happen differently on the identical and immovable basis of the subject. "Subjectivity," Gadamer writes, "is just a fragmentary mirror."[108] Insofar as it understands, the subject puts itself into play as such. It is for this reason that, with regard to the subject who understands, I have spoken here of a "non will," an *Unwille*—which in German means both "not wanting," but also "unwilling" and "annoyance"—that is, of a renunciation of subjective identity.[109] Understanding does not mean that the subject quantitatively augments and accumulates its own knowledge; rather, the subject knows, and even before that understands, in a different way each and every time. In this understanding differently, it finds itself to be always different, not the same, namely something universal, it understands itself as an individual. Therefore, it understands itself always differently. The differentiating of understanding strikes the self of the subject all the more. Here emerges indeed its renunciation to the point of the dissolution of its own ipseity. Thus self-understanding is not auto-understanding, it is not affirmation and reaffirmation of the self, but is, on the contrary, the self-abandonment almost to the point of sacrifice. In this sense, Hegel speaks of a complete "sacrifice" (*Aufopferung*) "akin to death."[110] One understands when one renounces the self, when one dies as self. Hence, understanding appears to be intimately connected with death. The effort, the exertion of understanding—when, for example, Gadamer says: "I *will make an effort* . . ."—is here in this affective dimension of suffering, pain, and mourning. It is the affective dimension of *finitude*. What exhausts and engages in understanding bears this finitude, that is, this being always finite and hence the indefiniteness of what one understands. Understanding means then putting all understanding at stake, renouncing what remains after every understanding, not only and not so much of the other, as of the self. In understanding, the self is asked to be always other, and therefore not to conserve itself. But it is also the self who no longer wants to conserve itself in that apparent identity, which nevertheless exhibits its finitude clearly, the self prefers a nonidentity that allows it to constantly overcome itself in the difference of being other. Understanding, as understanding differently, is thus the way of freedom that is disclosed to the self beyond its finitude.

Freedom constitutes an unavoidable moment within understanding differently, starting from the play-space that under the star of every new understanding is granted to everyone. The *Spielraum*, in the sense indicated by Nietzsche, is that space, that margin of freedom that makes it possible to understand the self and the other differently. Freedom granted to any individual, as individual, for understanding differently, is a freedom not only in relation to that which is understood, and to the self as the always different subject of understanding, but also and above all in relation to other individuals. In fact, by speaking and understanding everyone grants to the other, even if tacitly, this freedom to *understand oneself*. And in this way everyone understands each other. This means that, even relying on and giving themselves over to the always different understanding, individuals always find a common point that is sufficient to orient themselves toward one another—one *for* the other, one *with* the other. In the space of understanding differently, a difference is opened up, which is first of all a difference between an individual and the other; thus every individual, who articulates his or her own individuality through understanding, will not only be for the other one among others. In the freedom of their understanding differently, individuals are not indifferently substitutable. Rather, and moreover, in their reciprocal dependence they are one for the other, one with the other. The different ways in which the other understands puts the self and its understanding into play; provoking it, colliding with it, and irritating it, it forces it to understand in a yet again different way. But the collision is also a push. Therefore, the other's understanding in its difference can be irritating but also liberating. It can suddenly disclose the open space of freedom beyond the finitude that is ultimately the anguish and the distress of not-understanding and misunderstanding. Freedom is here then not only and not so much a freedom toward the other, as a freedom through the other. But because of this, freedom, while it is disclosed, is also and at the same time limited.[111] The limit is the other in its difference and its understanding differently. Difference is thus the margin, the play-space, where freedom fulfills itself in understanding.

Being free to understand differently does not mean being free to not understand. In other words: One cannot escape understanding. This suggests also that one cannot even escape the difference that understanding carries with it. One seldom reflects on how much in this life understanding creeps in, gets into, and imposes itself, soliciting and demanding an understanding, be it involuntary or voluntary, fleeting, rapid, hasty or attentive, deep, meditative.[112] Examples are innumerable: a billboard, a red stoplight, the sound of a foreign word, the sight of a pleasant face, the letters of a book on display in the window of an antique dealer's. In all of these examples, one is already involved in understanding that pushes us to continue the game, to understand more, even if differently.

Yet for hermeneutics, at the beginning there is always an understanding that comes to be articulated and differentiated in the movement of dialogue. Understanding (*Verstehen*), which is initially taken for granted (*selbstverständlich*), is the accord (*Einverständnis*) of the language, of the common language that communalizes. As Wittgenstein says, however, understanding in language and with language is not a concordance in the meanings of words, and therefore in the definitions, but rather a concordance in judgments.[113] Nevertheless, it is in judgments or, better, in the sentences of individual speech that individuality makes its way by understanding, modifying, and differentiating. The more one articulates individuality, the more one marks the difference, the more discordance breaks forth in the commonality of language, which modifies itself in its identity, which is otherwise only provisional. The meanings that seemed immediately understood lose their immediate understandability through "judgments" and vice versa. Thus, every time one stops to ascertain the supposed agreement, one also needs to ascertain disagreement, and every time that one searches for agreement in order to continue speaking, one is unavoidably thrown back on disagreement.

10. ON ACCORD AND DISCORD

If language occurs in the openness of a historical language, and in this is fulfilled as speaking, speaking *for* the other and speaking *with* the other, then *the being-there of language is in dialogue*.[114] Hölderlin's poem—"since we have been a dialogue . . ."—has to be interpreted in a radical sense.[115] Not only are we always already in dialogue and speak from that infinite flow, in that infinite flow. Moreover: we are dialogue. Dialogue is the hermeneutic universe in which we breathe, in which we live. The reality of language is in the pneuma that unites I and you, is in the we.[116] Starting from the we, the foreignness between the I and the you cannot be absolute. The common we, which brings us together in language, limits the foreignness. But the common we, which brings us together, is the *we of the common word* that precedes every I and every you.

Presupposing communality in speaking and understanding is a trait that already distinguishes classical hermeneutics, where the reflection on communality is indissoluble from that on language. Communality, for Schleiermacher, must be brought back to the "communality of language."[117] For the spoken word also belongs well to the one who listens and, in turn, utters it. Thus, Humboldt writes that the word is potentialized when "the self-coined word is echoed from a stranger's mouth."[118] In short, and once again, language is the property of no one. In order to clarify this, it is necessary to quote a passage of Rosenzweig: "The word does not remain at all the ownership of the one who utters it; the one to whom it is addressed, the one who hears it, the one who takes it up, they are all co-owners; the foretokens of the word regard the latter, as and even to a further extent than what was experienced by the one who uttered it in origin."[119] The co-ownership or communality *of the word* is the condition of speaking and understanding. This means that the one who speaks, speaks for the other and with the other, even if tacitly, has already convened to share this co-ownership; although unknowingly, has already reached an accord with the other even before with himself. Here lies the political dimension of the linguistic community. The word, already communal at the beginning of the dialogue, becomes increasingly communal in the course of the dialogue.

It is in this sense that Gadamer's words are to be understood when he recalls—in a way not altogether different from Schleiermacher—the unity of a "shared language," affirming that "understanding one another first of all means coming to agreement" and that *"agreement is more originary than disagreement."*[120] This is far from unsophisticated optimism. In line with the hermeneutic understanding of language, there is here the idea that speaking is articulating the previous communality that the shared language guarantees. The communality is that of the orientation of the world articulated in a language. Speaking-with-others is hence not the place of confrontation or of the exchange of already formed opinions. On the contrary, moving from the communality of a language, and of the world articulated in language, the shared thinking constitutes itself in shared speaking. And this previous *communality* develops further because in speaking one further renders communal that of which one speaks. This is the reality of human *communication*, that is, of dialogue. "The commonality between the partners is so very strong that the point is no longer the fact that I think this and you think that, but rather it involves *the shared interpretation of the world which makes moral and social solidarity possible."*[121]

In order to seek agreement one needs to continue speaking. The unlimited availability for dialogue, which characterizes hermeneutics, is motivated by the trust placed in language and in its capacity to *communalize*. But this does not mean that dialogue succeeds. On the contrary, agreement is never guaranteed and understanding is never fully accomplished. Dialogue can never succeed, if succeeding is understood as concluding itself, closing itself off in a tacit, definitive accord. Dialogue is never closed. This does not mean that, putting aside its potential infinity, dialogue does not have a successful unity. This happens not when one has learned something new, but rather when one encounters in the other something that, in one's experience of the world, one has not yet encountered. This something that remains in us, changes and modifies us. "Dialogue possesses a transformative power."[122] Hence, dialogue succeeds when the I is modified through the you, but also when the you is modified through the I. "Genuine dialogue transforms the viewpoint of both."[123] Paradoxically, the more dialogue succeeds, the less it closes itself off, that is, the more disagreement reemerges. It does not close itself off if the word that the I addresses to the you and that the you addresses to the I leads to a new openness from which, through new questions and new answers, the dialogue can continue.[124]

Every word discloses an *infinity* of further possible words.[125] Because there is always still another word to say or to let be said. Every word, thanks to its virtuality, tacitly points back to the openness in which one continues to speak. Thus, speaking proceeds in dialogue. Hence, it follows that dialogue "*has an inner infinity or has no end.*"[126] Even in that limit case that is the soul's inner dialogue with itself, for Gadamer *dialogue is infinite*.[127]

Yet the flow of dialogue can be interrupted by a word that breaks the agreement and produces disagreement and it is the moment of misunderstanding and not-understanding. Regarding this experience, Gadamer speaks of a "collision" (*Anstoß*).[128] The foreign, which is such because it is incomprehensible, because it surprises, provokes wonder, disconcerts, and irritates. The Greeks called it *átopon* in the sense that it disorients and dislocates because it does find a place within the usual schema of experience.[129] Suddenly, the apparent familiarity with which one moves in a language and with the other in a language is impaired. The presupposition of the communality of words and the sharing of their meanings becomes problematic. This does not rule out resorting to repeated interpretations in order to search again for the agreement—without excluding disagreement and "the renunciation of shared meaning."[130] Here understanding becomes a *task*. Wanting to understand intervenes in the flow of understanding, starting from the incomprehensibility of the *átopon*; but it is a wanting to understand that, however *reflexive*, reflects the unreflected wanting to understand that corresponds and is specular to the wanting to say. It is then, as Schleiermacher says, a question of "degree" (*Abstufung*).[131] Wanting to understand, then, takes the previous difference between the one who speaks and the one who understands at its word, without claiming to overcome it.

Nevertheless, starting from the infinity of dialogue, the interruption that is produced does not prejudice the infinite openness of the dialogue for hermeneutics. The interruption is indeed only momentary; it is a suspension that is already a prelude to the resumption of the dialogue. Here the dissonance between deconstruction and hermeneutics must be grasped: If deconstruction stresses the creativity of *interruption*, hermeneutics, over and above every interruption, invokes the *uninterrupted* dialogue.

11. HEIDELBERG 2003: STARTING FROM THAT INTERRUPTION

In Heidelberg, Derrida again takes his start from the dialogue that was interrupted in Paris, from that interruption, from that "strange caesura" that seems to have marked the "improbable debate."[132] But why prolong a debate that has already been interrupted? And furthermore, why continue a debate that was almost unanimously considered "improbable"? Perhaps one should revise such a judgment, above all within the new constellation that takes shape in philosophy after Gadamer? This is the question, which more than any other, echoes in the words of Derrida.

The interruption is evoked by beginning again from the third and final question put to Gadamer, the one about the rupture, "the interruption of rapport, a certain rapport of interruption, the suspension of all mediation."[133] Thus Derrida starts again from that singular beginning that was and is the interruption. It was not an "originary misunderstanding," as some interpreted it.[134] Rather, it was "a sort of prohibition," the "inhibition of a suspension," and "the patience of indefinite expectation, of an *epochē* that made one hold one's breath, withhold judgment or conclusion."[135] Thence began the dialogue that was destined to be an *interior* dialogue, to continue within both of them, perhaps without words, and without voice, silent and seemingly mute. This destiny has not, therefore, decreed its failure. The testimony is also in the voices of those philosophers who have taken on the burden of continuing it. Yet the interruption, more than impeding it, has actually permitted and favored it. Both Gadamer and Derrida cultivated the dialogue in themselves, saving the "hidden meaning" of that interruption, and did it uninterruptedly. Interruption, as Derrida had understood it at that time, has revealed itself to be "the condition of comprehension and understanding."[136] The secret of that dialogue has been the *Unheimlichkeit*: a singular uncanniness tied to an intimate familiarity. And that dialogue still remains *unheimlich*. Therefore, far from having been an unsuccessful dialogue, it "succeeded" much more "than if it had been a harmonious and consensual dialogue," leaving "an active and provocative trace," promising a more to come.[137]

12. "THE WORLD IS GONE . . .": DIALOGUE AFTER DEATH

But Gadamer, the philosopher of an epoch of many upheavals, is no longer.[138] The timeless melancholy, already felt in Paris, is now infinitely aggravated by death. "A jamais."[139] And this A jamais re-echoes the *Adieu* that Derrida dedicated to Levinas in 1996.[140] The melancholy is also the sad and overwhelming certainty that one day death will separate us, that one day one of two friends will watch the other die. "The dialogue, virtual though it may be, will forever be wounded by an ultimate interruption."[141] It is in front of this ultimate interruption that Derrida found himself; the first interruption simply preceded and anticipated it, enveloping everyone in the mourning of a relentless future. But this final interruption is a separation unlike any other: the separation between life and death. Without an end, thinking will endlessly seek to decipher this enigmatic seal. *What will come to pass after the seal that death has stamped on dialogue?* Will dialogue continue? Will it be a dialogue after dialogue? Will it be a dialogue after the interruption of dialogue? Will it always be an *uninterrupted dialogue?* Will it perhaps be an *inner dialogue?*

Dialogue continues, following the trace in those who survive. The survivor will once more leave the word to the lost friend, letting his voice echo within himself. Alone—so he was destined—he will carry him within himself. Alone he will take up the burden of continuing the dialogue even beyond the break and interruption, through the break and interruption, and he will preserve his memory.[142] The uninterrupted dialogue, starting from that first "apparent" interruption, beyond and after the dialogue in the world that, as Derrida admits, has always been in French, will continue to be an inner dialogue—far from the inner monologue, since it precedes it and makes it possible.[143]

This promise and commitment are expressed in the verse of another friend, a common friend of Gadamer and Derrida, a friend who brings them together: Paul Celan. *The world is gone, I must carry you.* The theme of death, of the ultimate interruption, intertwines itself with the theme of the dialogue in Derrida's discourse, but also, in the wake of Gadamer, with that of poetry. Two of Gadamer's works, to which Derrida continually refers, form the background here: *Gedicht und Gespräch* (*Poetry and Dialogue*) and the preceding book *Who Am I and Who Are You? On Paul Celan.*[144] The dialogue continues through the poetry of Celan. It is "in order to speak to him,"[145] in order to still speak to Gadamer, that Derrida interprets Celan. The homage to an interpretation is perhaps also an homage to the way in which Gadamer has understood it—thinking of the poetic text—as *Zwischenrede*, as speech that interposes and interrupts, as a necessary "interruption" of dialogue.[146]

The world is gone. I must carry you. Following a hermeneutic principle applied by Gadamer in his book on Celan, Derrida isolates, with an interruption, the final verse of the poem *Grosse, glühende Wölbung*, taken from the cycle *Atemwende*.[147] *The world is gone. I must carry you.* This is the sentence to which Celan decided to give the last word, as if it were an almost eschatological signature.[148] Separated, like an aphorism, isolated and insulated, it speaks of the absolute solitude when the world is no longer here, when it is gone. One cannot pronounce it, at the eschatological border, at this extreme limit, if not after the most marked interruption, after having withheld and resumed breathing, after a "breath-turn."[149] Derrida, in turn, after the pause of expiration, makes it almost the sentence of his memorial lecture. Between the duty and the promise this is "the truth of the verdict on the edge of the end of the world."[150]

What is the death of the other? The death of the other is the "world after the end of the world."[151] Every time, and every time in a unique, irreplaceable, and infinite way, death is not the end of something or of someone *in* the world, but is rather, and very much more, the end *of* the world. Death "marks each time, each time in defiance of arithmetic, the absolute end of the one and only world, of that which each opens as a one and only world," the end of that which is or can present itself as the origin of the world for that unique living being who is no more.[152] The survivor remains alone. Being beyond the world of the other, he is also beyond and before the world itself. He is deprived of the world—within and outside the world. "*Die Welt ist fort*: the world has gone, already, the world has left us, the world is no more, the world is far off, the world is lost, the world is lost from sight, the world is out of sight, the world has departed, farewell to the world, the world has died."[153] The world—in three views of the world—is distant, suspended, or annihilated. The survivor feels like the only one responsible, destined to carry the other and his world, both disappeared, responsible and without world (*weltlos*), beyond the end of the world.[154]

13. THINKING, CARRYING, TRANSLATING

But what does "carrying" mean? What does *ich muss dich tragen* (I must carry you) mean? What is the importance, the gravity, of this word? Thinking it requires weighing it up and pondering it. The question echoes Heidegger's: *Was heisst Denken?—What is Called thinking?*

> To that which is thought and to its thoughts (*Gedanken*), to the Gedanc, belongs the thanks (*Dank*). But perhaps these echos/resonances of the word *Denken*, thinking, in the *Gedächtnis* and in the *Dank*, memory and thanks, are just an exterior and artificial trick. . . . Is thinking a thanking? What does thanking mean here? Or is thanking perhaps grounded in thinking?[155]

The proximity of *Denken* and *Danken*, of thinking and thanking, underscored by Heidegger, is taken up again by Celan.[156] But this proximity is lacking in French and in all romance languages, in which questions like the one posed by Heidegger turn out to be difficult to translate.

Derrida, through an etymological figure, which he almost opposes to *Denken-Danken*, approaches the French terms *penser* and *peser*, *to think* and *to weigh*—to ponder, to compensate, to counterbalance, to compare, and to examine. *Examen* in Latin is the hand of a scale to which justice is entrusted, perhaps the justice of a judgment on what gives itself to be weighed and carried. In order *to think* and *to weigh* it is thus necessary *to carry*, to carry in itself and on itself. That between thought and weighing, thought and gravity,[157] is a "friendship" that holds true in romance languages.

When the world is dead with you, I must carry you, you alone in me and in me alone. On me. On me and in me, since there is no longer a world to support us, as ground, as earth, as earthly and worldly territory, there is no longer a world as mediation. What remains is only the "abyssal altitude of a sky."[158] It is the orient of the sky toward which thought orientates itself, rising up from the earth in the future and in the coming of the *ought*. But one can also overturn the order of the *if, then*. There is not, nor can there be any longer, a world that is for us foundation or alibi, from the instant when I speak to you and am responsible for you or in front of you. Remaining alone in the world, in front of you, who now depends on me, I must carry you and take you upon myself, I must assume the responsibility to which I must answer in front of you and for you.

Carrying speaks the language of birth: A mother carries her child in the womb. But carrying also speaks the language of death: One carries one's mourning. It is with Freud, Husserl, and Heidegger, that Derrida sharpens the value of "carrying" that means the interiorization of remembrance, but not an inclusion of the other in oneself. Above all, it is not an appropriation. "*To carry* now no longer has the meaning of 'to comprise' [*comporter*], to include, to comprehend in the self, but rather *to carry oneself oneself toward* [*se porter vers*] the infinite inappropriability of the other, toward the encounter with its absolute transcendence in the very inside of me, that is to say, in me outside of me."[159] I must carry the other, but the other must carry me. The I and you, as Gadamer said, are inverted, as are the author and reader, all of the protagonists of a poem, the virtual signers and counter-signers.[160] On account of this uncanny and strange carrying, I am dislocated by the infinitely other in me, and I am alone, alone without world, either as foundation or mediation, alone with the other and for the other, with you and for you. The immediacy of this abyss binds me, commits me, and promises me to the other with the "I ought"—"I ought to carry you." Another reading of *cogito* and *sum*: Before thinking, and before being, I carry. *Before being myself, I carry the other.*

I remain before you and in front (*devant*) of you, obligated and indebted to you; I must keep myself within your reach, I must be what you cling to. "Always singular and irreplaceable, these laws or injunctions remain untranslatable from one to the other, from some to others, from one language to another, but that makes them no less universal."[161] Carrying, therefore, reveals itself a transporting, transferring, and *translating*—all the more the untranslatable. It is the "violent sacrifice of the passage beyond."[162] Here more than ever, in the passage, in the search for an orientation in thinking—and perhaps for a new thinking of the world, after the world is no more—there is a need for the other, a need to carry the other, to be carried by the other. *For no one bears life alone—Denn keiner trägt das Leben allein.*[163]

14. THE BLESSING OF THE HAND, THE BLESSING OF THE POEM

To think of Gadamer seems to mean first of all addressing him once again and once again letting him speak. But how? The proximity of "thinking and poetizing" in which surfaces a thread of the proximity between the two philosophers—as Gadamer himself suggests—indicates the passage.[164] It is a passage that, showing a disconcerting affinity with the "passage beyond," leaves one inter-dicted: It is the test of translation.[165] Just like death, poetry also exhibits the limit of translatability. Even here there is an untranslatable that nonetheless demands to be translated, transported, carried—said. *The limits of language*—according to the title that Gadamer gave to his essay—are perceived much more in the front of poetry that, still leaving the demand for the "right" word unsatisfied and insatiable, evokes human finitude and the extreme limit of death.[166] The experience of the poetic word continuously recalls translation. "The poem no doubt is the only place propitious to the experience of language, that is to say, of an idiom that forever defies translation and therefore demands a translation that will do the impossible, make the impossible possible in an unheard of event."[167] The limit of the untranslatable, toward which poetry leads, is that limit in which one experiences "the particularity and foreignness of language."[168]

In order to open up this path, Derrida considers the final verse of Celan's poem *Wege im Schatten-Gebräch,*[169] which Gadamer had already isolated in his interpretation.[170]

Wege im Schatten-Gebräch	Paths in the shadow-rock
deiner Hand.	Of your hand
Aus der Vier-Finger-Furche	Out of the four-finger-furrow
wühl ich mir den	I grub for myself the
versteinerten Segen.	Petrified blessing.

The theme of the final verse is that of the blessing: *Out of the four-finger-furrow I grub for myself the petrified blessing.* It is impossible not to think of another famous poem by Celan, one that Derrida here recalls: *Benedicta.*[171] The blessing is not given, but is rather sought after and beseeched; indeed, it seems to be wrested from the hand. It is as if the blessing, while exerting pressure, were trying to open a hand already closed on itself and on its meaning. *Wühlen* means searching for, by rummaging, to extract, to try to remove by rummaging, to wrest; Gadamer insists on this movement that Derrida views as a subversive, curious, and impatient impulse. It wants to wrest a blessing from the benedictory hand, which is such because, although it offers the message to be read, it takes it away from the reading, because it retains the blessing in itself. Gadamer subsequently proposes a subversion of the scene of reading, which is also a subversive scene, that of the poem itself: "from the hand of the one who bestows the blessing to the hand upon which. For the one who reads it, a message of blessing and hope is concealed."[172] Offered by the benedictory hand, the blessing is sought after with despairing fervor. As if a blessing could only be wrested. As if a blessing on which one can count, a verifiable, calculable blessing were no longer a blessing. Should not a blessing—as Derrida therefore wonders[173]—always remain "improbable," in order for it to be a blessing? "Improbable" reminds one of the Paris debate, suggesting continuity and perhaps something more.

The blessing is first of all that *of* the poem. The poetic text is a double blessing because it blesses the other and lets itself be blessed by the other. But there is also a specular reflection, which is self-telic and self-referential: "The poem speaks *of itself*, of the scene of writing, of the signature and of the reading that it inaugurates."[174] Yet it does not stop at itself and simultaneously grants a blessing to the other. It is under the sign of this blessing that Derrida wants to inscribe the moment in which he commemorates the philosopher who is no longer. The benedictory hand that seems to open itself is perhaps that of Gadamer. Gadamer's hand merges with that of the poetic text. In both cases, the text, of the hand and of the poem, appears to be a "lattice of interrupted and folded lines" of "breaks" that, to the one who deciphers them, are visible as lines, *interrupted and internal*, destined like the text to refuse, escape, and disappear.[175] Without this risk for interruption, without this "improbability," without this impossibility of an ultimate proof, which must remain endlessly, there will be no reading, giving, or blessing.[176] This is the right that has to be recognized to the text, the right to remain in indecision, to keep indecisive and undecidable that which cannot be decided on. Defended by Gadamer, the "right to leave things undecided" is taken up with force by Derrida.[177] The frontier, the *external* limit that surrounds the text, is the suspensive interruption that alone permits the possibility of the blessing and the advent of interpretation. Thus, when the world distances itself and runs away, it can happen that the poem, like a hand, greets and blesses, and carries the other, carries "you." "This poem is the 'you' and the 'I' that is addressed to 'you' but also to any other."[178] The "immediate unreadability" of the text is the "resource" that allows it to bless, to give, to give something to think about, to read, and to understand—that allows it to speak.[179] It is the "resource"—or the blessing—of hermeneutics, no less than of deconstruction.

The deconstructive and disseminating reading of Derrida thus moves toward the trace of the poetic text, toward the irreducible remnant (*Singbarer Rest*) of unreadability, destined to survive in an uninterrupted process, both infinite and finite, to the decipherment of all the undersigners and readers to come; this remnant and excess of unreadability is what has made hermeneutics possible and is made possible by hermeneutics. Thus, with the same move by which he carries himself toward the trace of the poem's unreadability, Derrida also moves toward hermeneutics. By attempting to be "faithful" to the hermeneutical demand, but also to that singular alterity that hermeneutics has within itself and that carries it beyond itself, Derrida tries to decipher the constellation of Celan's poem *Grosse, glühende Wölbung*, the configuration of the stars in that "great, glowing vault."[180]

On the Jewish landscape, through which Derrida travels, appears the ram with his "stony face," the animal of sacrifice and holocaust—the image of the infinite revolt of all the scapegoats, all the substitutes, of the rams of every holocaust—whose horns are the shofar, sounded on Rosh Hashanah, the first day of the year, and on Yom Kippur, the day of atonement and of Great Forgiveness. It is between these two fatidical days that the scripture of God can carry some and not carry others in the Book of Life. On these days, one recites: "May you be inscribed in the Book of Life . . ." Here every Jew feels at the edge of the whole, at the edge of everything, between life and death, rebirth and end, between the world and the end of the world, the mournful annihilation of the other or of oneself. Carrying here means, in the Jewish sense, which Derrida seems to follow, inscribing and writing.

15. STARS AND CONSTELLATIONS

From the heart of its "solitude" the poem writes, underwrites, and pre-scribes.[181] Compared with everything that passes and flees, like existence, the poetic word, enunciating and witnessing itself, "stands firm in itself," in its irreplaceable uniqueness and in its absolute solitude. But its solitude, self-telic and self-referential, while speaking of itself does not exclude the other. This self-referring is always an appeal to the *other*—be it only to the other as inaccessible in itself. Thus, it "in no way suspends the reference to the inappropriable."[182] It is no coincidence, then, that here there echoes the question: "Who am I and who are you?" "Your irrefutable testimony" is already mine, because it is much less one's own than it can be of others.

The poem is the *subjectum*, and there is no other subjectivity. This is how it is for Derrida, in much the same way that Gadamer outlined with regard to the play of art: "The '*subjectum*' of the experience of art, that which remains and endures, is not the subjectivity of the one who experiences the work but the work itself."[183] This work's sovereignty, which makes the poem the said of a dictation or a *Diktat*, is nonetheless the sovereign authority of a question that, demanding a responsible response, opens up the dialogue. The *Gedicht* refers back to the *Gespräch*, and here Derrida refers to Gadamer. Referring in the sense that he returns the word to him and takes it up immediately after. It is a way of opening an access and a passage; it is the possibility of throwing a bridge between the two banks of hermeneutics and deconstruction. This sovereign and eminent passage is the poem. But not just any poem, but one that bears a signature: *Paul Celan*.

Even though it is signed and undersigned, the poem *pre-scribes* a poetic dictation to which no living speech can ever correspond, because it "stands in itself," autonomous, "at once" independent of the conscious and intentional wanting to say of the signatory, cut off, separated, and abandoned like a trace, like every trace that is abandoned to its destiny. Left to itself, deprived of the origin, but also of the end, an orphaned child because of the interrupted filiation, and hence emancipated through the double interruption, this wandering trace, unforeseeable, untranslatable, and almost unreadable, is destined to survive because of its "immediate unreadability," passing from one to the other, to the decipherment of all the readers to come, of all the signers and counter-signers, in an "infinite process."[184]

For Gadamer the infinite is that of dialogue. Gadamer insists on this infinity also in his last essays, above all where in his thought the "limits of language" come to light in connection with the limits of human finitude. On the one hand, there is no dialogue that reaches its end before having led to a real agreement; but on the other, there is no dialogue that really reaches an end, because a real agreement contradicts the essence of individuality. The limits of human finitude, of temporality, of the discursivity of our saying, prevent the dialogue from having an end.[185] Thus, "the dialogue that we are is an endless dialogue. There is no last word, just as there is no first word."[186] Every word is always already an answer, because for Gadamer it is the question that inaugurates the suspension and marks the interruption. In that sense, "questioning means to establish an opening."[187] Even the greatest poetry, that of Celan, asks a question, for Gadamer the question *par excellence*: "Who am I and who are you?"[188] But the question, even the one posed by the poetic text, always occurs within the dialogue. It is that interruption from which the infinite process of dialogue takes up its own movement. In other words, for Gadamer, the dialogue of poetry is always dialogue. The poetic text inscribes itself into the constellation of dialogue. It only lets the star of a new interpretation shine.

Things are different for Derrida, or rather, things are the other way round. The process is infinite, but it cannot *not* interrupt itself. The trace of the poem, which is untranslatable, translates itself *infinitely*—*until* it is out of breath, breathless, like Celan's pilgrim-poet who, out of breath and holding his breath, reaches the "breath crystal" of the poetic word. The process is interrupted because at a certain point one remains out of breath. The break, which could be in turn infinite, is the break that precedes the "breath turn," the *Atemwende*. Once again it is to finitude that infinity is brought back. But before being the temporal and discursive finitude of saying, the one indicated by Derrida is a natural finitude, neither artificial nor intentional, it is the human inability to speak without taking a breath, and to hold one's breath. This finitude, which holds interruption within itself and which interrupts, reclaims the infinite process.[189] But at the same time, the finitude traces and delineates it in a discontinuous way—with twists, turns, and hairpin bends. How could one not think of the sound raised by the shofar? How could one not bring to mind the breath that passes, twists, and modulates itself through the swirls outlined by the ram's horn? How could one not think of the "melody of the spirals," another turning around, or perhaps the "breath turn" before all the turns?

Thus, the process and its infinity are not important, nor is retaining the infinity of dialogue. It is much more important for Derrida to retain interruption, because interruption, just as it happened in Paris, maintains that secret of *Unheimlichkeit*, that strange and distant proximity, which is the condition for dialogue. The future of every new interpretation, that is, of every new movement of dialogue, is tied to the interruption that is meditative and suspensive in itself. The suspension is part of the interruption and has to be read as indecision. "Interruption is indecisive, it undecides."[190] Because it interrupts and suspends, the indecision holds attention's breath, keeps it alive, alert and vigilant, ready to lend an ear, hanging on the very breath of the other word and of the word of the other, in order to set out for wholly other paths. Gadamer already recognizes the right to indecision, and grants it to the poem.[191] It is the poem then that does not decide.

The poem does not decide due to its immediate unreadability, through which it also says the unreadability of the world. The unreadable is not here what is opposed to the readable; by remaining unreadable, the poem discloses infinite possibilities of reading. In this remnant, in this irreducible surplus, Derrida points to the difference between hermeneutics and the disseminal "reading-writing" [*lecture-écriture*].[192] This is because hermeneutics, which aims to unfold the implicit and explicit folds of meaning, the ambiguities, the semantics and rhetoric, the idiomatic resources of language and of the poet, the intentional wanting to say of the latter, aims precisely to not let that remnant be unread and unreadable—that remnant that nonetheless escapes from every hermeneutic context. If, on the other hand, one were to eliminate this remnant, one would eliminate hermeneutics itself. The disseminal "reading-writing," therefore, comes to the rescue and aids hermeneutics by safeguarding that remnant and pointing to it. Without the "singable remnant,"[193] the *Anspruch* and also the provocation that sings and makes one sing in every poem, the latter would not even be able to survive. The remnant is the trace of the poem. The wandering trace articulates, or rather interrupts, the answer that hermeneutics gives to the question of the poem, and that continues from meaning to meaning, and from truth to truth. For hermeneutics, the disseminal experience manifests and takes on the evidence of an interruption, of a break, almost a wound, the hiatus in the poem itself of a wound whose lips will never be able to close. The word remains "circumcised."[194] Although it continues infinitely, the process now appears discontinuous, both infinite and finite. More than infinite, starting from the interruption, it is *uninterrupted*.

But the interruption is not a new "star," good or evil, under which a dialogue is born.[195] The interruption tears open the sky and discloses a new "constellation."[196] The trace of the poem, which carries the hiatus, the break, the ellipsis inscribed within itself, opens unforeseen and unforeseeable constellations. It multiplies the horizons and the skies, studs them and disseminates them with stars, promises an infinite multitude of stars, under which one can read and re-read the poem. A multitude, like the offspring which, after the interruption of the sacrifice of Isaac, God promises to Abraham (*Genesis* 15, 5).

Once again, both in hermeneutics and deconstruction, unity and difference, difference and unity, reassert the secret of their bond, of their elusive cross-reference. Between the two infinites, and therefore infinitely other, beyond finitude and because of finitude, above and beyond the end, beyond the final interruption, dialogue continues, uninterrupted, in the poem, and with the poem. The trace left by Celan keeps the dialogue open. His words, like many interruptions, disclose unforeseen openings and unprecedented passages. But the breath of the poet does more than just support the bridge suspended in the air between the two infinites. The "breath turn" is for both much more. It is a turn yet to come, beyond hermeneutics and deconstruction. As a privileged interlocutor, an elected witness of the one and the other, Celan offers his words so that one speaks to the other. Both find themselves here "in the environs of the poetic," where poetry can, in dialogue, stray into philosophy and provoke an oscillation that, beyond every metaphysical opposition, is not that of a synthesis.[197] Celan is this *tertium datur*; more than a point of convergence, he is a point of orientation. He is the East to which both hermeneutics and deconstruction, in different ways, point. He is the morning star that has yet to rise in the sky. His *Schibboleth*, the sign of alliance, of division and sharing, waits for them at what is perhaps the opening of a new philosophy.

NOTES

1. Wilhelm von Humboldt, *On Language: On The Diversity of Human Language Construction and its Influence on the Mental Development of the Human Species*, ed. Michael Losonsky, trans. Peter Heath (Cambridge: Cambridge University Press, 1999), 63. Translation modified.

2. In the French edition, the texts are compiled in the *Revue internationale de philosophie*, (*Herméneutique et néo-structuralisme. Derrida—Gadamer—Searle*), no. 151, 1984, issue coordinated by Manfred Frank which also includes essays not directly concerned with the debate: Hans-Georg Gadamer, *Le défi herméneutique*, 333–340, a shorter version of the reworking developed in *Text und Interpretation*; Jacques Derrida, *Bonnes volontés de puissance (une réponse à H.G.G.)*, 341–343; Hans-Georg Gadamer, *Et pourtant: puissance de la bonne volonté (une réplique à J.D.)* 344–347. The German edition, from the same year, is larger and was published in a volume edited by Forget with a much larger influence: *Text und Interpretation*, ed. Philippe Forget (München: Fink UTB, 1984); the volume contains an introduction by P. Forget, the texts of Gadamer and Derrida, and contributions from F. Laruelle, J. Greisch, P. Forget, and M. Frank.

3. Taken indirectly from Derrida's presentation, "Three Questions to Hans-Georg Gadamer," in *Dialogue and Deconstruction: The Gadamer–Derrida Encounter*, eds. Diane P. Michelfelder and Richard E. Palmer (Albany: State University of New York Press, 1989), . . . This expression is used by Forget in the title of his introduction "Leitfäden einer unwahrscheinlichen Debatte" in *Text und Interpretation*, 7–23.

4. Diane P. Michelfelder and Richard E. Palmer, eds. *Dialogue and Deconstruction: The Gadamer–Derrida Encounter* (Albany: State University of New York Press, 1989). The gap between the American edition, on the one side, and the French and especially the German, on the other, is therefore five years. The American edition is different from the German, because, beyond the two new articles by Gadamer "Destruktion and Deconstruction" and "Hermeneutics and Logocentrism," from 1985 and 1987, respectively, it on the one hand no longer contains the essays by F. Laruelle and J. Greisch, and on the other, presents a new reflection of Forget, besides the contributions of F. Dallmayr (and a letter from Gadamer to him, also published in German with the title *Dekonstruktion und Hermeneutik*), J. Simon, J. Risser, Ch. Shepherdson, G. B. Madison, H. Rapaport, D. G. Marshall, R. Shusterman, D. F. Krell, R. Bernasconi, J. Sallis, J. D. Caputo, N. Oxenhandler, G. Eisenstein. The great number of the new contributions testifies to the lingering echoes of the debate in America.

5. See Hans-Georg Gadamer, "*Destruktion* and Deconstruction," in *Dialogue and Deconstruction: The Gadamer–Derrida Encounter*, eds. Diane P. Michelfelder and Richard E. Palmer (Albany: State University of New York Press, 1989), 102–113. Hans-Georg Gadamer, "Hermeneutics and Logocentrism," in *Dialogue and Deconstruction: The Gadamer–Derrida Encounter*, eds. Diane P. Michelfelder and Richard E. Palmer (Albany: State University of New York Press, 1989), 114–125. Hans Georg Gadamer, "Letter to Dallmayr," in *Dialogue and Deconstruction: The Gadamer–Derrida Encounter*, eds. Diane P. Michelfelder and Richard E. Palmer (Albany: State University of New York Press, 1989), 93–101. Hans-Georg Gadamer, "Hermeneutics

Tracking the Trace," in *The Gadamer Reader: A Bouquet of the Later Writings*, ed. Richard Palmer (Evanston: Northwestern University Press, 2006).

6. Hans-Georg Gadamer, "Hermeneutics Tracking the Trace." See also Gadamer, "Hermeneutics and Logocentrism," 114.

7. There are many places where Derrida refers to this difference and it is clearly not possible to mention them all. For example, see Jacques Derrida, "Fors: The AnglishWords of Nicolas Abraham and Maria Torok," *The Georgia Review* 31: 1 (1977), 64–116; "Scribble (Writing/Power)," *Yale French Studies* 58 (1979), 116–147; "Schibboleth," in *Word Traces*, ed. Aris Fioretis (Baltimore: John Hopkins University Press, 1992).

8. A large crowd also attended because of the theme, but the discussion had little lasting effect on the debate between the two philosophers. See Günter Zehm, "Wenn es um Heidegger geht, reicht der Hörsaal nicht aus" in *Die Welt*, February 8, 1988, 3.

9. See Jacques Derrida and Gianni Vattimo eds., *Religion* (Oxford: Polity Press, 1998).

10. Jacques Derrida, "Rams. Uninterrupted Dialogue—Between Two Infinites, the Poem," in *Sovereignties in Question. The Poetics of Paul Celan*, eds. Thomas Dutoit and Outi Pasanen (New York: Fordham University Press, 2005).

11. Gadamer has insisted on this shared derivation. See Hans-Georg Gadamer, "*Destruktion* and Deconstruction," 108–109; Hans-Georg Gadamer, "Hermeneutics and Logocentrism," 124; Hans-Georg Gadamer, "Letter to Dallmayr," 93; Gadamer, "Hermeneutics Tracking the Trace."

12. See Georg W. Bertram, *Hermeneutik und Dekonstruktion. Konturen einer Auseinandersetzung der Gegenwartsphilosophie* (München: Fink, 2002), 11.

13. This dialogical manner of posing the question, although already anticipated in the introductory essay by Michelfelder and Palmer, has not been greatly followed. See, *Dialogue and Deconstruction: the Gadamer–Derrida Encounter*, 2.

14. Hans-Georg Gadamer, "Text and Interpretation," in *Dialogue and Deconstruction: The Gadamer–Derrida Encounter*, ed. Diane P. Michelfelder and Richard E. Palmer (Albany: State University of New York Press, 1989), 27.

15. Jacques Derrida, "Three Questions to Hans-Georg Gadamer," in *Dialogue and Deconstruction: The Gadamer–Derrida Encounter*, ed. Diane P. Michelfelder and Richard E. Palmer (Albany: State University of New York Press, 1989), 52–53. The plural "good wills" chosen by Derrida indicates a proximity between this text and the talk held immediately after entitled Jacques Derrida, "Interpreting Signatures (Nietzsche/Heidegger): Two Questions," in *Dialogue and Deconstruction: The Gadamer–Derrida Encounter*, ed. Diane P. Michelfelder and Richard E. Palmer (Albany: State University of New York Press, 1989), 58–71.

16. See Josef Simon, "Good Will to Understand and the Will to Power: Remarks on an 'Improbable Debate,'" trans. Richard E. Palmer, in *Dialogue and Deconstruction*, 162–175; see also Philippe Forget, *Leitfäden einer unwahrscheinlichen Dibatte*, 7–23.

17. Hans-Georg Gadamer, *Truth and Method*, trans. Joel Weinsheimer and Donald G. Marshall (New York: Crossroad, 1989), 297.

18. See in particular Hans-Georg Gadamer, *Gadamer on Celan: "Who am I and Who are You?" and Other Essays*, trans. Richard Heinemann and Bruce Krajewski (Albany, NY: State University of New York Press, 1997). On this, see James Risser,

Hermeneutics and the Voice of the Other. Re-reading Gadamer's Philosophical Hermeneutics (Albany: SUNY Press, 1997), 159–208. In Gadamer's encounter with Celan, Risser sees a difference with respect to *Truth and Method* because the voice of the poet reveals itself as the voice of the other, which is absolutely not assimilated.

19. Cf. Hans-Georg Gadamer, "Text and Interpretation," 30.

20. Ibid., 31.

21. Ibid., 34.

22. Ibid., 35.

23. Ibid., 43. On this point, see Chapter V, § 2.

24. Ibid., 27–28.

25. For a precise, albeit quite one-sided, commentary, see Josef Simon, "Good Will to Understand and the Will to Power: Remarks on an 'Improbable Debate,'" in *Dialogue and Deconstruction: The Gadamer–Derrida Encounter*, eds. Diane P. Michelfelder and Richard E. Palmer (Albany: State University of New York Press, 1989).

26. Hans-Georg Gadamer, "Text and Interpretation," 33–34. Translation modified; my emphasis.

27. See Jacques Derrida, "Three Questions to Hans-Georg Gadamer," 53.

28. Immanuel Kant, "Groundwork of the Metaphysics of Morals," in *Practical Philosophy*, ed. Mary J. Gregor, *The Cambridge Edition of the Works of Immanuel Kant* (New York: Cambridge University Press, 1999), 50–52, 86.

29. Ibid., 52.

30. See Jürgen Habermas, "The Hermeneutic Claim to Universality," in *The Hermeneutic Tradition: from Ast to Ricoeur*, eds. Gayle Ormiston and Alan Schrift (Albany: State University of New York Press, 1990).

31. Jacques Derrida, "Three Questions to Hans-Georg Gadamer," 53.

32. The concept of "interruption" is taken up again in § 11 of this chapter.

33. Jacques Derrida, "Three Questions to Hans-Georg Gadamer," 53.

34. See Hans-Georg Gadamer, "Reply to Jacques Derrida," in *Dialogue and Deconstruction: The Gadamer–Derrida Encounter*, eds. Diane P. Michelfelder and Richard E. Palmer (Albany: State University of New York Press, 1989), 55–57.

35. Ibid., 55. (My emphasis).

36. Plato, *Gorgias* 458a.

37. Hans-Georg Gadamer, "Hermeneutics and Logocentrism," 119. See also Gadamer, *Truth and Method*, 385.

38. Hans-Georg Gadamer, "Reply to Jacques Derrida," 55.

39. Ibid.

40. Ibid. For the German version, see "Und dennoch: Macht des guten Willens," in *Text und Interpretation*, 59.

41. Ibid., 57.

42. See Jacques Derrida, *Speech and Phenomena: And Other Essays on Husserl's Theory of Signs*, trans. David Allison (Evanston Ill.: Northwestern University Press, 1973), 22.

43. On this, see § 10 later in the chapter.

44. Hans-Georg Gadamer, "The Boundaries of Language," in *Language and Linguisticality in Gadamer's Hermeneutics*, ed. Lawrence K. Schmidt (Lanham, MD: Lexington Books, 2000), 12. (Translation modified).

45. See Plato, *Cratylus*, 434b-c; Aristotle, *De Interpretatione*, 16a, 19.

46. On this issue, see § 9 later on in the chapter.

47. Hans-Georg Gadamer, "Reply to Jacques Derrida," 56.

48. Hans-Georg Gadamer, "Reply to Jacques Derrida," 56.

49. Ibid., 57.

50. See the critical position assumed by Habermas in his encounter with Derrida in Jürgen Habermas, *The Philosophical Discourse of Modernity*, trans. Frederick G. Lawrence (Cambridge, MA: MIT Press, 1993), 161–184. Jürgen Habermas, *Postmetaphysical Thinking*, trans. William Mark Hohengarten (Boston: MIT Press, 1996). And, in particular, "The Unity of Reason in the Diversity of Its Voices," 115–148. Gadamer makes particular reference to this latter work, pointing out the "excellent critique" performed by Habermas on Derrida, in "Zwischen Phänomenologie und Dialektik. Versuch einer Selbstkritik" in *Gesammelte Werke 2: Hermeneutik II* (Tübingen: Mohr (Siebeck) UTB, 1999), 23.

51. See Martin Heidegger, "The Origin of the Work of Art," in *Off the Beaten Track*, eds. Julian Young and Kenneth Haynes (Cambridge: Cambridge University Press, 2002).

52. The limit of infinite dialogue is life Itself. See Plato, *Republic*, 450b. On this very issue, see Donatella Di Cesare, "Das heilende Wort der Philosophie," in *Begegnungen mit Hans-Georg Gadamer*, ed. G. Figal (Stuttgart: Reclam, 2000, 126–136).

53. Hans-Georg Gadamer, "*Destruktion* and Deconstruction," 113. Translation modified.

54. See Jacques Derrida, "Three Questions to Hans-Georg Gadamer."

55. See Jacques Derrida, *Of Grammatology*, trans. Gayatri Chakravorty Spivak, Corrected Edition ed. (Baltimore: Johns Hopkins University Press, 1997), 19.

56. Gadamer not only defends, and will continue to defend, Heidegger's position; he nonetheless never ceases to question himself on the "sense," With regard to his defense of Heidegger, see Hans-Georg Gadamer, "Text and Interpretation," 24; "*Destruktion* and Deconstruction," 105, 109, 113; "Letter to Dallmayr," 93; "Hermeneutics Tracking the Trace."

57. Hans-Georg Gadamer, "Hermeneutics and Logocentrism," 115–116.

58. Ibid., 116. See also Hans-Georg Gadamer, "Hermeneutics Tracking the Trace," 129.

59. Hans-Georg Gadamer, "Hermeneutics and Logocentrism," 121.

60. Hans-Georg Gadamer, "Letter to Dallmayr," 98.

61. See Hans-Georg Gadamer, "*Destruktion* and Deconstruction," 106.

62. See Hans-Georg Gadamer, "Hermeneutics Tracking the Trace."

63. See ibid.

64. Hans-Georg Gadamer, "Text and Interpretation," 27. On the metaphor of the bridge, see also Chapter III, §3.

65. Friedrich Nietzsche, "On the Truth and Lies in a Nonmoral Sense," in *Philosophy and Truth: Selections from Nietzsche's Notebooks of the Early 1870's*, ed. Daniel Breazeale (Atlantic Highlands, NJ: Humanities Press, 1979), 85.

66. Wilhelm von Humboldt, *On Language: On The Diversity of Human Language Construction and its Influence on the Mental Development of the Human Species*,

ed. Michael Losonsky, trans. Peter Heath (Cambridge: Cambridge University Press, 1999), 69.

67. See Jacques Derrida, *Of Grammatology*, 73. Jacques Derrida, *Positions*, trans. Alan Bass (Chicago: University of Chicago Press, 1982).

68. Hans-Georg Gadamer, "Man and Language," in *Philosophical Hermeneutics*, ed. David Linge (Berkeley, CA: University of California Press, 1976), 65.

69. G. W. F. Hegel, *Phenomenology of Spirit*, trans. A.V. Miller (Oxford: Oxford University Press, 1977), 308.

70. See Chapter IV, §9.

71. See Hans-Georg Gadamer, *Truth and Method*, 396, 404.

72. Maurice Merleau-Ponty, *Signs*, trans. Richard McCleary (Evanston: Northwestern University Press, 1964), 97. Translation modified.

73. Wilhelm von Humboldt, *Grundzüge des allgemeinen Sprachtypus* in *Gesammelte Schriften*, ed. A Leitzmann (Berlin: Behr, 1906), vol. V, 373.

74. See Hans-Georg Gadamer, "Reply to Jacques Derrida," 55.

75. Hans-Georg Gadamer, "Language and Understanding," in *The Gadamer Reader: A Bouquet of the Later Writings*, ed. Richard Palmer (Evanston: Northwestern University Press, 2006), 107.

76. Hans-Georg Gadamer, "Man and Language," 64.

77. But an analogous distinction can also be found in the difference between "what is talked about" (*das Beredete*) and "what is said in the talk" (*das Geredete*) in Martin Heidegger, *Being and Time*, trans. John Macquarrie and Edward Robinson (San Francisco: Harper and Row, 1962), §35, 211–214.

78. Edmund Husserl, *Logical Investigations*, trans. J. N. Findlay, II vols., vol. I (London: Routledge, 1970), 192.

79. In "*vouloir dire*," resounds the impossibility of saying all what one wants to say; here lies the difference intrinsic to the "*vouloir dire*." "Derrida insists on this 'difference'—writes Gadamer—and I fully agree with him," Hans-Georg Gadamer, "Hermeneutics and Logocentrism," 118; see also Hans-Georg Gadamer, "Hermeneutics Tracking the Trace."

80. See Hans-Georg Gadamer, "Phänomenologie, Hermeneutik, Metaphysik" in GW10, 107, and "Zwischen Phänomenologie und Dialektik—Versuch einer Selbstkritik" in GW 2, 5.

81. Hans-Georg Gadamer, "Man and Language," 66.

82. Hans-Georg Gadamer, *Truth and Method*, 103.

83. See Hans-Georg Gadamer, "On the Problem of Self-Understanding," in *Philosophical Hermeneutics*, ed. David Linge (Berkeley, CA: University of California Press, 1976).

84. See Jacques Derrida, *Speech and Phenomena: And Other Essays on Husserl's Theory of Signs*, trans. David Allison (Evanston: Northwestern University Press, 1973), 33–34.

85. See ibid., 71–73.

86. Ibid., 74. See also Jacques Derrida, "Form and Meaning: A Note on the Phenomenology of Language," in *The Margins of Philosophy* (Chicago: University of Chicago Press, 1982), 155–173.

87. See Jacques Derrida, "White Mythology," in *Margins of Philosophy* (Chicago: University of Chicago Press, 1982), 213.

88. Friedrich Nietzsche, *Writings from the Late Notebooks*, trans. Kate Sturge (Cambridge: Cambridge University Press, 2003), 34 [253], 16.

89. Friedrich Nietzsche, "On the Truth and Lies in a Nonmoral Sense," 83.

90. Friedrich Nietzsche, *Nachgelassene Fragmente: Herbst 1885 bis Herbst 1887*, ed. G. Colli and M. Montinari, vol. VIII, 1, *Werke* (Berlin: De Gruyter, 1974), I [182], 47.

91. Ibid.

92. Friedrich Nietzsche, *Writings from the Late Notebooks*, 2 [148], 90.

93. Friedrich Nietzsche, *The Will to Power*, trans. Walter Kaufmann and Reginald J. Hollingdale (New York: Vintage Books, 1968), §385, 207; §643, 350.

94. Friedrich Nietzsche, *Nachgelassene Fragmente: Herbst 1885 bis Herbst 1887*, I [182], 46–47.

95. Ibid. See also, Friedrich Nietzsche, *Beyond Good and Evil*, trans. Judith Norman (Cambridge: Cambridge University Press, 2002), §27, 29. Translation modified.

96. Friedrich Nietzsche, *Writings from the Late Notebooks*, 7 [60], 139.

97. Although one can renounce the interpretation, because of the difficulty of being understood, it needs "to be sincerely thankful for *the good will to a certain refinement of interpretation.*" See Friedrich Nietzsche, *Nachgelassene Fragmente: Herbst 1885 bis Herbst 1887*, I [182], 46–47. (My emphasis).

98. Simon has written on the theme of understanding "without interpretation" by Nietzsche, even though his discourse goes in a different direction from that I have proposed here. See Josef Simon, *Verstehen ohne Interpretation? Zeichen und Verstehen bei Hegel und Nietzsche*, in *Distanz im Verstehen (Zeichen und Interpretation II)*, ed. Josef Simon (Frankfurt: Suhrkamp, 1995), 72–104, and in particular, 72–80.

99. See Günter Figal, "Die Komplexität philosophischer Hermeneutik" in *Der Sinn des Verstehens* (Stuttgart: Reclam, 1996), 11–31.

100. See for example, F. D. E. Schleiermacher, *Hermeneutics: The Handwritten Manuscripts*, ed. Heinz Kimmerle, trans. James Duke and Jack Forstman (Missoula: Scholars Press, 1977). Wilhelm Dilthey, "The Rise of Hermeneutics," in *The Hermeneutic Tradition: from Ast to Ricoeur*, ed. Gayle Ormiston and Alan Schrift (Albany: State University of New York Press, 1990), 102–103.

101. See Martin Heidegger, *Being and Time*, trans. John Macquarrie and Edward Robinson (San Francisco: Harper and Row, 1962), §32, 190.

102. For example, see Jochen Hörisch, *Die Wut des Verstehens. Zur Kritik der Hermeneutik*. Frankfurt: Suhrkamp, 1988; see also Susan Sontag, *Against Interpretation, and Other Essays*. New York: Farrar, Straus, and Giroux, 1966.

103. See Hans-Georg Gadamer, *Truth and Method*, 260–261. And already in Heidegger, *Being and Time*, §4, 28.

104. Hans-Georg Gadamer nevertheless spoke both about *Sichverstehen* and also *Selbstverstehen*, which could be translated respectively with "self-understanding" and "auto-understanding." The latter term, namely *Selbstverstehen*, was and is "misleading"—as Gadamer himself observes—because it brings to mind a certain

self-awareness, or rather one unflinchingly sure of itself, while in fact it is a matter of exactly the opposite, that is, a self-understanding that is always destined to fail. See Hans-Georg Gadamer, "Letter to Dallmayr," 97. See also Hans-Georg Gadamer, "Hermeneutics and Logocentrism," 119.

105. The relativity that characterizes difference in hermeneutics, and therefore foreignness, in no way leads to a reduction or devaluing of it. Those who advance an absolute and absolutely external concept of "foreign" seem unjustified. See Bernhard Waldenfels, *Der Stachel des Fremden*, Suhrkamp, Frankfurt 1990 and *Topographie des Fremden*, Suhrkamp, Frankfurt 1997. On this point, see also G. W. Bertram, *Hermeneutik und Dekonstruktion*, 75–77.

106. Hans-Georg Gadamer, *Truth and Method*, 295. Translation modified.

107. Ibid., 297. Translation modified.

108. Ibid., 276. Translation modified.

109. See Josef Simon, *Philosophie des Zeichens* (Berlin-New York De Gruyter, 1989), 152.

110. G. W. F Hegel, *Phenomenology of Spirit*, trans. A. V. Miller (Oxford: Oxford University Press, 1977), 307.

111. See Tilman Borsche, *Freiheit als Zeichen. Zur zeichenphilosophische Frage nach der Bedeutung von Freiheit*, in *Zeichen und Interpretation*, ed. Josef Simon (Frankfurt Suhrkamp, 1994), 117.

112. On the role of understanding in life, see Chapter VII, §9.

113. See Ludwig Wittgenstein, *Philosophical Investigations*, trans. G. E. M. Anscombe, 2nd ed rept. ed. (Oxford: Blackwell Publishers, 2000), §242, 88.When analytic philosophy, referring to Wittgenstein, attempts to reflect on the valid rules as conditions for understanding, it totally neglects the fact that already for Wittgenstein understanding occurs in the judgments that not only modify themselves, but can likewise modify the meanings and thus the very condition for understanding.

114. See Hans-Georg Gadamer, "Die Vielfalt der Sprachen und das Verstehen der Welt," ed. Gesammelte Werke: Ästhetik und Poetik I (Tübingen: Mohr (Siebeck) UTB, 1999), 343. See also Hans-Georg Gadamer, "Die Unfähigkeit zum Gespräch," in *Gesammelte Werke 2: Hermeneutik II* (Tübingen: Mohr (Siebeck) UTB, 1999), 207. This thesis returns again and again in Gadamer's work.

115. Friedrich Hölderlin, "Conciliator, You that no longer believed in . . ." in *Poems and Fragments*, trans. Michael Hamburger (New York: Anvil Press, 1994), 444–453.

116. Hans-Georg Gadamer, "Man and Language," 65–66.

117. Friedrich Schleiermacher, *Hermeneutics: The Handwritten Manuscripts*, ed. Heinz Kimmerle, trans. James Duke and Jack Forstman (Missoula: Scholars Press, 1977). Translation modified.

118. Wilhelm von Humboldt, *On Language: On The Diversity of Human Language Construction and its Influence on the Mental Development of the Human Species*, ed. Michael Losonsky, trans. Peter Heath (Cambridge: Cambridge University Press, 1999), 56.

119. Franz Rosenzweig, "The Builders: Concerning the Law" in *On Jewish Learning* (Madison, WI: The University of Wisconsin Press, 1955), 73.

120. Hans-Georg Gadamer, *Truth and Method*, 406, 180. See also, "Language and Understanding" (my emphasis); and "Phänomenologie, Hermeneutik, Metaphysik" in *GW* 10, 100–109.

121. Hans-Georg Gadamer, "Language and Understanding," 96.

122. Hans-Georg Gadamer, "Die Unfähigkeit zum Gespräch," 211. Translation modified.

123. Hans-Georg Gadamer, "Language and Understanding," 96. Translation modified.

124. Hans-Georg Gadamer, "Hermeneutics Tracking the Trace."

125. See Hans Georg Gadamer, "On the Truth of the Word," *Symposium 2*, no. 6 (2002): 115.

126. Hans-Georg Gadamer, "Man and Language," 67.

127. Hans-Georg Gadamer, "Wie weit schreibt Sprache das Denken vor?" in *GW* 2, 199–206.

128. Hans-Georg Gadamer, *Truth and Method*, 268.

129. Hans-Georg Gadamer, "Language and Understanding." Hans-Georg Gadamer, "On the Scope and Function of Hermeneutical Reflection," in *Philosophical Hermeneutics*, ed. David Linge (Berkeley, CA: University of California Press, 1976), 22. On this topic, see Chapter VII, §10.

130. Hans-Georg Gadamer, *Truth and Method*, 181.

131. Friedrich Schleiermacher, *Hermeneutics: The Handwritten Manuscripts*, ed. Heinz Kimmerle, trans. James Duke and Jack Forstman (Missoula: Scholars Press, 1977), 192.

132. Jacques Derrida, "Rams. Uninterrupted Dialogue–Between Two Infinites, the Poem," in *Sovereignties in Question. The Poetics of Paul Celan*, eds. Thomas Dutoit and Outi Pasanen (New York: Fordham University Press, 2005), 136.

133. Ibid., 140.

134. Ibid., 137.

135. Ibid., 136.

136. Ibid., 139.

137. Ibid., 137.

138. See ibid., 135.

139. Ibid.

140. See Jacques Derrida, *Adieu to Emmanuel Levinas*, trans. Pascale-Anne Brault and Michael Naas (Stanford University Press, 1999).

141. Jacques Derrida, "Rams. Uninterrupted Dialogue–Between Two Infinites, the Poem," in *Sovereignties in Question. The Poetics of Paul Celan*, eds. Thomas Dutoit and Outi Pasanen (New York: Fordham University Press, 2005), 139.

142. See ibid.,140.

143. "One speaks often and too easily of interior monologue. Yet an interior dialogue precedes it and makes it possible." See ibid., 136, 138. See also Derrida, *Speech and Phenomena: And Other Essays on Husserl's Theory of Signs*, trans. David Allison (Evanston: Northwestern University Press, 1973), 78.

144. See Hans-Georg Gadamer, *Gadamer on Celan: "Who am I and Who are You?" and Other Essays*. Also Hans-Georg Gadamer, *Gedicht und Gespräch* (Frankfurt: Insel, 1990). On this issue, see Chapter V.

145. Jacques Derrida, "Rams. Uninterrupted Dialogue–Between Two Infinites, the Poem," in *Sovereignties in Question. The Poetics of Paul Celan*, eds. Thomas Dutoit and Outi Pasanen (New York: Fordham University Press, 2005), 141.

146. Hans-Georg Gadamer, "Hermeneutics Tracking the Trace [On Derrida]," 404–405.

147. See Jacques Derrida, "Rams. Uninterrupted Dialogue–Between Two Infinites, the Poem," in *Sovereignties in Question. The Poetics of Paul Celan*, eds. Thomas Dutoit and Outi Pasanen (New York: Fordham University Press, 2005), 141; Paul Celan, "Great, Glowing Vault," in *Breathturn* (Los Angeles: Sun and Moon, 1995), 233; See Gadamer, *Gadamer on Celan: "Who am I and Who are You?" and Other Essays.*

148. See Jacques Derrida, "Rams. Uninterrupted Dialogue–Between Two Infinites, the Poem," in *Sovereignties in Question. The Poetics of Paul Celan*, eds. Thomas Dutoit and Outi Pasanen (New York: Fordham University Press, 2005), 157.

149. See more on this in Chapter VII, §2.

150. Jacques Derrida, "Rams. Uninterrupted Dialogue–Between Two Infinites, the Poem," in *Sovereignties in Question. The Poetics of Paul Celan*, eds. Thomas Dutoit and Outi Pasanen (New York: Fordham University Press, 2005), 152.

151. Ibid., 140.

152. Ibid.

153. Ibid., 149.

154. But Derrida asks, looking above all to Heidegger, if the "world" should not therefore be rethought beginning from its *Fort-sein*, from its no longer being there, and in its turn the *Fort* should not be rethought starting from *Ich muss dich tragen?* See ibid., 36; see also Martin Heidegger, *The Fundamental Concepts of Metaphysics: World, Finitude, Solitude*, trans. Will McNeill and Nicholas Walker (Bloomington: Indiana University Press, 1995).

155. Martin Heidegger, *What is Called Thinking?* trans. Fred D. Wieck and J. Glenn Gray (New York: Harper & Row, Publishers, 1968), 139.

156. See Paul Celan, "Speech on the Occasion of Receiving the Literature Prize of the Free Hanseatic City of Bremen," in *Selected Poems and Prose of Paul Celan* (New York: W.W. Norton, 2001), 395.

157. Jacques Derrida, "Rams. Uninterrupted Dialogue–Between Two Infinites, the Poem," in *Sovereignties in Question. The Poetics of Paul Celan*, eds. Thomas Dutoit and Outi Pasanen (New York: Fordham University Press, 2005), 142.

158. Ibid., 158. A passage when Celan speaks of Lenz comes to mind: "Whoever walks on his head, ladies and gentlemen, whoever walks on his head has heaven as an abyss beneath him." Paul Celan, "The Meridian," in *Selected Poems and Prose of Paul Celan* (New York: W.W. Norton, 2001), 407.

159. Jacques Derrida, "Rams. Uninterrupted Dialogue—Between Two Infinites, the Poem," in *Sovereignties in Question. The Poetics of Paul Celan*, ed. Thomas Dutoit and Outi Pasanen (New York: Fordham University Press, 2005), 161.

160. See more on this in Chapter V, §6.

161. Jacques Derrida, "Rams. Uninterrupted Dialogue—Between Two Infinites, the Poem," in *Sovereignties in Question. The Poetics of Paul Celan*, ed. Thomas Dutoit and Outi Pasanen (New York: Fordham University Press, 2005), 162.

162. Ibid.

163. Derrida ends his commemoration with this verse by Hölderlin.

164. See Hans-Georg Gadamer, "Letter to Dallmayr," 93.

165. See more on this in Chapter III.

166. See Hans-Georg Gadamer, "The Boundaries of Language," 18. See Chapter I, §8.

167. Jacques Derrida, "Rams. Uninterrupted Dialogue–Between Two Infinites, the Poem," in Sovereignties in Question. The Poetics of Paul Celan, eds. Thomas Dutoit and Outi Pasanen (New York: Fordham University Press, 2005), 137.

168. Hans-Georg Gadamer, "Grenzen der Sprache," in Gesammelte Werke 8: Ästhetik und Poetik I (Tübingen: Mohr (Siebeck) UTB, 1999); "Boundaries of Language" in Language and Linguisticality in Gadamer's Hermeneutics, ed. Lawrence K. Schmidt (Lanham: Lexington Books, 2000), 16.

169. Paul Celan, "Paths in the Shadow Rock" from Poems of Paul Celan, trans. Michael Hamburger (New York: Persea Books, 1988).

170. See Hans-Georg Gadamer, Gadamer on Celan: "Who am I and Who are You?" and Other Essays, 95–96.

171. See Paul Celan, "Benedicta," in Selected Poems and Prose of Paul Celan (New York: W.W. Norton, 2001), 174.

172. Hans-Georg Gadamer, Gadamer on Celan: "Who am I and Who are You?" and Other Essays, 95.

173. Jacques Derrida, "Rams. Uninterrupted Dialogue–Between Two Infinites, the Poem," in Sovereignties in Question. The Poetics of Paul Celan, eds. Thomas Dutoit and Outi Pasanen (New York: Fordham University Press, 2005), 143.

174. Ibid., 144.

175. Hans-Georg Gadamer, Gadamer on Celan: "Who am I and Who are You?" and Other Essays, 95. Translation modified.

176. Jacques Derrida, "Rams. Uninterrupted Dialogue–Between Two Infinites, the Poem," in Sovereignties in Question. The Poetics of Paul Celan, eds. Thomas Dutoit and Outi Pasanen (New York: Fordham University Press, 2005), 145.

177. Ibid.

178. Ibid., 153.

179. See ibid., 147.

180. Paul Celan, "Great, Glowing Vault"; See Jacques Derrida, "Rams. Uninterrupted Dialogue–Between Two Infinites, the Poem," in Sovereignties in Question. The Poetics of Paul Celan, eds. Thomas Dutoit and Outi Pasanen (New York: Fordham University Press, 2005), 153.

181. Ibid., 151.

182. Ibid., 147.

183. Hans-Georg Gadamer, Truth and Method, 102.

184. See Jacques Derrida, "Rams. Uninterrupted Dialogue–Between Two Infinites, the Poem," in Sovereignties in Question. The Poetics of Paul Celan, eds. Thomas Dutoit and Outi Pasanen (New York: Fordham University Press, 2005), 146. See also Gadamer, "Hermeneutics and Logocentrism," 123–124.

185. Hans-Georg Gadamer, "The Boundaries of Language," 16.

186. Hans-Georg Gadamer, "Letter to Dallmayr," 95.

187. Hans-Georg Gadamer, "Hermeneutics and Logocentrism," 124; Gadamer, *Truth and Method*, 375.

188. Hans-Georg Gadamer, "The Eminent Text and Its Truth," in *The Horizon of Literatur*, ed. Paul Hernadi (Lincoln: University of Nebraska Press, 1982), 346. On this see Chapter V.

189. Jacques Derrida, "Rams. Uninterrupted Dialogue–Between Two Infinites, the Poem," in *Sovereignties in Question. The Poetics of Paul Celan*, ed. Thomas Dutoit and Outi Pasanen (New York: Fordham University Press, 2005), 146.

190. Ibid.

191. See §14.

192. Jacques Derrida, "Rams. Uninterrupted Dialogue—Between Two Infinites, the Poem," in *Sovereignties in Question. The Poetics of Paul Celan*, ed. Thomas Dutoit and Outi Pasanen (New York: Fordham University Press, 2005), 149.

193. Paul Celan, "Singable Remnant," in *Breathturn* (Los Angeles: Sun and Moon, 1995), 101; see also Jacques Derrida, *Schibboleth*, 68–69.

194. Jacques Derrida, *Schibboleth*, 101–105, 109–110.

195. See Hans-Georg Gadamer, *Truth and Method*, 383.

196. Jacques Derrida, "Rams. Uninterrupted Dialogue—Between Two Infinites, the Poem," in *Sovereignties in Question. The Poetics of Paul Celan*, ed. Thomas Dutoit and Outi Pasanen (New York: Fordham University Press, 2005), 153.

197. Jacques Derrida, *Schibboleth*, 80; Hans-Georg Gadamer, "Hermeneutics Tracking the Trace [On Derrida]," in *The Gadamer Reader: A Bouquet of the Later Writings*, ed. Richard E. Palmer (Evanston Ill.: Northwestern University Press, 2007), 404.

SEVEN

UTOPIA OF UNDERSTANDING

> In rivers north of the future
> I cast the net you
> haltingly weight
> with stonewritten
> shadows.

> —Paul Celan[1]

1. U-TOPIA, TOPIA, UTOPIA: ON GUSTAV LANDAUER

In the *Libellus* on the *nova Insula Utopia*, which Thomas Moore submitted to press in Louvain in 1516, *Utopia* is the proper name for the place of an ideal community. For there—and not only in Moore's work—the name *Eutopia* appears as well. The reference here is to the highest good represented by the "community," which is designed in the new being together. But the unreality of the design—which contrasts with the criticized reality—and the distance of the place are the motivations behind the preference accorded to the name "utopia," formed in Greek from the negation *ou* "non-" and from the substantive *tópos* "place"; hence, it means a *non-place*, a place which is not, which is not yet. Later, the almost definitive substitution of the *eû* with the *ou* will indicate the negativity perceived in the name "utopia"—a negativity destined to be interpretable and indeed to be interpreted in various ways.

Raised to a common name for different forms, from Plato's *Republic* to Campanella's *City of the Sun*, and on to Bacon's *New Atlantis*, utopia is defined negatively through the sharp opposition to reality, since it names all that is unreal, or better still, not real: ideas, dreams, desires, chimeras, inventions, fictions, and imaginary voyages to the fabulous and fantastic non-place, beyond the in itself rational and perfect place of reality. The *beyond*, which is different and distant, foreign to reality and unrealizable, succumbs to reality and is thus refuted in its name. This, for example, is what happens with Leibniz.[2] Seen in this way, the non-place named by "utopia" reveals itself to be a place that is positively and concretely identifiable, and whose negativity lies not so much in its nonreality, as in its opposition to reality. As such, the non-place appears defined and definable: a philosophically contradictory place, equivocal and suspect, politically dubious and dangerous, poetically unrepresentable.[3]

The negative or pejorative meaning begins to fade when the static opposition between reality and unreality breaks down, in the moment when unreality is understood as not-yet-reality, as a future possibility. The dynamic connection emerges in history. Not because the future is deduced from the present, or even from the past. But because the past already contains the beyond-yet-to come of the future—not, however, according to an evolutionary line, but according to a leap, an interruption, a revolution.

In the political-philosophical reflection on this topic, Gustav Landauer constitutes an indispensable point of reference. He remains such even in Celan's *Meridian*.[4] What is revolution? In order to answer this question, Landauer distinguishes in his essay *Revolution* between "topia" and "utopia."[5] Topia is the entirety of all those forms of communal life that have acquired a relative stability. But stability is called into question, and the equilibrium becomes precarious, when utopia takes the place of topia. Differently from the topia, utopia does not belong to the realm of communal life, but rather to that of individual life. Landauer defines utopia as "a combination of ambitions" that, although they are initially isolated and heterogeneous, can nevertheless, in a moment of historical crisis, come together in a communal form, that is, in the tendency to create a new topia.[6] Thus, every topia is followed by a utopia and the latter, in turn, is followed by another topia, according to an incessant rhythm that marks the history of the world. Revolution is the utopic passage from the old to the new topia, it is "the space between two topias."[7] But in itself the passage marked by utopia is destined never to be realized. Utopia never fully becomes "actual (material) reality": The new topia, intervening to save it, determines instead the demise of utopia.[8]

Yet one cannot speak of a real end, just as one cannot speak of a real beginning. Utopia is anarchic—from *an arché*—it is *an*, that is, the negation of the *arché*, of "domination," but at the same time also of the "beginning."[9] ". . . history has no beginning. This is implied in the notion of *Geschehen*. If there is a beginning, there is an end. *Geschehen* has no end, however. Neither is there historical beginning."[10] On the contrary, there is neither beginning nor end of historical happening: We would not know where to write the word *end*. In every topia, the elements of the preceding utopia come together with the surviving elements from the preceding topia. In an analogous interweaving of past, present, and future, every utopia arises both from the reaction against the existing topia and from the powerful remembrance of all the known utopias that have come before. Although utopia seems to fade and wane, nonetheless, even where stable topias dominate, it continues to live in an underground way, and to search in foreign lands for a passage that will allow it to re-emerge and that can be indicated by a name: "revolution." In this sense, revolution is not a period of time, but is the principle that always goes "further," that pushes "beyond."[11]

This revaluation of utopia, which, starting with Landauer, runs through the entire political-philosophical reflections of the twentieth century, from Bloch to Adorno, is carried out through a new relation between past and future that can no longer be reduced to a simple opposition between reality and unreality. We understand the past—Landauer says—only in terms of how we are today, we understand it from the point at which we stand, as if it were "our way."[12] Seen in this light, the past is never something statically defined and accomplished, but is rather a becoming. This not only means that the past appears different, because it is considered differently: Moreover—even though it may sound paradoxical—the past modifies itself along with us. Thus, "the past itself is future. It is never finished, it always becomes. It changes and modifies as we move ahead."[13] In every moment, the past runs and passes by, precipitates into the future, and thus always appears to be in movement.

The barrier between past and future falls. The past makes itself readable and understandable only in light of the future and for the future, because the future is the future of the past, in which the past realizes itself by becoming present. On the other hand, this is possible because, beyond every barrier and every separation, the stirrings of the future are already present in the past. According to Bloch, in every shaped reality there is present an "unresolved utopian tension."[14] By way of this tendency, the distinct boundaries between real and possible appear problematic, doubtful, uncertain, and fluid. Indeed one strays in on the other. The question about the reality of things is the question about the star of their utopia, about their future possibility. Without these utopic stirrings that constitute a part of it, one would not be able to understand the real in its transitory presence. The being of the present refers to the not-yet-being of the future to be understood. *The future is the hinge of understanding.* The utopic tendency, as it results from the latency of history, appears time and time again as the "most essential reality" and even as the very "anticipation" of reality.[15]

In the name of the future—and of the not-yet-being—new light is shed on the present and the past. Each time they make themselves readable and comprehensible in a different way. Thus, in respect to the moment of its first appearance on the philosophical scene, twentieth-century utopia takes on an opposite value, and thus the relation between reality and unreality is inverted. From *u-topia*, the absence of place, the absence of reality, unreality *par excellence*, measured with the limited reality of *topia*, along the lines of the future, utopia unexpectedly reveals itself to be the opening of the place beyond the border in which reality is anticipated.

2. CELAN, POETRY, AND THE "REVOLUTION OF THE BREATH"

The utopic power of poetry, already underscored by Landauer, is also affirmed by Bloch.[16] Celan, however, is the one who brings together poetry and utopia. He does it both in the transversal reflection on the poetry found in his poems, as well as in the reflections contained in his few and elliptic prose-writings.

"Aber auch die Dichtung eilt uns manchmal voraus. La poésie, elle aussi, brûle nos étapes."[17] In its preceding us, in its rushing ahead of our steps, by forging ahead, in its anticipating and overcoming us, poetry describes the utopic movement from place to non-place. It is this utopic movement that Celan redescribes. By sustaining it and following it, in order to redescribe it, Celan encounters the meridian, the imaginary yet truly terrestrial and planetary line that, by traversing the poles and intersecting the tropics, returns each time in an open and infinite circularity.

First and foremost, the poem is *speaking for the other*. By this directing from the self to the other, it shows a centrifugal dimension and, by fleeing from the center in order to anticipate and predict a new center, it also reveals an eccentric dimension. The poem continually moves outward from the center of the here and now where it could stop and settle down, simultaneously revoking it as a center. In its eccentricity, the poem is prefigured as an exit from the self. Yet it is not simply an exit, because it moves decidedly toward the other.

Whereas the poem marks distance and estrangement—why else would it direct itself toward the other?—it also projects and prepares for an encounter. For Celan, the poem is precisely this: *encounter*. It is an encounter already in a completely elementary sense, in the way a handshake is. "I cannot see any basic difference between a poem and a handshake," writes Celan to Hans Bender.[18] But the *encounter* recalls Buber's *Begegnung*. The poem, even in its solitude, which sets it on the way, and precisely for this, is situated *"in the secret of an encounter."*[19] But how does the poem prepare the encounter and open up the dialogue? There is a preliminary condition that comes before every message, before every gesture, even before the handshake, which comes before every beckoning. Its importance rests not in its meaning, but in its invoking. It constitutes the first step of the turning toward and reaching out to the other, like calling for attention.

What opens the poem to the encounter is *attentiveness*—Celan here takes up Benjamin's idea, who had in turn taken up Malebranche's[20]—as the "natural prayer of the soul": that extreme welcoming and extreme giving, in short, that extreme hermeneutic capacity that requires a concentration "on our dates," on our days, months, and years, that marks the existence of the other as well as our own existence.[21]

Yet, if attentiveness is the opening of the poem, will it be able to translate itself immediately into words? Will it not rather rest in the concentrated silence of listening? Before directing itself and running toward the other, a rest, an interruption is required of the poem. It is that pause between inhalation and exhalation that precedes the *Atemwende*, the sudden inversion, the turn of breath. It can be both infinite or can last for only an imperceptible instant. However, it will be enough for the breath to turn itself around before condensing into the crystal of the poetic word. Poetry is first and foremost this inversion. *Dichtung: das kann eine Atemwende bedeuten*—"Poetry: that can signify a breath turn."[22] With the breath, all the hope that always accompanies a mutation, an overturning, a revolution, condenses and holds itself to the point of explosion. "No one can say how long the breath-pause—the longing and the thought—will last."[23] Before running out of air from holding one's breath, the poem gives it back by inverting it into a word that, screamed or whispered, is a new word, a word that is indeed a "counter-word" (*Gegenwort*).[24] This inversion is also, and above all, a subversion, a revolt, and a revolution. *Atemwende* should be translated as "revolution of the breath."[25] Thus, the poetic word is the counter-word and poetry is revolution.

Celan is not the first poet to propose this connection. The Russian poets play a major role here. In acknowledging this, Celan addresses his "fellow traveler" Osip Mandelstam. What is revolution for Mandelstam? Or, in light of the elective affinity they share—what is revolution for Celan? "For him revolution—and here a chiliastic trait particular to Russian thought stands forth—is the dawn of the different, the rising up of the humble, the exaltation of the base—an overturning on a truly cosmic scale. The revolution lifts up the earth by its hinges."[26] The word that arises from the inversion of breath, the word that bursts forth from the subversion, which is condensed, concentrated, and rapid—as with everything in a revolution[27]— is the poetic word that discloses the exit in the direction of the other.

3. BREAKING THE SILENCE: VOICE AND THE ABSOLUTE VOCATIVE

The "step" outside and forward, the exit from the self, is *speaking*. Here, in speaking, language reveals itself as *breath, direction, and destiny*.[28] It first of all reveals itself as breath because, in the presence of the "strangeness," of the "abyss," and of the "head of Medusa," it can fall silent.[29] That which Celan also calls the "Majesty of the absurd" can take one's breath and the word away, provoking a fearful silence.

Thus, the word is a word "torn from silence," an *argumentum e silentio*.[30] If it is "torn," if it is "wrested from silence" (*erschwiegen*), it is because the one who speaks, perhaps without knowing it, perhaps without wanting to, has not tacitly given in to that "strong bent toward falling silent" that seems to belong to poetry.[31] If silence is not the limit of language for Celan, the delimitation and the external line from which this begins (because there is always a filigree of silence in language), nonetheless silence does not have the magic of the unsaid and indeed it does not have any magic at all. The unsaid is the residue of silence in language, it is that which is not said, that not yet said which waits to be said and awaits saying. This is far from the apotheosis of silence that can be easily found in the literature and philosophy of the second half of the twentieth century. For Celan, silence is a "burden," before one's own the silence of the other, and even more that of the foreigner or of foreignness.[32] Moreover: silence is the foreigner and the foreigner is silence. Since the foreigner has remained silent, has not been articulated in word, has not become language, it escapes understanding, and it is the incomprehensible as such. It is precisely because the silence is strange in its incomprehensibility, that it is a "collision," a "strike." "The silent strike against you, silent strikes."[33] The counter-word of poetry is therefore an opposition to this strike, a rebellion against silence. Even from a purely phenomenological perspective, speaking is speaking into the silence (*in die Stille*), it is a breaking of silence, that is, tearing, breaking, cleaving it, in a certain way, opening it.[34] Speaking is marking the silence, articulating it—one could even say translating it.

When the breath is not cut short, it turns itself around and, looking for a way, for a way out, finds the voice and becomes voice. For Celan, who perhaps has here in mind the homophony in French between *voie* and *voix*, the voice is the way, way out or the way of freedom.[35] The importance of the voice for Celan cannot be emphasized enough, and because of this he sits within the Jewish tradition.[36] Poems make their way through paths opened up by voices intercalated with silence, wrested from silence.[37] While speaking finds the way out through the voice, it appears to be an intercalating, or better, a stuttering. As for Hölderlin, even for Celan speaking is, in its primal modality, a stuttering childhood of language.[38] Its primal modality here means the way in which poetry makes its way with the voice. The primary modality is poetic because the poet seeks out the word by stuttering. And in this seeking he runs up against the limits of language. Here, at the limits of language, speaking emerges—as it had appeared in Hamann—as nothing other than a stuttering that mimics the stuttering of others, a restuttering of the stuttering that those already ignore. In this sense, for Celan it is language that stutters: "And so it stutters, on and on."[39] And because the poet, who is a "guest" in language, as well as in the world of that language, can only reproduce the world through his stuttering, experiencing in this, once again, his own irreducible foreignness, his being exiled in language.[40] In exile, the "distance from the I" (*Ich-ferne*) is realized that for Celan characterizes modern art, and especially modern poetry.[41]

The word that the poet stutters after is directed to the other. His breath has a direction, it is a direction. Crystallized in the word, the poet directs himself to the other, distances himself from the I. This is the step forward. Separated from itself, forgetful of itself, by estranging itself in the word, the I becomes entirely word. Even before: It becomes entirely a sign. In this sense Hölderlin says: "we are a sign. . . ." The I signals donation of a sign to the point of making itself entirely a sign. It is a matter, as Levinas writes, of a "singular de-substantiation of the I."[42] The first step of speaking to the other is this directing and addressing itself of the I, desubstantiated in the breath and in the direction of the breath, this absolute vocative that precedes every word and every content of the word. The emblem of every act of speaking is in this *absolute vocative*.[43] The poem uncovers the speaking for the speaking, the proximity for the proximity, the proximity of the word as pure invocation, as almost only a still articulating attentiveness and prayer turned toward immediate contact, as that of a handshake. It is the proximity of the word that is already a response, because it anticipates and runs ahead of the question that by its being beyond the I entirely for the other, signals, with this far from obvious surplus, the overcoming of the I in a word that is always for the other. "*Poems* are also *gifts—gifts* to the attentive. Gifts bearing *destinies*."[44]

4. JANUARY 20: THE DATE AND THE CIRCUMCISED WORD

Poetry, by following its direction and destination, by running toward the other, neither forgets nor denies its own provenance—the destiny in which it is written and inscribed, the star under which it is born. Thus, every poem carries with itself the trace of its provenance, of its destiny, of its star: the *date*. "Perhaps what's new for poems written today is just this: that here the attempt is clearest to remain mindful of such dates?"[45] Remaining mindful of the date means freeing the poem from every presumed a-temporality in order to emphasize its extreme temporalization. Thus, Celan asks in a question, which is almost an observation: "But don't we all date from such dates? And what dates do we ascribe ourselves to?"[46] Every date marks both the destiny in which everyone is inscribed and the time from which—and after which—everyone writes. This is because language—one could say with Rosenzweig—"is time-bound, time-nourished."[47] Speaking enacts itself from the inescapable uniqueness of a point in time. What would be the sense in abstracting from this point and from this uniqueness in which language, in order to be actualized, must inescapably individualize itself? Thus, every poem must remain mindful of its own date and carry within itself the trace of that date.

But what is a *date*? Derrida chooses this question as the guiding thread in his reading of Celan, in whose poetry he sees both a reflection on the date and a poetic setting-into-work of dating.[48] The one is not separable from the other. The date that appears in Celan's poetry is more than just historical memory—in the sense of "remaining mindful"—and is a warning in remembrance of *"that which happened"* and for which language has found no word.[49] The question of the date, as Celan poses it, assumes exceptional philosophical importance for Derrida. Thus, the date, with its enigma, seems to resist exceptionally every philosophical theorization. The date is the event that happens only once and that nevertheless reproduces and indeed multiplies itself in the self-repeating of the calendar; the date is the unrepeatable that repeats itself in the recurrence of the memory and of the anniversary. "It is necessary that in the date the unrepeatable [*unwiederholbar*] repeat itself, effacing in itself the irreducible singularity that it denotes. It is necessary that, in a certain way, the unrepeatable divide itself in repeating itself, and in the same stroke encipher or encrypt itself."[50] As a trace of what has been lost, as the metonymy of the unreachable event, the date that poetry remembers and commemorates, readable only by rendering itself unreadable, is another way of saying the *différance* that cleaves writing open, the wound carved and inscribed from the origin, the incision of the tongue, its circumcision. The Jewish ritual of circumcision, which runs through all Celan's work, is not only the *Schibboleth* of an origin, but the open wound of a circumcised writing. If every word is circumcised, the poetic word, the one opened and held open by Celan, is circumcised in an eminent sense.[51] Thus, the poetry of Celan is for Derrida a "tropic of circumcision."[52] In this tropic, the date, in its plural uniqueness, opens up a wound on madness and the abyss of madness. "A *date is mad, that is the truth*."[53] But that abyss and that madness are the abyss and the madness of language itself. If poetry dates from the uniqueness of an event, and sets the date into work in order to dwell there in memory, this dwelling at the margin and on the verge of the abyss, the dwelling in the language and living it, has nothing secure or reassuring. Perhaps it is not even a dwelling, but rather a wandering together with the wandering of language. For the country that is your mother's "wanders everywhere, like language."[54] Celan's dates constellate his wandering. Yet the poetic setting to work of the date allows that a date belonging to the poet is a date for the other, the date of the other, it lets the date—repeatable in its uniqueness which commemorates heterogeneous recurrences and infinitely extraneous and distant events—to be given and the poet transcribes and promises himself in the date of the other. Because of this wandering will therefore not be solitary, and the date will be the point of encounter with the other no less than with oneself. It will be, in the *Meridian*, the "secret of an encounter."[55]

The word "date" indicates much more than a simple point in time. From the classical Latin *data(m)*, date is the past participle that appears in the expressions *datam litteram* or even *datam epistulam* and means "letter given, consigned (on that day, the day indicated)," from Latin *dare*, namely "to give, hand, offer, present, bear, consign, gift, bestow, donate." That every poem has a date, that it is dated, means then that starting from that date the poem is *given* and *gifted*—to itself, for the destiny that lets it be, and to the other, toward which it is destinally addressed. However, the date inscribed in every poem is not merely its possibility of being, but also its possibility of not being, its annihilation before it is. The date can also mark the abyss in which the breath is cut off and the word falls silent. January 20th is the date in which the poetry of Celan is inscribed, scribed, and to which it is assigned. Which January 20th? The January 20th that marks Celan's destiny is January 20th, 1942, the date of the Wannsee Conference where the "final solution" was decided on. Hence, before it existed, the poetry of Celan had been caught in a "straitening" (*Engführung*)—according to the title of the last poem contained in the collection *Sprachgitter*—at the crossroads between its annihilating silencing in the place of the annihilation, which, as Szondi suggests, is absolutely real, is a Nazi Lager, and the inversion of the breath that manages to pass through that straitening and that anguish by singing that place as the place of absolute horror.[56] But in being "thrown" into the straitening of January 20th, Celan's poem is not different from any other poem. "Perhaps we may say that every poem has its '20th of January' inscribed?"—Celan asks.[57] And Derrida sees in January 20th "something like the essence of the poem."[58] As an inalienable property, the date, January 20th, can be transcribed, exported, deported, ex-appropriated, reappropriated, and repeated in its absolute singularity. Every poem has its January 20th. "But in spite of the generality of the law, the example remains irreplaceable."[59]

5. SPEAKING EVER YET

The effort sustained by the poem not to fall silent, to continue to exist "at the margins of itself," is indicated by Celan in the unceasing transition from "Now-no-more" (*Schon-nicht-mehr*) to the poem's "Ever-yet" (*Immer-*

noch),[60] from a gesture of renunciation and silence to a gesture of audacity and language. "But this ever-yet could be only an act of speaking."[61] In the "Ever-yet" the breath and the yearning of every speaking, of every wanting to speak, condenses—ever yet. And all the more in poetic speaking. Thus this is not "simply language" (*Sprache schlechthin*), nor "correspondence" beginning from the word, but is rather "actualized language," it is act, *enérgeia* "set free under the sign of radical individuation."[62] But the ever-yet of the poem, the individual and radically individualized speaking, can be found only "in a poem by someone who does not forget that he speaks from the angle of incidence of his very being, his creatureliness."[63] The ever-yet, the audacity to speak, can only come forth under this angle of incidence. Osip Mandelstam is the example *par excellence* of the audacity of the ever-yet, because the poet *knows that he is speaking* under the angle of incidence and inclination, starting from the point where the star of his own existence becomes apparent, and he *knows to speak* from that angle by individualizing his own speaking in a radical way, until the limits of language, pushing the language to its most extreme limits.[64] Here language bears the individual trace of individuation. The poem would therefore be the "language-become-form of a single individual."[65] This language of the poem, which by "following its inmost nature, its presentness and presence" stretches itself into time, stretches out, in its singular solitude, into the other. "The poem is lonely. It is lonely [*einsam*] and on the way [*unterwegs*]."[66]

"Yet the poem does speak! It remains mindful of its dates, yet—it speaks. Indeed it speaks only in its very selfmost cause."[67] The poem speaks in spite of the date, January 20th, of the memory of that date, rooted in that single event. For the poem speaks if it recalls that date, if it refers back to that date, the date in which it writes, of which it writes. And while it speaks, it carries the word *beyond* the date.[68] Thus, it makes the impossible possible: dividing and sharing a singularity. Starting from the date, and thanks to the date, the poem speaks *in causa sui*, as one would say in the juridical terms used here by Celan: *in seiner eigenen, allereigensten Sache*. The German word *Sache* means "controversy, cause, reason for contention."[69] Without giving in to that absolute singularity, that inalienable property that has summoned it, which has con-voked it, this inalienable, this inappropriable must speak and speaks of the other, *in causa alteri*, to the other. Speaking is this ex-appropriation *par excellence*. Thus, speaking breaks the silence of the pure singularity. If silence preserves ownership, where language bursts forth, ownership fades away. While it speaks of that singularity, the poem, by articulating it, makes it readable, audible, and understandable, *beyond* the pure and absolute singularity of which it speaks, and directs and destines it to the other.

This *beyond* distinguishes the centrifugal movement of speaking *to the other*, of speaking *for the other*—perhaps something more than such a movement. The flight outside of the center is marked by the respiration, the direction, the destiny, while language becomes form. Poetry—as Celan had already said and repeated—"hurries ahead."[70] Albeit through by-ways, its audacity rushes ahead of our steps, forging ahead, anticipating us by overcoming us. "'Speed,' [das Geschwinde] which was always 'outside,' has gained speed [Geschwindigkeit]."[71] Similarly, Rilke speaks of the speed of the poetic word. He evokes it as an angel: "Über uns hinüber kann der Engel."[72] The angel of the word surpasses us and is always in front of us.[73] To follow the angel of the word is to sustain the yearning breath of the ever-yet. While it is uttered, in the breath turn, the poetic word, addressed to the other, is all of a sudden already above and beyond, beyond the I, is already with the other. It is the step outside and beyond which poses and exposes the I to the other and prepares it for the "secret" of the encounter. The encounter in itself is both a secret and a mystery, a Geheimnis.[74] The word recalls the Unheimlich, the "uncanny" that preceded it and the Heimkehr, the "return" and the "repatriation" that will follow it. It is the point of caesura between the two—of both it holds their respective secret; it is simultaneously far and near, foreign and familiar. Geheimnis, "secret," is another way to say breath turn. The Hebrew word for "breath" is ruah, which however also means "spirit."[75] The turn of breath is therefore also that subversion, that turning around of the spirit, which makes the impossible possible: that the breath of the I becomes the word of the other, that the breath speaks perhaps in the name of the "Wholly Other."[76]

6. THE LANGUAGE-GRILLE

The poet who follows the angel of the word, who accomplishes the audacious passage of the ever-yet and speaks under his angle of incidence, translates himself in the language. Speaking is translating.[77] It is translating oneself in the language of the other. While it directs itself toward the other, but before reaching the other, the breath that crystallizes itself encounters language. Thus, the "secret of the encounter" first fulfills itself in the encounter with language. Until the moment of this encounter, language is still breath, direction, and destiny. Only after the encounter will it be figure as well. The one who speaks under the sign of the "radical individuation," while he is aware of speaking under his angle of incidence, at the same time knows that he speaks "mindful of the limits drawn by language," limits that are just as much "the possibilities opened by language."[78]

The poem, which solitarily and ceaselessly directs itself toward the other, searches for a passage out of the straitening. More than a simple passage (Übergang), this exit is a passing through (Durchgang). It is a passage through the language-grille. The metaphor is Celan's and, besides being the title of one of his most famous poems, it is also the title of one of his collections: *Sprachgitter*. But what does "grille" mean? And why would language be a "grille"?

If one thinks of a grille, one thinks of a prison grille, or even, as was perhaps the case with Celan, the grille of an enclosed order.[79] In any case, "grille" indicates first a closure. Thus, the grille should close off, impede, or block passage. If this were so, the speaker would be shut in, encaged, and locked up in language. Language would be a prison. It is not uncommon to find in philosophical thought this conception of language. Approaching "grille" as a "structure" does not help, because structure, especially the way it has been understood by structuralism, refers to something static and fixed. Instead, there is another metaphor, a metaphor used by Humboldt that can help to clarify Celan's. With regard to language, Humboldt speaks of a *web*. Language appears as a "web of analogies."[80] The one who speaks is caught in the web, in the weft that he has not woven, and that has sprung forth from a dialogue to which he has not taken part. From this aspect, language is totally foreign and seems to envelope and entrap the one who speaks. But being caught up in a web does not mean being imprisoned. From the opposite aspect, and on closer inspection, the web is a web of analogies that are becoming crystallized but that can always become fluid again, analogical nexes that, by their nature, and because of the difference that always remains near to identity, emerge as open nexes. Thus, they simply offer an articulation that is neither closed nor definitive; the one who speaks can continually modify it and subsequently language is no longer totally foreign to him. But without the web, without the grille of language, the articulation itself, in its flexibility, would not even exist.[81] Hence, the paradox of a metaphor that stands for the metaphor, since the grille of language is the metaphor for the metaphorical grille, for the language's web of metaphors. It is the paradox of a *liberating closure*. The barrier of the grille is here the condition of freedom. The limits are as much possibilities. The grille of language discloses the only way to reach the freedom of speaking.

The grille, however, is a grille, and all the more so "for a poet who is Jewish and yet writes in German."[82] As Celan writes in his *Bremen speech*, language is "not lost," but had to "pass through."[83] Or better, by overturning the order of the *if–then*, insofar as it managed to "pass through," language is not lost. But the violence of that *passing through* can be grasped already in the obsession with which *hindurchgehen durch* is repeated three times, and also taken up twice more by Celan: *Sie ging hindurch*, "it passed." It is the violence of speaking that with the counter-word offers resistance to the power of language, which forces the grille and passes through it. Finally, by passing through, through "the event," it can come back to the light, even "enriched," *angereichert*—where by assonance Hitler's *Reich* is buried. The grille of language has not stopped and does not stop the speaking, the yearning of speaking, its ever-yet. Through and thanks to the grille, beginning from the grille of language, speaking can be individualized and become figure. This means, furthermore, that it is not language that speaks. As Heidegger wrote, *die Sprache spricht*, "language speaks."[84] Celan knew this all too well. In the famous yet complex *Gespräch im Gebirg* of 1960, prompted in 1959 by a missed encounter in the Engadine with Theodor W. Adorno,[85] and modeled after many literary and philosophical precedents, from Büchner to Nietzsche, from Kafka to Buber and to Mandelstam, in the context of Jewish wandering Celan describes a dialogue in the mountains, between a Jew and his son, where the themes of the I, the you, language, God, and Nature are tackled. Already deeply influenced by Buber's philosophy and by the Jewish thoughts on dialogue, Celan puts at the linguistic and philosophical center of the text the antinomy of two forms of language, namely, the personal and interpersonal.[86] The antinomy is between the language of the I and the language of the you, the language of dialogue, and "a language for you and not for me," namely a language "with no I and no Thou, pure He, pure It, you see, pure They, and nothing but that."[87] To the "neuter language," as Levinas rightly called it, by perceiving the Heideggerian resonance of the language that speaks and gives dwelling to Being,[88] Celan opposes the language of persons, of personal pronouns, of the I and the you, of the I that says I to the you and can say "do you hear me? Do hear me"[89] It is the language that says, repeats and demands: "Do you hear me?," *Hördstdu?*—translation of the Hebrew *Shemah*, "Hear," prayer and dictum of Judaism: *Shemah Israel*. The language is not the language of the neuter, it is neither neuter nor neutral; it is for me and for you, and it would not be without me and without you, without I and without you, it would not be if the I were not to speak it and if the you were not to speak it, and if, by speaking it, they would not direct it, the I to the you, the you to the I. Only in this dialogue, as with the dialogue in the mountains, can the language of the I, and that of the you, individualize itself and become poetry. For Celan, poetry springs forth from dialogue.

But although it permits individuation, language also marks the distance between the I and the you. Precisely because the I and the you are articulated in language and through the grille, the grille remains to indicate the distance and the foreignness: "nobody is *like* the other." As Celan underlines, the "like" is illusory and deceptive.[90] This is also what he wanted to express in his poem *Sprachgitter*. He wanted to say the difficulty of speaking and understanding each other.[91]

> (Were I like you. Were you like me.
> Did we not stand
> Under *that one* trade wind?
> We are strangers.)[92]

One should not delude oneself as to the *wie*, the "how." The conditional emphasizes this. The parentheses nonetheless mark an interruption which might also be a hope, turned against that ending: "strangers," *Fremde*. There is, in fact, a saving, redemptive word: *Passat*. The German *Passat*, or *Passatwind*, names the trade wind and thus can be translated as "wind." But *Passat* evokes *Passa*, the German expression for the Hebrew *Pessach*. The favorable trade wind is that which blows at Passover, the feast of passage after the exodus, the feast of liberation. But that wind is the same wind and the strangeness is only in a community.

7. STRAITENING, ANGUISH, ANXIETY: ON THE LIMIT SITUATION

Every word that opens up a passage, which removes straitening and anguish, can be saving and redemptive. The German word *Enge*, which appears in Celan's poem *Engführung*, means "straitening," "narrow passage," "pass," "gorge," and thus "straitness," "narrowness," but also "anguish." On the other hand, *Enge* also has an etymological affinity with *Angst* that, besides the meaning of "fear," also has the philosophically well-known and noteworthy meaning of "anguish." *Enge* is therefore a keyword not only in Celan's poetry. Alongside its physical value, the word also has a psychical value: It indicates both the straitening of the body and of the soul. In Hebrew the word for *eng*, "narrow," "strait" is *tzam*, hence *Mitzrajim*, meaning "Egypt." The title of Celan's poem *In Ägypten* is the translation of the Hebrew *B'mitzrajim*, namely "In Egypt," in the place of oppression and slavery, of anguish and exile (*Exodus* 3, 7).[93]

Straitening, straitness, anguish—the limits between the meanings of these words are fluid—are experienced where there is a limit, where one runs up against the limit of a limit situation. But what is a "limit situation"? The concept can be traced back to Karl Jaspers as one of the pillars of his philosophy.[94] Man's existence is always situated, irrevocably inserted into a particular situation with which one identifies—for Celan, it is January 20th. One can step out of a situation, but only by entering into another. If the situation changes, what does not change is the being-in-a-situation.[95] The straitening and anguish—Jaspers speaks of *Enge*—in which existence is always situated, defines the *human condition*.

There are nevertheless situations for Jaspers that can be neither transformed nor overcome because they are connected with the precariousness and finitude of existence. Jaspers calls them limit situations (*Grenzsituationen*): "Situations like the following: that I am always in situations; that I cannot live without struggling and suffering; that I cannot avoid guilt; that I must die–these are what I call limit-situations."[96] But in this sense, one can say that every situation is a limit situation, and every limit situation is a situation. Such an objection, albeit tacitly, is raised by Heidegger.[97] One could then ask: Which is the limit between the situation and the limit situation? The limit, the boundary, is unstable. Put otherwise, there is no limit from which one can define a limit situation, and thus there is no objectivity. Every situation is lived, in fact, in an individual form. Thus, what is a situation for one person can be lived by another as a limit situation, and vice versa, what is a limit situation for one may be lived by the other just as a situation. Heidegger draws attention to the latter case. Extreme, extraordinary, and exceptional situations can be lived simply as situations, and not as limit situations; the human being hides from itself its own being-in-a-situation, and even more its own being-in-a-limit-situation, because otherwise, if it were continually confronted with the limit of its own being and of its own being-human, the human being could not go on living.

Despite the intrinsic ambiguity in the limit-situation, one can say that between multiple and disparate situations, to which human life can be linked, limit situations are those that, when lived, lead to a *limit*. For Jaspers, the concept of "limit" becomes relevant in relation to the concept of "situation." In a nonmetaphorical sense, the limit of the limit situation is, for Jaspers, a "wall" against which one collides and "founders."[98] As such, the limit is *per definitionem* insurmountable, even if it is definable only individually—that which is a wall for one may not be a wall for another. Thus, this means that the limit is neither a static nor an absolute concept, but rather a relative, relational, and dynamic concept.[99] The limit is not definitively given, once and for all, and in the same way for everyone. But what happens when each of us, in our own individual way, collides with the limit? In the very moment that one collides with the limit of the limit situation, one also collides with the limit of one's own existence in its finitude. Every attempt to overcome the limit, to get over the wall, to transform the situation, is destined to founder.

8. THE OTHER OF THE LIMIT, THE LIMIT OF THE OTHER: THE YOU IS THE LEVER OF THE I

At the wall of the limit, the human being is completely alone in his foundering. All of a sudden his knowledge vanishes, the word falls silent, and the voice fades away. A lonely and isolating silence takes over. And since the silence is absolute, so, too, is the solitude. The limit situation stands at the limit of language. It is already in the neighboring region of a silence incapable of language. Here, in this region, which is foreign to time and foreign to language, the human being is closed in and constricted. And, as with all that surrounds the human being, even the human being becomes foreign to time and foreign to language—the human being becomes inarticulate.

It does not allow itself to be articulated and converted into words. This is a silence that overwhelms and dismays, insofar as it is a "frightful falling silent" of absolute solitude, whose breath has been taken away, together with the very capacity to speak.[100]

Here, alone and silenced, at the wall of the straitening, the human being can be suffocated, asphyxiated, oppressed, it can be annihilated. The human being has been annihilated in the places of annihilation. However, the limited and limiting anguish of the limit situation presents an ambiguity, or even a sort of antinomy. Depending on the perspective, the limit is, on the one hand, an internal barrier, and on the other, an external wall and even an exterior door, a door that grants passage and exit onto an open and free space. At the wall's limit, the breath can be inverted. After the pause of inhalation, albeit infinitely long, the yearning to speak, grown in anguish, can burst forth. It can pass through the straitening and direct itself to the other. If there were, however, no other, there would not be the breath's turn. For the silenced I could in no part of itself, find the strength to breathe. Rather, closed, immersed and absorbed in itself, it would breathe its last breath.

But the "limit implies that there is some other."[101] The other is therefore always already given in the limit situation. The experience of the other at the limit, taken not as an internal barrier of existence, but rather as the point of opening of the possibilities that are offered, is the peculiar trait of the limit situation. The other is the quidditas of the limit. When it reaches the limit, while experiencing the other as a you, existence articulates itself as an I. And no matter how the other is perceived, as a foreigner, but also as hostile and adverse, it is always the other who draws the I out of the anguish of its situation in order to grant it access to the vastness of saying and letting be said, of speaking and of understanding, that is, to the opening of the dialogue.

Dialogue responds to the fundamental—foundational and thus abyssal—disposition of life that is anguish and anxiety. In order to escape its own anguish toward the vastness that is always foreign, the I is forced to take distance from itself. In this centrifugal movement, in which it collides with the limit of the other, of the stranger, and undergoes this collision, the I loses its own center. Paradoxically, however, it is the stranger and the other who help the I to rediscover its center. This paradoxical event takes place in dialogue. Turning toward the you is for the I the condition of relocating itself, of relocating the center of its own self, of reestablishing its own equilibrium. But for the destinal eccentricity of the I, the center is never the former center and is thus always different. It differs through time, through language, and in dialogue. It is a "wandering, empty, hospitable" center.[102] Thus the I, through the you always understands itself differently.

The encounter with the you elevates the I above its own anguish and therewith above its own limitations. The you is the lever of the I. Not only because the I, in the always familiar foreignness of the you, experiences its own limit, but also because in the escape from the center, in the centrifugal movement of speaking, the I is, thanks to the you and with the you, always already beyond itself: in the common, shared word. The breath that, cut short, was about to go out forever, directed at and destined to the other, in the yearning of the ever-yet, becomes the word of the other. On "breath paths" the word migrates from one mouth to another.[103] One turn around follows another: that of the other. And the identical is restituted, but in a different way. Taken, taken-with, and repeated, in the mystery of an identity that defers, the word becomes a common, shared word.

9. UNDERSTANDING TO LIVE,
LIVING TO UNDERSTAND: AUSCHWITZ

Withdrawing from understanding is withdrawing from language. And as with the philosophical tradition one speaks of a "natural instinct" for language, it would also be legitimate to speak of a natural instinct for understanding.[104] But, in order to better focus this instinct, one could perhaps speak of a *vital instinct of understanding.*

Etymologically, "vital" is connected with the Latin *vita,* "life." Beyond this immediate connection, by which "vital" refers to everything that concerns "life," the meanings that can be discerned in the semantic field of "vital" are twofold and correlated: Vital means "full of life," "full of life force," and thus also "able to give life,," that is, vital in the sense of "relative to life," hence, in a figurative form, "important," "necessary," and "indispensable," where it is implicit "for life."[105]

That understanding is a vital instinct means, above all, that understanding is indispensable for living, that without understanding one cannot live and, furthermore, it means that understanding is able to instill life, to transform it, and to enlighten it. In both cases—even though the one is not really separable from the other—understanding is part of life and, indeed, it is the most essential part of human living.

At a second glance, the link between living and understanding is actually not surprising. What is surprising is that this link has not yet been stressed. Clearly, it could not have been stressed in the entire philosophical tradition that, dominated by rationalistic optimism, has never drawn understanding into question. But things are different in contemporary philosophy where understanding, as is well known, has a leading role. In respect to the traditional way of taking understanding for granted, philosophical hermeneutics—starting with Schleiermacher and Humboldt—

placed the accent on not-understanding. As is well known, the not-understanding experienced in the hermeneutics of sacred texts, namely, in texts written in foreign and ancient languages that are difficult to interpret, becomes a revelatory symptom of the much broader not-understanding that always occurs in the dialogue of daily life and that thus claims universality. Even though with Heidegger first, and then with Gadamer, the situation changes, and understanding constitutes the starting point, not-understanding remains in the constellation of hermeneutics—it could not have been otherwise—and thus marks the way in which understanding is understood.

Nevertheless the "not-" of not-understanding has gained more and more relevance. The renunciatory trait of this negativity has circulated widely throughout contemporary philosophy and not-understanding has found a theoretical justification, or even just a practical one, in the most diverse forms and manners. But the risk here could be great. For not-understanding is not taken as the limit of understanding, is not seen in relation to understanding, correlated to it, that is, in its relativity. On the contrary, just because it is absolutized, albeit only inadvertently, and only in order to be safeguarded, not-understanding risks to be hypostasized. The hypostatization of not-understanding—ultimately the flip side of the traditional obviousness of understanding—can have disastrous consequences.

It is a short step from not-saying to denying—and in history one has come to deny the facts. Also in this regard the prejudice has dominated and continues to dominate according to which there would be nothing to understand. Evil would be precisely a nothing, outside of being, outside of that which is, that which could be said and that which could be understood. This negation is actually a way of taking part in the large enterprise of extermination. The Hebrew word *Shoah* means, at is well known, annihilation, destruction, ruin. Evil has wanted not only the termination of consciousness and the death of bodies, but also the total negation of understanding.

Becoming entrenched in not-understanding, or even in not wanting to understand, under the banner of Nietzsche's *amor fati*, and of a presumed respect for what in the human being is individual, and what, if it were understood, would be offended, can be dangerous and even deadly for life.[106] Taking the limit of not-understanding as a trench means to separate oneself from the past, to close oneself off from the future, and to hold oneself in a present taken as "destiny." Hence, it means to escape language and therefore to escape dialogue, but also the dialogue of history; it means to escape history. And no matter how grotesque it might sound, recent history already seems to have given way to this becoming entrenched in not-understanding and of having provoked a crisis of understanding. How can one presume to understand "what has happened"? What would even be understandable in the absolute strangeness of what Paul Celan called "the Medusa's head"? To the silence that Adorno prescribed to poets, should there not correspond a similar silence of not-understanding? Should one not agree, then, that one is here dealing with an *unsayable incomprehensible*? In this way, does one not run the risk of granting Auschwitz a mystical privilege and of worshiping it in silence?[107]

This question must be addressed today above all to philosophy, because philosophy has interpreted radical evil as the opposite of thought; thus it has contributed in a decisive way to banishing Auschwitz to the domain of mystery, of that which is inexplicable, unsayable, and incomprehensible. But rejecting Auschwitz as something outside of its own sphere of competence, philosophy has at the same time renounced its duty and admitted its loss. Even the questions, which were more debated in recent years, of guilt and forgiveness, reaffirm the limits between the anti-world and the world, and are at least attempts to think evil by transforming it into good. But in this way philosophy not only misses its target; it misses also the opportunity to invert its course, the possibility perhaps of that new post-metaphysical beginning for which it has been searching for long a time.[108]

The absence of philosophy in the face of Auschwitz leads to us ask: Why not begin again—starting from Auschwitz—in a new and different way? Why not begin again from the anti-world of the world? And why not ask the philosophically relevant question of *understanding* precisely with respect to Auschwitz? Understanding Auschwitz: Why not begin again from here?

An answer to this question, but also to the question of not-understanding and of understanding, could perhaps come from an inversion, from a *hysteron—próteron* of the argument. Just where not-understanding and not-being-understood have been deadly, where the not-understanding has shown itself in all its mortal capacity, just there, and all the more there, understanding is required, demanded and invoked.

Auschwitz, the proper irreplaceable name, the metonymy for "what happened," to which Celan does not give a name, is the event that one must not call "unique," insofar as that would abstract it from history, and that one could call then—following Emil Fackenheim[109]—an "unprecedented" event—so that one is pushed to search for precedents in the past and to be vigilant so that it will not become a precedent in the future. As epochal event, wound, break, that marks a first and an after in the history of the world, Auschwitz is a challenge issued to philosophy. It is a challenge, not only because it leads it to revise its own concepts, from that of death to that of freedom, from that of moral law to that of reason, to mention but a few. It is a challenge not only because it strongly points out previously unthought concepts that have still remained outside of the philosophical inventory.

Auschwitz is a challenge above all, because, starting from the human being who is no longer human, who is dehumanized and inhuman, of both, the victim or the executioner, starting from their inhuman condition, it forces philosophy to rethink radically the human condition.[110] It forces it to ask again, once again: What is a human being? *Se questo è un uomo* (*If this is a Man*)—this is the title of Primo Levi's book that appeared 1947. Levi's question concerns the "Muselmann," the hungry prisoner, who is close to death. The etymology of "Muselmann" is still unclear: The word is traced back to the fatalism or to a particular way the prisoners had to bandage the head, which reminds one of a turban. For all intents and purposes, it meant the Jew who was dying, the human being decomposing within the camp.[111]

Planet Auschwitz is the anti-world at the limits of the world. As the Buchenwald survivor David Rousset called it for the first time, it is the "concentrational universe" that contains in itself, unexplained and explained with transparent crudeness, all the concentrational and totalitarian universes to come. Auschwitz is the *"extreme situation" par excellence*—as Bruno Bettelheim called it in 1943 after fleeing from the Nazi camp. It is the limit situation of all human or even inhuman limit situations, from which one should try to view the world again, in a new way, by rediscovering the connection between the anti-world and the world.[112] Many witnesses have lived and recounted Auschwitz as limit situation, at the edge of the world, and at the limit of the human.

It is to the limit situation of speaking and understanding or, better, of not-speaking and not-understanding in Auschwitz-Monowitz that Primo Levi bears witness. In his book *The Drowned and the Saved*, published in 1986, shortly before he took his own life in 1987, there is a chapter entitled *Comunicare*, "Communicating."[113] Levi describes with great precision the limit situation of the anti-language in the anti-world of the world, in the concentrational universe of the camp. A "total linguistic barrier" rises here implacably in a way that is unlike the "normal world" where, even in the encounter with the most foreign and distant languages, it is always a matter of a more or less, and "the almost not-understanding each other can even be as amusing as a game."[114] This linguistic barrier is as *total* as the totalitarianism that it established through the not-understanding, the not-wanting-to-understand, the not-making-oneself-understandable, the not-wanting-to-make-oneself-understandable. The mechanism of power institutes itself here. And the barrier, total and totalitarian, does not tolerate games and does not make any room for games: It is a "life sentence."[115] Very simply: *The one who does not understand, dies.*

At Auschwitz, the Babel of the twentieth century, the language of the camp is a rudimentary and skeletal variant of the *Lingua Tertii Imperii,* the German of the Third Reich.[116] However, in *Lagerjargon*, in the jargon of the camp, German is contaminated by Yiddish, Polish, Silesian, and Hungarian. But knowing or not knowing German is the watershed between life and death. The Italian prisoners who had just arrived and who did not understand, who did not have time to understand, drowned after just a few days "in the stormy sea of not-understanding."[117] At first glance, they died from hunger, cold, fatigue, or illness; but, looked at more closely, they died from the "*collision*" with the linguistic barrier. The SS, like all brutish people, do not distinguish between those who do not understand their language and those who do not understand at all. According to a common model in the ethnic manipulation of language—or as Derrida would say of *lógos*—the one who cannot understand German is a "barbarian" who babbles and does not speak. If he insists on speaking, or even on babbling in "his non-language," he must be silenced. Since he does not even have a language, he is not even a "*Mensch*, not a human being."[118] Only the one who understands, even if just a little, and answers in an articulate way to those angry German barks, "establishes the semblance of a human relationship."[119]

But, it is no more than a semblance. In the universe of the concentration camp, the communication shows, besides the total linguistic barrier, another characteristic: the use of the word, which makes a human being human, falls into disuse. For Levi it is a sign: "for those people we were no longer human beings."[120] Language becomes then an instrument that serves only to give orders to a dehumanized being who is treated like an animal. Speaking to this no longer human being would be like recognizing his or her humanity—precisely the humanity that must not be recognized and actually removed; speaking to this no longer human being would be to take it and to understand it as other than oneself. Therefore, the language in the camp is reduced to a dozen or so "variously assorted but *univocal* signs . . . , be they acoustical, tactile, or visual."[121] But those univocal signs, emptied of all semantic content and reduced to mere designations, mean a lot: They are the extreme, ferocious transformation of the other into the self, the final episode of Western cannibalism in which the self definitively absolves itself from the other.

And because there is no longer a need to speak, there is not even the need to translate. The interpreter no longer has a use. In the camp of Mauthausen, the rubber whip was called "*der Dolmetscher*," the interpreter.[122] In fact, everyone understands the language of the whip and it becomes useless and stupid to translate and interpret it. Therefore, starting from here, one ought to meditate more than ever on the value of translation and interpretation for human life. This whip is the word reduced and lowered to a thing; it is the word humiliated and revoked in the thing; it is the dead word,

and indeed it is the death of the word. It is the annihilation of language and thus the annihilation of the human. As Levi notes, "where violence is inflicted on the human being, it is also inflicted against language."[123]

In the memory of the survivors, and of Levi in particular, the first days in the camp were like a "black and white film, with sound but not a talkie."[124] From the bottom of that continuous and deafening noise, from that background din, the human word no longer emerges. It is possible only to pull out mere fragments from the indistinct and the unfelt. Levi compares these fragments of words to potato peelings: They serve to satisfy the hunger for speaking, the intense need for communication. In the cruel laboratory of the camp, this need is tested in a violent way. One dies from a lack of communication—understood, however, not only as information. The one who is not informed, or who does not know the orders, prohibitions, or prescriptions, dies. But above all, one dies at Auschwitz from a lack of communication. And communication is saying and letting be said, speaking and understanding. One dies from a lack of dialogue. Levi has in mind the almost untranslatable German word *Angesprochensein*. He renders it in the following way:

> This "not being talked to" had rapid and devastating effects. To those who do not talk to you, or address you in screams that seem inarticulate to you, you dare not speak. If you are fortunate enough to have next to you someone with whom you have a language in common, good for you, you'll be able to exchange your impressions, seek counsel, let off steam, confide in him; if you don't find anyone, your tongue dries up in a few days, and your thought with it.[125]

Not all suffer in the same way from this *eclipse of the word*. But accepting it marks the beginning of the end, the approaching of definitive indifference—before the death of the Muselmann. Those who can defend themselves by begging or inventing news and information—the pretext of information for communication—have "sharpened eyes and ears to seize and try to interpret all signs offered by men, the earth, and the heavens."[126]

At Auschwitz, one dies in the collision with the total linguistic barrier, one dies by not understanding the other who no longer wants to be other, but only self. One dies because understanding is taken away, if language is made into a mere instrument of power, oppression, and death. What remains of language at Auschwitz is, on the one hand, the deafening noise of the almost inarticulate screams, and on the other, the suffocated stuttering, almost a gasp that is going out. It is this stuttering, this gasp, of which Celan writes in his poetry, as a wound inscribed in the German language. His "obscure writing," as Levi calls it, is the echo of this nonlanguage.[127]

At Auschwitz, however, not only the not-understanding, but also the not-speaking leads to death. Levi provides the terrifying example of Hurbinek, the three-year-old child born secretly and never taught a word. Through his intense and explosive need for the word that pulsated throughout his body, through his wheezing and his suffocated babble, Hurbinek says much more than all scientific experiments and all philosophical speculations could ever say about the necessity of the word for human beings.[128] It is not only necessary to speak the word to the other, but also necessary to listen for the word from the other as a sign of attentiveness and welcome. To put it briefly, and this is the decisive point: Where there is no absolute vocative, there is no life. With a gesture opposed to that of Nietzsche, a gesture that belongs within an ethics of the here and now, Levi claims: "to refuse to communicate is a failing."[129]

But through the difficult transition from the anti-world of Auschwitz to the world, in order to bring the anti-world back to the world, and to push the world toward the limit of the anti-world, it emerges that not-understanding, and no-being-understood can signify death. They can mark the limit between life and death, even in those world-situations that thus appear to be limit situations. Not understanding the anguish, the straitening, the dire straits of living can be deadly. And in this anguish the word of the other can be liberating and saving. Not understanding one's own pains of love can mean dying from them. Literature, and not just romantic works, abounds with these unforeseen, incomprehensible, and tragic events. Many other examples, even more banal, could be mentioned, which fill everyday life.

In all circumstances of life, understanding is vital: It gives life and is indispensable for life. Therefore, in every understanding life is at stake. The concentration camp, as limit situation, sheds light on this point that has great philosophical relevance, insofar as it marks the dividing line between diverse, and even opposed, philosophies. On the one side are those philosophies, based on a scientific-analytic model, which, because they are convinced that there can be a subject capable of objectively knowing itself and the world, consider understanding to be a superfluous and dangerous remainder of knowing. On the other side, are those philosophies that, explicitly appealing to understanding, think that knowledge is never pure, purified, and cleansed, but is always contaminated, deviated, and misled by the understanding that precedes it and to which knowledge belongs. For the latter philosophies, especially for hermeneutics, life is at stake in every knowing because it is first at stake in every understanding.

But it is not only life, in its simple possibility of being or not being, which is at stake in understanding. Moreover, as becomes clear in the concentrational universe described by Levi, understanding acts on life and influences it. For understanding is always a "self-understanding"—that, thanks to the other, is always an understanding of the self as other from oneself, that is, an understanding differently—understanding renders life more aware and more worthy of being lived.[130] But before granting life such a dignity, understanding, just because it understands by differentiating itself, acts on the beyond that is peculiar to life. In order to live—in order to survive—life must always be a living beyond. By its centrifugal movement, understanding sustains living in its stretching *outside* and *beyond*. Understanding acts on living and surviving, because it is by understanding that the limit of that strait is overcome, in which life seems to be held firm and closed in within itself, from which it cannot come out by going beyond itself. Thus, the movement of understanding supports the movement of life that overcomes itself in order to survive. Understanding is indeed life realizing itself.

This going beyond the movement of speaking, and beyond the movement of understanding, is the very going further and beyond living, or better still, it is the very movement of living that thus coincides with speaking and understanding. Because of this the breath of life gains nourishment from speaking and understanding. Living in order to understand means then following and supporting the further and the beyond of the word that is also the further and beyond of life by its stretching itself. For life, the way to continue or, better, to survive, is not to conserve itself, but to understand itself differently, and therefore to become different by continually overcoming itself.

If understanding is vital, as it emerged in the anti-world of Auschwitz, but as it also emerged in the transition from the anti-world to the world, because understanding is a matter of life and death, then it is possible to invert the relationship between living and understanding. Radicalizing the position of philosophical hermeneutics, it would be possible to say that one lives in order to understand, that even the you of the text needs to be understood, and indeed to be interpreted. Thus, it becomes clear that here, in the interpretation of this poetry, life and death are at stake, that without this poetry that speaks to you, speaks for you, speaks in your name, and that is the word that was searching for you, living would not have been worth the trouble, living would not be worth the trouble.

10. *ÁTOPOS*: THE STRANGER OUT OF PLACE

The vital instinct for understanding reacts to a shove that comes from the outside. Gadamer insists on this concept of "collision" (*Anstoß*) as a way of clarifying how understanding can be set in motion.[131] Otherwise the question would remain obscure, or one would be forced to assume that understanding sets itself in motion autonomously. In this concept of "collision," which also marks Gadamer's distance from Heidegger, there must be seen the particular contribution of philosophical hermeneutics to the reflection on understanding. The collision of the incomprehensible intervenes in that which, once understood, and almost forgotten, is seen as obvious and taken for granted. Insofar as it strikes what is understood, the shove is another way of saying the interruption. This concept was not unknown to Greek philosophy, from which Gadamer retrieves it. "The Greeks had a very fine word for that which brings our understanding to a standstill. They called it the *átopon*."[132]

In Plato, *átopos*, the one who is *without a place* or *out of place* (i.e., foreign, strange, extraordinary) is often said about Socrates. Thus *átopos* is the one who, incomprehensible in his foreignness, surprises, irritates, and provokes disconcertment and wonder. Briefly put, it is the philosopher—if wonder, *thaumázein*, is the *páthos* from which philosophy begins.[133] Wonder marks the threshold between what is customary, usual, and ordinary, and what is not customary, unusual, and extraordinary. Socrates, that is the philosopher, is the one who is seized with astonishment and provokes astonishment, who stands on the threshold, in the between, and thus, by not belonging to one side or to the other, is outside, placeless, *átopos*. In his incomprehensible foreignness he irritates because, having renounced the place, any place, and having hence lost all orientation—in Wittgenstein's words: *ich kenne mich nicht aus*, "I don't know my way about"[134]—is, in turn, disorienting.

But the *atopía*, Socrates' strangeness, which provokes disquietude and turmoil, is in Greek philosophy a limit concept, at the limit of philosophy, or even foreign.[135] Thus, philosophy must be guided by the *lógos* of reason. And just as the *lógos* excludes the barbarian from Greece, it also excludes all that is foreign, alien, and strange. This notwithstanding, in the Platonic dialogues it is the foreigner who suddenly breaks in and interrupts the course of philosophizing. Apart from the case of Socrates, who is the foreigner *par excellence*, the figure of the *xénos* comes on the scene at decisive moments and asks questions that open up new perspectives. Such is the case of Diotima of Mantinea in the *Symposium*—and that the foreigner is a woman is certainly not without significance. But perhaps the most emblematic case is that of the Eleatic stranger in the *Sophist*. By pressing and asking unavoidable questions, the stranger pursues Parmenides, the father of the doctrine that was supposed to be the basis of philosophy itself: that of the identity of Being. Accordingly, being is *ésti*. The stranger not only dares to press him, but also to deal him the final blow. From the stranger, who does not hesitate to commit parricide, comes in fact the insane, scandalous, and subversive question, the question that marks a turning point and subverts philosophy, namely the possibility of *being-other*. By forcing *not-being* in a certain way to be, and *being* in a certain way to not be, the stranger says that: "not-being is not something opposite to being, but only something different."[136] From this moment, the *héteron*, the being other and different, even if through many occurrences, will be a conquest of philosophy reached through an expropriation of the identity of being realized by the stranger?

But for the Greeks, masters of ethnocentrism, the foreigner is *absolutely* outside, from the *éthnos*, from the *pólis*, from the *lógos*. The foreigner is determined first of all starting from the place, or from the non-place, is exterior and external, that is, outside the center, or better, from a place taken as center; he is determined starting from the property, or the not-propriety, be it a thing, a quality, or an identity. That is, he is a foreign because he does not possess what everyone else possesses; he is determined starting from his way of being, doing, and speaking, he is the strange, extravagant one who is out of tune with the alleged collective harmony. Finally, he is determined starting from an order which is supposedly normal, is therefore the extraordinary or the out of the ordinary that marks the boundary of that order and, indeed, by managing to cross the boundary, is out of the ordinary, is the excessive, the exception, the exceptional. Thus, one could say, in the loosest and most conventional way, that the foreigner is the one who comes from afar, the wandering Jew, who has another nationality, another language, who has no property, the drifter, the gypsy, the refugee, the one who is alien and alienated, the one who comports himself in a bizarre way, like a child or a madman, the one who is exceptional and original, inspired, a revolutionary, a poet, a philosopher. Nonetheless, it is impossible to describe him, even in broad strokes, because the foreigner, for his peculiar ambivalence, escapes every description even before every definition. The latter is always negative, and in the negative. As the determining limit oscillates, between inside and outside, so too the figure of the foreigner oscillates, fluctuates, moves, and changes. And by turning themselves upside down, the very criteria that serve to distinguish him from the nonforeigner, modify themselves. Looked at more closely, the foreigner is indeed the criterion itself, the criterion for defining the identity of the *idiótes*, of the owner, who is the opposite of the *xénos*, the foreigner, that is, the identity identical to itself and the property deprived of meaning (i.e., the obvious and plain idiocy of normality). This does not mean that because of this the foreigner has not been fascinating and seductive, but only in the form of exoticism, of the *éxo*, of what is on the outside and must remain outside.

In Greek philosophy, the foreigner, the stranger, the *xénos* and the *allótrios* are neither concepts nor keywords; in a philosophical-linguistic sense, even before a logical or epistemological sense, only the *héteron* is admitted, what is other in relation to what is the same, to the *tautón*.

The *lógos* of reason, characterizing what is common to the Greeks, marks a vertical, rather than a horizontal, difference in relation to the barbarians. Only in modern philosophy, when reason begins to decline itself in the forms of language and history, does the subject decenter itself and the global order thus lose its center. If estrangement and alienation rises to a concept in the Hegelian and Marxist traditions, the stranger nevertheless remains a difference to be removed and overcome in view of the universal. Only in the twentieth century, and by diverse ways, the one forged by phenomenology, but, above all, the one opened up by philosophical hermeneutics, does the stranger penetrate into the heart of one's own. It is precisely the last voices of contemporary philosophy, and even more decisively those of deconstruction, which let the stranger call into question one's own in its most intimate, originary, and unquestioned properties.

The stranger is therefore accepted at the beginning of Western philosophy only as the extraordinary and, at best, ec-centric stranger, namely Socrates. But the atopia of Socrates is also a great merit that should be ascribed to Greek philosophy, and in particular to Plato. Thus, the foreigner, the stranger, is ultimately the philosopher himself. By coming from the non-place, which cannot be localized, from an elsewhere that is at the limit, and indeed is the limit of the *pólis*, the philosopher crosses the *pólis* "beholding from above the life of those below."[137] He is *ápolis*, the displaced *par excellence*, expatriated in his homeland, homeless at home, outsider and outlaw, the dissident, dissentient, who diverges, deviates, and transgresses. This is precisely the singularity Alcibiades attributed to Socrates.[138] In the city Socrates lives with others, although he does not live like others. Even his way of speaking—and this is not surprising—is different from the others, straying into the strange, odd, unusual. When he goes on trial, Socrates himself recognizes: "I am a dangerously clever speaker."[139] He knows that he is being accused of this: His digressions are as much transgressions. But he does not disavow his style and, by emphasizing rather his being not only "extraordinary" (*deinós*), but also "foreign" (*xénos*) to the use of speech (*léxis*) in the trial, he demands to be treated *as if* he were really a foreigner whose foreign tongue differs in voice (*phoné*), manner, and trope (*trópos*).[140] Linguistic singularity, which is the sign of an actually lived strangeness, is reclaimed as foreign origin. I am stranger to you, hence treat me as a foreigner.

Atopia is recovered as heterotopia.[141] The non-place, which does not fall into the order, which withdraws itself and puts itself at the limit, is not a *non place*, which is not, which does not exist, but is rather a place which is *other*, and, by not finding room within the *tópoi* of the order, refers back to an outside, outside of the order, and which, starting from this outside of its out of place, puts the order, its center, and its alleged uniqueness into question, it dislocates, decenters, defers it, and makes it one among the possible orders. The atopia of Socrates, as Plato describes it, is therefore this political moment of extreme tension within the *pólis* in which the strangeness of the individual opposes and counterposes itself to the normalization of the order, to the homologization, to the totalization—the anarchic moment, because the strangeness, as image of elsewhere, coming from elsewhere and referring back to elsewhere, denies the *arché*, both as origin and dominion. *Atopia*, as *heterotopia*, out of place and against time, discloses in the collision with the topia the open beyond the border where the place yet to come is anticipated, and thus reveals itself as *utopia*.

Utopia is the question addressed from the foreigner that, if it were to be identified in the immobility of one place and the fixity of one time, would because of this cease to be utopia. What provokes it is the shove of the *átopon, of* which hermeneutics speaks, the interruption of which deconstruction speaks. The strangeness, however, is not an absolute outside. It is an outside that can also come from within, a sudden idea, an obsession, an experience that surprises and astonishes at the limits of one's own strangeness: in the body that perceives itself, in the name that hears itself being called, in the gaze that looks at itself. Thus, as it arises from the heart of philosophy, strangeness arises as well from the heart of the I and does not spare it: The I is an other, is strange and foreign to itself, in the strongest places of its identity, in birth, in language, and in death.[142] The strangeness penetrates and pervades ipseity. The point of departure will no longer be the *cogito* of the *ego*, but rather the elsewhere of the stranger, perhaps even the stranger within me.

Coming from elsewhere, the stranger is the unforeseeable unforeseen, it is the incomprehensible not yet understood that, springing from an irrevocable past, breaks in with a promise of the future. The Jewish tradition can be drawn on here, because in it the I, its own image reflected back to it by way of the other, has always seen itself as foreign.[143] One could mention here the guest *par excellence* who arrives unannounced, uninvited and unanticipated, like a thief in the night, namely, the Messiah.[144]

11. THE TENT OF ENCOUNTER

The incomprehensible that surprises and astounds, which leaves us open mouthed, speechless, will be articulated in words so that the I, overwhelmed by anguish and by fear at the wall of silence, at the limit of not-under-standing, will not succumb in the limit situation, will not suffocate in the distress and the strait where the breath expires, will not fall silent in the renunciation of the now-no-more. To speak, even just stuttering the incomprehensible, is the way out, the step outside and beyond. With the turn of the breath what is unforeseen, unexpected, and disquieting in the incomprehensible, is articulated in a promise always already expected. The audacity of the ever-yet, the audacity to speak, is a messianic audacity. But the ever-yet of the I could not exist without the you. Only because the I experiences the other of the you in the limit, does it manages to turn, by accomplishing in itself a half turn, from the closedness of the strait toward the open and free space, it manages to address the you. In this way, it prepares the encounter and prepares itself for the "secret" of the encounter.

The word that has articulated the incomprehensible and, by crossing the strait, has turned toward the open and free space, is a promise of freedom. "We will now perhaps find the place where the strangeness was, the place where a person was able to set himself free as an—estranged—I? Will we find such a place, such a step?"[145] The I, freed from the word that has carried it beyond, is an estranged I. And it could not have freed itself, if it had not estranged itself. It has done it by speaking. For its breath has articulated itself by passing through a word that was not its own, that was always already the word of the other. The first step toward freedom is also the extreme step of estrangement, it is the step of estrangement and of extreme expropriation. The I, stretching itself out by speaking, reaches the most distant and foreign place for itself, the place of the extreme strangeness, that of language. Yet just here, and only here, the breath of its most intimate existence, by giving voice to the incomprehensible, can articulate, syllabilize, and translate itself by passing through that grille that is, nonetheless, the condition of freedom.[146] And its speaking, which makes its way in the language, can individualize itself, can become figure and trope, and thus bear the trace of its individuality and freedom.

But this freedom is not only for the I. "Perhaps here, with the I—the estranged I set free *here* and in *such wise*—here perhaps yet some Other becomes free?"[147] With this question, asked at the heart of *The Meridian*, Celan reveals, in a sort of phenomenology of the word, what he is able to grasp in poetic praxis, and expresses at once the hope which, in spite of the "perhaps," still dwells in his poetry. It is the hope that the poetic word in its being always *beyond the I* could be always *for the other*. This word is the excess of a gift.[148] The remainder, the excess of the more, of the beyond, is what in the word can liberate and make free. With a speed that forges ahead, and is always already beyond the I, the poem makes for this other that it imagines to be "reachable, free-able, perhaps empty," and simultaneously turned toward the poem.[149] In the poem's tending and protending toward there is the attempt to draw out an "Over-against," a *Gegenüber*[150]—according to the I and the You of Buber's philosophy with which Celan was well acquainted.[151] While it searches for an attentive and vigilant you that listens to and perceives its voice, the poem becomes dialogue, passionate or desperate, but dialogue nonetheless.

But is it really dialogue? And why on earth should its word, the poetic word, that of the I which after having been estranged, has freed itself, not only reach but even liberate the other? Is this not, more than just a hope, an unheard-of demand? And what could motivate it, if that word has January 20th inscribed in it, the date of its absolute singularity? How could the freedom that springs from a speaking, which is individuated starting from a unique and inappropriable event—"here and *in such wise*"—be divided and co-divided (i.e., shared), even be freedom for the other and of the other?

The answer lies in a word that stands *for* the word: Zeltwort, "tent word."[152] In Celan, the word *Zelt*, "tent," occurs at least ten times. But even alone it is rare that he does not refer, although indirectly, to the word. It could be taken as one of the many metaphors that constellate his poems. But why should the word be a tent? The numerous commentaries on Celan's work fail to provide an interpretation, be it satisfying or not. In the main, *zeltlos* is read, albeit with justification, in the sense of "defenseless." Like in the concentrational universe, so too in the technological universe, which is equally *ungeahnt*, unforeseen and unsuspected, the human being is without a tent and hence defenseless.[153] Thus *zeltlos* is another way of saying Heidegger's homelessness, the loss of homeland, of the land, and of home, the sense of *Unheimlich*, because there is no longer a *Heim*. The one "who, shelterless in this till-now undreamt-of sense and thus most uncannily in the open, goes with his very being to language."[154] And in language he seeks, if not a fixed dwelling, at least a shelter.

The tent, which has to be planted, pitched, and constructed, is the tent of exile in the desert. In the Torah, *'ohel*, "tent," is not just any word. The tent is the "tent of the encounter" להא דעומ, *'Ohel Mo'ed* (*Exodus* 28, 43). It is therefore the Tabernacle that can also be indicated by נכשמ, *mishkan*, "dwelling," the place in which God dwells with His people. The expressions, which are synonymous in Hebrew, can be combined when saying *Mishkan 'Ohel Mo'ed*, "the Dwelling of the Tent of the encounter" (*Exodus* 39, 32). But what is the Tent of the encounter? In the Torah, the Revelation of God on Mount Sinai is the paradigm of every Revelation. The event, unique and unrepeatable, is the event of language. God makes Himself heard through a voice—"you heard a voice . . . , but saw no image; there was only a voice" (*Deuteronomy* 4, 12)—and manifests Himself not to a singular individual, not only to Moses, but to the whole community, to the entire Jewish people. The event is an act of communication and is the encounter between the emanating voice and Moses who welcomes and interprets it. Beyond the various ways in which the voice of God was understood in the Talmudic and kabbalistic traditions, and even in Jewish philosophy, there emerges almost everywhere the importance of the communicative event, of the encounter: if the voice that emanates in permanence were not grasped and understood, there would be no Revelation. The work of Moses, who was stutterer, is that of translating—which here means understanding—from one language to another, that is, of articulating the heavenly voice into human words (*Exodus* 4, 10). The voice, in its absolute semantic indeterminacy, in its pure virtuality, which precedes every articulation, is a promise of sense.[155] After Sinai, the voice continues to manifest itself, accompanying the Jewish people during their wandering in the desert. But they could no longer hear it. The voice could be still received, but only in the Tent of the encounter, that Holy Tent, that Sanctuary that the Jews carried with them in their wandering. The Tent, at the center of their camp, could easily be taken down and put up again. The Tent was the Dwelling of God, of His *Shekhinah* in exile.[156] When the cloud, which indicated His Presence, leaves the Tent, this was the sign that it was time to leave (*Exodus* 40, 36–37). The Tent was divided into three contiguous parts: in the first two, the access was allowed only to the priests; in the third, the *Kodesh ha-Kodashim*, "the most holy place," only the high priest could enter and only on the day of *Yom Kippur*. Thus there was the Ark of the Covenant, which contained the Ten Commandments; on the propitiatory of the Ark were two cherubs, carved in fine gold, whose faces were turned toward each other (*Exodus* 25, 17–20). Moses could enter the Tent, but not the third part. It is in the tent that God speaks to him, in those encounters, gatherings, and meetings, as he had promised him: "There I will meet you and there, from above, I will speak to you . . . from between the two cherubim" (*Exodus* 25, 22). And as it is later said: "When Moses entered the tent of the encounter to speak with him, he heard the voice addressing him from above the propitiatory on the ark of the commandments, from between the two cherubim; and it spoke to him" (*Numbers* 7, 89). Although the event on Sinai was unique, the voice has never stopped speaking. Indeed, it continues to speak, even in the desert, and it will continue without interruption, uninterruptedly, until the end of time. Revelation is permanent. Instead of *vaydaber* "He was speaking" here there appears the reflexive *middaber* "He was speaking to himself," which is a sign of respect for God's speaking that must be self-reflexive. Besides the many interpretations of this verse, from Rashi to Sforno, from Leibowitz to Levinas, and besides the way in which God's speaking is understood in the Jewish hermeneutics, what needs to be underlined here is that the inarticulate and undifferentiated voice, with neither beginning nor end, which speaks, or speaks to itself, by announcing itself as the promise of sense that Moses can articulate by stuttering, would give rise, in its self-reflexivity, to an impersonal communicative act and thus to an impersonal Revelation, if a mere detail would actually not change all. The heavenly voice that comes from above passes *between* the two cherubs before going out into the Tent of the encounter. The between that at the same time separates and

unites the two cherubs, the space where the voice from the anonymity of
the sky falls by declining itself in human speech in the Tent, is the space
of an interpersonal relation, between an I and a you. Thus, one can say
that only in this *between* can the divine Word be heard, articulated, and
understood. But one could also say that for the Torah the word that exists
between an I and a you is divine.[157] The Tent of the encounter, the place
where God, the God of exodus and history, has decided to dwell among His
people in exile, the Dwelling of His *Shekhinah*, is the place of the dialogue
that can occur and occurs at the threshold, at the entrance, at the opening:
"I will meet you and speak to you" (*Exodus* 29, 42).

The "tent" speaks of an encounter; but even before that, it speaks of
the desert, of the blinding sun, of the lack of shade and shelter. It speaks
of exile and wandering. The tent is destined to migrate with the people
who wander in search of an orientation; it is destined to be nomadic. In
fact, the tent is the sign, the signal, and the injunction to wander. For
Celan, the Tent is all of these things. It is constructed on "sand," without
foundations, unstable, insecure, precarious, provisional, and ephemeral—
always revocable.[158] Tomorrow it will be elsewhere. And it will have to
be remade. This is the source of the command: "Pitch the Tent!"[159] Every
time it is taken down, it will have to be reassembled and reconstructed.
Together. It is therefore always another, even though it is the same Tent.
It stands alone on the immense expanse of dunes, surrounded by solitude
and silence because in the distances of the desert it is difficult to hear the
voice. There is no immediate proximity. Immediacy is lost. The separation
and distance are infinite. In this infinity of wandering, where there are
no well-worn paths, but only traces, the Tent stands, planted precariously,
where there are no plants or trees, in a place that is and will always be a
no-place, or better, an out-of-place. For, it is always destined to be elsewhere,
even further away, in an expanse without center like that of the desert. In
this expanse, the place, out-of-place, is always only that of the Tent. But
the Tent is nevertheless a dwelling, it offers shelter, first from the sun, it
gives shade. And, beyond the mirage, it is the sole good of the exiled, the
separated, the estranged, the expatriated, the "Tentmakers"[160] who, after the
exodus, cross the desert, moving toward the Promised Land.

12. ". . . THE LANGUAGE THAT WANDERED WITH US"

For Celan, the Tent is made of language. The Tent is the word. There
are no other goods, no other shelters, and no other dwellings. "Our sole
good is the word"—writes Jabès, who is extraordinarily close to Celan even
in understanding the word as a Tent.[161] This sole good, the shade of the
Tent opened by a word, is moreover borrowed, because, as Celan writes in

"Conversation in the Mountains," "how could he come with his own when God had made him a Jew?"[162] Thus, the only shade that can be found in the desert is that of the word borrowed from the language of the other, which is nomadic and wanders with the nomads.

> We here, we
> Glad for the passage, before the Tent
> Where you baked desert bread
> From wandered-along language[163]

The Tent is therefore a light Tent, a "wordmembraned oiltent"[164]—where oil and skin, sacred components of the Tabernacle, refer explicitly to the 'Ohel Mo'ed, to the "Tent of the encounter." The shadow projected by the Tent, which offers shelter from the blinding light, is therefore the shade of the word. This optical metaphor is not new. It accompanies the word, and the way of understanding it, through the entire philosophical tradition where, nonetheless, the word is light and brings clarity where there would be otherwise the obscurity of the indistinct. The same metaphor, inverted and thus with antimetaphysical resonances, appears often in Heidegger. Celan certainly retrieves the Heideggerian sense of this metaphor when he speaks of Sprachschatten, of the "language shade" or of the word that, like a tree, "promises shade."[165] But Celan inserts this metaphor in a different constellation, in which its sense becomes completely different. The positivity of the promised and projected shadow of the word does not lie so much in the infinity of the unsaid, but rather in the shelter that it offers, even if that shelter is also in the difference between the said and the unsaid, in opacity. The shelter is what really matters in the word-Tent of Celan. And it is a shelter for you and for me—it is for us.

That the Tent is made of words also means that the Tent's material is not just any material like fabric, leather, or wood. It is a material that makes it solid and resistant while remaining fine, light, and airy. It is air. It is the breath, pnêuma, or better ruah, which is also the breath of life. But the breath, by articulating itself, has already crystallized; the material has already been worked over, indeed it is in part worn out, thus, it is borrowed. That material of which the Tent is made, passed through many deserts, and the history of many deserts, is the word that comes from the other, is of another, and of this other carries the trace. In the word there is already the other. There is the other who has spoken in this word and with this word. It is impossible to appropriate or fully possess it, unless one does not erase or pretend to erase the trace of the other and to erase the other. The word, coming from the other, is strange from the beginning. Perhaps, however, by changing perspective, according to the place of the Tent, one could say that the word, which comes from the other and in which the other speaks, is already from the beginning dialogical. This means that it already has a *dia-* in itself, a "crossing," a "between," and an opening. For in its internal dialogical structure, it is the word itself that opens up the dialogue. When I articulate and utter the word that comes from another, from a you, by speaking I am already engaged in a dialogue. For what I say is never completely mine, but always also of another. I say what is mine through the word of the other, I say the other in my word. The more I speak under my angle of incidence, the more I manage to leave a trace of what is mine, my trace, in the word. But the proper and the strange are inextricably interwoven in the word, and the word is actually their oscillating boundary. Thus the Tent, which is made of words, is woven of proper and strange, and only because of this can it be called the Tent of the encounter. This means that the encounter, in a certain sense, begins before the encounter, the dialogue before the dialogue. The dialogue begins even before an I turns toward a you, or a you toward an I. Through the *dia-*, the dialogical opening that scores and cleaves it from the inside, the dialogue already starts in the shadow of the word, in the shadow that the word promises to the you as well as to the I, because the I and the you are already in that promised shade. Thus, the Tent promises, anticipates, and by anticipating allows the passage of the word between the I and the you and makes dialogue possible. The shelter it offers is then this or, perhaps, nothing else than this. In the word of the you, the I has found its dwelling; in the word of the I, the you will find its dwelling.[166] There are no other dwellings, no other shelters. The words of one sustain and hold the other. The distance, however, remains, and the strangeness endures. The word stresses both. Thus, in the Tent of the encounter, the encounter is always separation. This is *Geheimnis*, the secret and mystery of the encounter. Your word will never be mine, and mine will never be yours. The shelter has lasted an instant, and the dwelling was not a dwelling. It was already a leave-taking, the injunction to leave. It was the word that commanded it. Although I believed, by pronouncing it, that it was mine, that it was my word, it has already left me. It was already directed toward the other—like a "boomerang."[167] Coming from the other, and already borrowed, the word is destined to return to the other. The word is nomadic by vocation—it migrates and departs. And like the Tent of the *Shekhinah*, it imposes wandering. It is the sign of exile.

13. THE TIME OF THE PROMISE

That sole good, the good of the language, which uproots because it is uprooted, because it has its roots in the air, that inappropriable property, the abode that is not an abode, ephemeral shelter like a puff of wind, is the only place for the expatriated I. It is a place-no-place, because it is the place of the behind and of the after-place, which contains the thousand places of a language, those of the past and those of the future. For the I that inhabits it, in the instant in which it inhabits it, it is the homeland, the dwelling, the house, its being at home, by itself—its very intimacy. This intimacy, which lasts only a breath's instant, is shared with those thousand places and millennia, is co-divided and shared with the you. It is, therefore, an intimate strangeness or an estranged intimacy. But the estrangement of the I in the word of the other is its step toward freedom. All the more so for the I of the poet who speaks, through the language grille, under his individual angle of incidence. No matter how profound his trace remains, the poet's speaking does not preserve the sovereignty and paternity of the creator. Self-forgetful, separated from himself, estranged, and hence free, liberated from a word that has chosen him, the poet lets the word, and thus lets the word speak alone. The word that springs forth from the audacity of its ever-yet is a promise of freedom for the you. As with every promise, it is, in its excess, also the remainder of a gift. And as with every gift, it does not even appear as a gift.[168] But what kind of gift is this? And with what kind of promise?

In the breath-turn, as Celan describes, the poem becomes dialogue.

> What is addressed takes shape only in the space of this dialogue, gathers around the I addressing and naming it. But what's addressed and is now become a Thou through naming, as it were, also brings along its otherness into this present. Even in a poem's here and now—the poem itself really has only this one, unique, momentary present—even in this immediacy and nearness it lets the Other's ownmost quality speak: *its time*.[169]

The turning of the I toward the other, not yet a you, is the absolute vocative that, by preceding every word, also precedes every temporalization. The event of speaking-to is, in its punctuality, a singular, unique, and unrepeatable event. But while this event occurs, *at the same time* another one takes place. For the you, not yet a you, to which the word is addressed, introduces itself in its being other. Therefore, two events happen simultaneously, separate in time, with different times, which cannot be given at the same time. It is the *impossible* simultaneity of two times—a logical and chronological contradiction. In the instant of that unrepeatable and punctual present, the only present of the poem, the other breaks in with what, in its being other, is ownmost: its time. That instant is then lacerated and lacerating time, and the present in its presence—which is still only the immediacy and proximity of the absolute vocative—cancels itself out. It cancels itself while it gives itself, indeed, while it gifts itself. Put differently: It gives time, it gifts it, by leaving time, leaving the time of the other to the other. This time of the gift, before every temporalization, is a gift of time. It is a gift without a present, a gift that, in its gratuity and unforeseeability, does not present itself. By leaving to the other what is its ownmost, its time, it leaves the other and the event of the other emerge, leaves the to-come of the other. And thus it leaves the word to the other. In the same paradoxical instant, in which it—messianically—leaves the advent of the other emerge, the time of the other, while it gifts it time, it gifts it the word. It is the other, the you, which speaks.

It is a doubly possible impossibility—that of the time of the other and of the word of the other. But how can it leave, give, gift the word to the other, if he has already borrowed it? If the word does not belong to him, is it not his property? But is not this the excess of the gift, that is, that what is gift and gifted is what cannot be possessed? And as it is for time, which nobody possesses, so too is it for language, which nobody possesses. And perhaps one can say, moreover, that language, by forbidding ownership, forces one to think the gift as gift, without the calculation of profit, without the reappropriation with surplus value, without capitalization. If language is a gift, the one who speaks is already involved and implicated in a relation of gifting. But precisely what it receives is never its own, is never its possession because language expropriates and, vice versa, what it will be able to give would never have been his, his property. This is the promise: the word, on which the I relies and which it now entrusts and pro-mises to the you, by permitting it to speak. The promised word is the word left behind. The word is left to the other by relying on the speaking and the understanding of the other. It is in this word of its time to come that the liberated you discovers itself as free. The word of the I is a promise of freedom for the you even before the I. And it does not matter whether the promise is kept.[170] Because to pro-mise, to pose by permitting and promising, recalls or reclaims the repetition of the unrepeatable in its singularity and inappropriability, and, indeed, it inscribes the repetition in that which could be taken for the originary word and, by exposing it to iterability, permits and promises the division and co-division, the sharing of a *Zeltwort*, of a "Tent-word." Celan writes, "Take this word, my eye speaks to yours! Take it, repeat it with me."[171] This disruptive instant, in which the promised word bursts forth, exceptional because it comes from an excess that belongs to no temporal continuum, is the instant in which the breath turn occurs. And it is the instant in which the *absolute vocative* reveals itself as a *performative absolute*.

Thus the I of the poet—the "accredited signatory" as Derrida says[172]— destines the poem to an other, gifts it, that is, leaves it, abandons it, above and beyond every addressee, every recipient, and every counter-signer to come. It abandons it without return, without interest, benefit, or profit, but also without a circular return, a returning home, a homecoming.

14. NORTH OF THE FUTURE

After his voyages to foreign lands, Ulysses, as is well known, returns to Ithaca, to his home, near to himself and near to his family. The longing for his homeland, the homesickness, had accompanied him throughout all his vicissitudes, indeed, it spurred him on from one adventure to the next, always looking forward to homecoming. His exile was only a temporary exile, perhaps not even an exile. It was a distancing from self in order to return to self, a movement from the proper to the strange, in order to come back to the proper. It was a Hegelian movement of reappropriation. Or, rather, one should say that the being-with-itself of the Idea in Hegel's Absolute Knowledge is Odyssean, because it follows the movement from the self to the self, passing through the other (but this *passing* is a problem), which characterizes the Eurocentric tradition and responds to the economy of return.[173]

With Celan's way there is no return. Even if this way is "circular," it will be a different circularity.[174] "I am back at the beginning"—he writes.[175] And this pushes him toward "topos research" in order to individuate the place where he began, that of his origin.[176] Already in his Bremen speech, Celan had traced a "topographical sketch" with the same purpose.[177] But the search, carried out "with an inexact because restless finger" and on a "children's map," a map he had had perhaps from childhood, but at the same time a map of his childhood, where, though by simplified and imprecise markings, everything is illustrated just as one does for children with large images and figures, is a vain search This place, or better "all of these places" are not to be found. Not because Celan did not look carefully, but because these places "do not exist."[178] And yet, they once did. There was a land in which "human beings and books used to live," and it was the land in which the Hasidim and "those Hasidic tales that Martin Buber retold for us all in German" were "at home."[179] Somewhere there was Czernowitz in Bucovina, between Romania, Russia, and Poland. It was the center of Eastern Judaism. But it has been erased; all those places have been erased, crossed out, suppressed, and annihilated. And not even a trace remains.

If the origin, and the *tópos* of the origin along with the origin, has been erased, topos research may no longer make any sense. What sense would it have, if the place that was sought after is no longer there, if it has become a non-place? What should one search for? Would it not be better to give up? Would it be better to choose the now-no-more? But the non-place is not simply a no place, the negation of a place. Rather, and moreover, it is an *átopos* that in its *Unheimlichkeit*, in its incomprehensible strangeness, interrupts the search, disorients it, lets it lose its point of orientation, its Orient, and renders useless the pointing with the finger and the eye toward that East on the geographical map. It demands indeed that the search itself become a-topical, that it starts from that non-place which is an out of place. If this has to be the point of departure, what should be the point of arrival, the goal, the returning place, if there is no return? Will it once again be a non-place, an inexistent place, inexistent or absent, an absence of place, or even an *ou-tópos*? Does not the path traveled by Celan, by his poetry and perhaps by poetry in general, appear to be a path from a non-place to a non-place? Is this not an "impossible path"? It is Celan himself who agrees on it.[180] And yet there does not seem to be another possibility outside of this impossibility, outside of this madness of a search that is simultaneously atopic and utopic. There seems to be no other way out.

Thus, Celan follows this path and readies himself for the exit. But this is not just any exit. Already marked by the messianic ever-yet, this exit, which by supporting the destinal eccentricity of the I reveals itself to be centrifugal, is considered by Levinas as the rupture, perhaps an absolute rupture, of the axis of Being. It is the exit "from Being to the other."[181] The exit toward the other is more adventurous and risky than any Odyssey, because there is nothing stranger, more estranging, or more foreign than the neighbor, that is, the other who is near, close by, in his immediate proximity. This exiting is a "stepping out of what is human, betaking oneself to a realm that is uncanny [*unheimlich*] yet turned toward what is human."[182] Perhaps it will be in this proximate uncanniness, in this uncanny proximity, that poetry will be able to set itself free.[183] In every topos research, the question of the *Woher*, "whence," and of the *Wohin* "wherein," is unavoidable; but, in the atopic and utopic topology, where Celan's poetry takes shape, this question of the origin and of the end is a "question 'staying open,' 'coming to no end,' pointing into the open and void and free."[184] It is the very opening of the question, the impossibility of responding, which refers to another, further opening. If there is no *Woher* and no *Wohin*, if the I no longer has an origin and no longer has a goal, the exit toward the other, in this diaspora, more than a deviation, is a change of direction, it is a leaving behind of the origin in order to turn toward the exodus, it is the exit "near to U-topia."[185]

The erasure of the originary *tópos*, the place of origin, the absurdly incomprehensible *átopos* of the non-place that is not, that is no longer, that is ciphered and deciphered together with the other as the other place, out of place in the places of the topos research, pushes it outside by pointing to the opening, which is beyond, of an *oútopos*, a utopic place that is not, that is not yet, of a place yet to come. The exile appears more originary than the origin. And from the sign of the *conditio judaica* exile becomes the sign of the *conditio humana*. This is how Celan reads exile. Being *Jewish*—the root עבר, *eber*, means "passing across"—is another name to say the impossibility of an originary identity, of a coincidence of self with self, the necessity of understanding oneself differently in wandering. Exile, therefore, is another, more originary way of thinking Being that is only in the difference. Radical homelessness, being totally void and devoid of roots, the elimination of dwelling, and thus the condition of the displaced, is taken up by Celan as the new condition of freedom. Because freedom, released from the *tópos* of a vanished origin, unchained from the gravity of a center that situates and fixes it, attunes itself to a place which, appealing from beyond memory, is immemorial and thus always also in the beyond to come.

Topos research can therefore be carried out, not, however, in the dark desperation of a lost place, but "in light of U-topia."[186] This means lending an ear, beyond itself and beyond the words, to a *Kommendes*, a *to come*. Therefore, it becomes understandable why Celan states: "I am back at the beginning."[187] This "at the beginning"—an allusion to that mother tongue and to that death which remains "*douloureusement*" his own[188]—does not mean Czernowitz and Bucovina, the places of his childhood that can no longer be found; rather, two years after, Celan confessed to his Romanian friend Petre Salomon: "With my meridian I am right there back at the beginning *avec, je le peux dire ici, mon vieux coeur de communiste*."[189]

The impossibility of finding what one is searching for inverts itself into the possibility of finding that for which one is not looking—"and . . . I find something"—Celan writes. Here the "impossible path" turns into the "path of the impossible."[190] It is the possibility of the impossibility of which Landauer had already spoken.[191] The turn of the path is fulfilled through the turn, the inversion of the breath, the subversion of the word, the revolution of the poem. The inversion of the breath marks the passage, also signaled graphically, from "U-topia" to "Utopia." The word appears written once, the first time, with a hyphen, and then, the two successive times, without a hyphen. Considering Celan's obsessive precision, it cannot be a simple coincidence. The two ways of writing refer to two different ways of reading the word, to two different meanings, and even to two different words. In the difference of the hyphen the entire history of the concept of utopia is condensed with the rapidity of the poem: from the no-place, which in its unreality is not, to the place which in its not-yet-reality, in its future possibility, is not yet. The hyphen marks the turning point of the breath, it stresses the exceptional brief instant between inhaling and exhaling, in which the breath, which could be cut off after that *u-*, or even extinguished, explodes in the passage from the now-no-more to the ever-yet, and the poem, revoking and recalling itself, affirms itself at its margin, which is, therefore, an eschatological margin. The hyphen, joining and separating the *ou-* of negation and the place of the *topía* thanks to that pause, through that scission and differentiation, which is also the interruption of an obvious reading, in a certain way negates the negation, erases the impossibility of the possibility by referring to the possibility of the impossibility. The hyphen is the trace of that messianic instant—for Benjamin the *Jetztzeit* of the revolution and the interruption of time[192]—in which by the bursting forth of the breath, the event to come can break in.

Utopia is the path of the impossible that opens onto the *Kommendes*, that *to-come, das zu keinem Ende kommende*, that which does not come to an end.[193] And thus it remains open. This opening is what seems to distinguish it. What is to come, beyond coming, is further and beyond the beyond-place of utopia that is not yet and which is ever-yet—the place that is always the penultimate, and never the ultimate, the last. If it were the ultimate, which also means the first, history, and with history also the messianic times, would be concluded, closed, and the world to come would already be here. Thus, following the veiled messianism, although not actually hidden by Celan, it is necessary to make a rigorous distinction between *future* and the *time to come*. Simply because even the future has a tomorrow. And if it were not to have a tomorrow, it would be defined on the basis of the present, as it has been defined in the philosophical tradition, namely as a *not yet*, as mere negative determination of the present. A future that does not take risks is a future that reproduces the present, which presents itself as a present future in the form—negative and privative—of the present. This is a future cautiously closed, and, because it is closed, it is solipsistic as well. Another future is the future of the other, open to the other, which remains open in the waiting for the other to come. However, for the irreducibility of the other, and the advent of the other, the future that is open to the to-come remains the most uncertain and thus also the most arduous. *North of the future*: it is the direction of utopia.[194] Nothing seems to be farther away than the rivers north of the future, nothing colder and quieter than those shadows, written by stones, metonymy of the Jewish mourning and the *Shoah*.[195] Yet, in those rivers, which trace their course away from the well-worn paths, in the beyond of a north—but for Celan, the "outlawed word," although "southbright," is nevertheless "northtrue"[196]—an "I" casts a net to a "you" that, albeit "hesitant," with stones dedicated to those shadows, helps to hold on to it. Casting a net is a gesture of waiting, it is a messianic gesture. The fisherman's net recurs in other poems by Celan in the context of a marine landscape, which is not so different from the one of the desert.[197] And the net always recurs with and within the same waiting: that of the promise—"the sea keeps its promise."[198] Here, north of the future, the promise is already kept by the you that holds fast to the net. The waiting will be a waiting together.

But the time to come is the time of the other and the to-come is always of the other, who comes from elsewhere. The waiting is the waiting of the other. The utopic movement takes shape as a movement toward the other. This direction that, forced to deviate from the return to the without-return, is addressed to the other, it is "Jewish," as Levinas writes.[199] In its going toward the other, it suggests another modality in front of the polarity between being and not-being in which philosophy has worn itself out. But what would this modality be, and because the modality changes, how would the poles be configured in a new atopic and heterotopic utopia?

If there is no longer a *Heimkehr*, a homecoming, because there is no longer a home, if the human being no longer dwells "poetically on this earth," if in the return the sacred and the word of the sacred is not resonant, but exile is an unavoidable and permanent condition, and the absence is unending, the distance too great to be crossed, then there will be no return, but only an *art Heimkehr*, "a kind of homecoming."[200] It will be a return that is not a return, a return without return, thus a paradoxical return, or, perhaps even a new way of understanding *Heimkehr*, "homecoming," and of understanding *Heim*, "home." If it is impossible to find what was searched for—like, for instance, Czernowitz on a small map—one can find what one was not seeking after. Thus, Celan writes: "I find something—like language—immaterial yet earthly, terrestrial, something circular, returning upon itself by way of both poles and thereby—happily—even crossing the tropics (and tropes)—: I find . . . a *meridian*."[201] After a hyphen, a colon, and three points of suspension, Celan finds then the meridian. In geography, the *circulus meridianus* is the imaginary line tracing the maximum semicircle that joins the two poles by perpendicularly bisecting the equator. Insofar as it is a semicircle, and therefore not a circle, it is a movement *without return* of a perfect trajectory. It departs from one pole, reaches the other pole, but it does not come back to itself, that is, to the first pole. It is not an error of Celan to speak of a "return to itself" with regard to the semicircle.[202] Returning to itself in this case clearly means going toward the other. The meridian is, in fact, "like" language. And like language intersecting tropes, the meridian also intersects the tropics.[203] These are the metaphors and tropes that in the topos research of poetry, in the light of utopia, have been "carried *ad absurdum*."[204] The lines that cut the language, those that make up its grille, the metaphors, in their identity alongside the difference, have been pushed to the absurd and to the extreme by poetry that has rendered the unrepeatable once again—another paradox—repeatable in its unrepeatability here and now. By crossing the lines of tropes, the meridian of poetry joins the two poles. But what poles are these? Poetry, as individualized and extremized language, and, indeed, nevertheless dialogical, joins the poles of the I and the you. And through poetry the meridian is like language, or better, language is like a meridian that is able to join and bring to an encounter. But here there echoes the older meaning of the meridian, that is, the "circle of midday" that marks the highest point reached by the sun at noon. This point of the sun's inversion cannot but remind one of the point of inversion of the breath, the *Atemwende*. But what is the noon of the meridian—the trope brought to the absurd by Celan? It is not so much the geographical-astronomical noon, the zenith of the celestial meridian to which there will always correspond the low point of the nadir, but rather the instant when the light comes and goes, that point between inhalation and exhalation. It is "the acute" of the today and of the here.[205] But "Everywhere is Here and Today."[206] The acute is therefore the utopian place of the encounter.

That the meridian is like language means that language is "immaterial," or that it has a particular materiality because its roots are "in the air," and it is terrestrial because it is "Breath-and-Clay."[207] This also means that language stands between earth and sky, it is terrestrial and celestial at the same time: "Language, language. Fellow-star. Earth-cousin."[208] Thus, the "truth" of the word not only wanders along "breath paths," but also "on star orbits."[209] Words are not only "sea-overflowed" but "star-overflown."[210] In Celan's linguistic utopia, the night, which corresponds to the sea and to the desert, is also the time when the stars can be seen. The "stars" are "cosmic paths" for which the gravity of the "nights" is translated into "the charge of our names."[211] The *tópos* of the star, the star of David and the star in the sky, from which innumerable meanings shine, is another metaphor for the utopian place of the encounter, and therefore for the word. To the imperative: "Pitch the Tent!" there echoes the analogous: "Place a star, place a star in the night!"[212] The star of the word rises from the night and is a human work. But language is also "planetary," with a foreign loan indicating the distance and the foreignness that nonetheless remains in its stretching out to all of the planets. Although language joins, it always separates. To the nearness of the native landscape Celan opposes the dialogical distance between the I and the you—the difficulty of the encounter.

But if there is no return, if the return is without return, what then will be the place of utopia? If not one's native land, will it be the Promised Land? Utopia's place is not the place of origin, but rather the place of promise. But it is not the earth, nor even a point on the earth, because the circular movement without return, the ellipses traced by the meridian, is without end. Thus, wandering can have no end. In the infinity of wandering, the promise is not the earth, but the word. The place of utopia is the promised word. The Tent-word of the encounter will be the place of return. Czernowitz in Bucovina, the land of the Hassidim, of their legends woven with dialogue, as Buber recounted them, the place that is no longer, the place no place, removed from the earth, reborn as the utopian place, as the place of a dialogue that will no longer be confined to the empirical and national here of a territory, but will be everywhere that there are an I and a you. If the utopian place is always the place of the other, the place to come of the other, the promise that comes from the other can be nothing but the word of the other. The return, without return, now appears to be a one-way. By breaking down the wall around itself and moving out toward the other, the I finds a dwelling, finds its home, finds its being close to itself, when it is close to the other and in the word of the other.

Thus, the I finds a dwelling in the word of the you. But this dwelling is as fleeting as the word. What sort of dwelling would that be? Can one really speak of "dwelling"? The poet's condition, "the man for whom language is everything, origin and destiny—in exile with his language"[213] becomes emblematic. The exile of the poet is the very emblem of human exile in the world, after the expulsion from the worldhood of the world and the scattering in the process of mondialization. If language is the only "homeland" that remains, it means that there is no longer a "homeland" because language is destined and destines to wander. Language offers no fixed dwelling. Thus, dwelling in language is not a dwelling, but only a shelter. Nonetheless, for the human being, "overarched by stars that are human handiwork," homeless, "without a Tent," exposed to a new and unforeseen opening, to a new and disquieting freedom, in the world mondialized through language, without homeland, without dwelling, what remains is only this shelter.[214] And it is the shelter offered by language. It is the shelter offered by the word of the you.

The word will never be a real dwelling; it has its by-ways and its escapes. It is a word-Tent, precariously pitched in the sand, insecure, provisory, ephemeral—always revocable. Even if it is the only place, it will always be out of place, a de-centered center in the expanse of the desert to be crossed before the promise. The Tent of the word will always be elsewhere, ahead, after, beyond, in the place of the beyond-place to come. It will rise for the instant of a whisper between the lost word and the promised word. The Tent of the word, the transient shelter, will ensure that the nomadic wandering does not cease until the utopia of the word to come. And in this wandering, it will continue to cross the desert of the promise.

15. THE WORD OF CONSPIRACY

The shelter, however, which lasts for only a whisper's instant, is nonetheless a shelter, a "kind of homecoming" for the I that finds itself in the encounter with the you. The word of the you resounds *as if* it were the word of the I and, vice versa, the word of the I resounds *as if* it were the word of the you.

This is what takes place in the Tent of the encounter. Indeed, this is what makes the Tent the Tent of the encounter. What is called "the secret of the encounter" is perhaps that which makes the impossible possible: to articulate the singularity of the word by making it understandable, beyond its singularity, to repeat the unrepeatability of the word, thus making it divisible, co-divisible, and shareable. The promised word, in its inappropriable intimacy, is the word left for and consigned to the other and to the repetition and iteration of the other—to its speaking and to its understanding. Grasped, understood, and repeated, the word appears to belong to the I no more than to the you. It appears, yet perhaps it is not. Nothing is *like* the other.[215] And the I is not *like* the you. The mystery of the word of the encounter is, however, the mystery of the identity that differs. The word itself is the limit between one's own and the foreign. But where does one's own end and the foreign begin? Where does what is mine end, and where does what is yours begin? Therefore, one must say that the word is neither yours nor mine. If it is neither yours nor mine, it will not even be neutral. After Auschwitz, one can speak only through the grammar of personal pronouns. Will there be a we? Will it be our word? Both mine and yours, that is, *communal*? But might not *communal* mean "as one"?[216] And have we not said that the "as" is illusory, not to mention the totalizing and totalitarian implications that the "one" could have?

The word articulated in the same wind, where the breaths are not, however, blended together, and the voices preserve their incommensurable singularities, is a word spoken, sung, and shouted "in one." The word is divided and shared only because it is *conspired*, that is, the result of a *conspiracy* which can last only for a whisper's instant. As a date or as a *Schibboleth*, it can be the encounter.

> Heart:
> Make yourself known even here,
> Here in the midst of the market.
> Cry out the shibboleth
> Into your homeland strangeness:
> February. No pasaran.[217]

According to an ancient or very ancient Jewish tradition, different, and often adverse, historical events go back to the same date. Thus, in the unrepeatability of the ninth of the month of *av* the following events occurred: the destruction of the First and the Second Temple, the quashing of Bar Kochba's uprising against Rome, the expulsion of the Jews from Spain, and even the beginning of the *Shoah*. In the cry *No pasáran* are condensed all the events of a February that Celan does not want to forget. The *Schibboleth* is here *No pasarán*, the rallying cry of Dolores Ibarruri and the International

Brigade during the Spanish Civil War. And February moves here from the bloody quashing of the workers revolt in Vienna in 1934, to the choosing of sides in Spain in 1936, ending with the relentless defense of Madrid in 1939. Like Benjamin's angel, Celan looks back at the different events that led up to his own catastrophe, which was not only his own, of World War II. Six years later another event is added to the list: February 13, 1962, eight protestors, who took part in the demonstration against the OAS, the extreme right-wing organization that opposed the independence of Algeria, were buried. As happened during the *Paris Commune* of 1871, the "peuple de Paris"—the *Schibboleth* of that Commune—filled the streets and squares. Celan writes another *Schibboleth* which this time bears the title *In Eins*, "In One."[218]

> Thirteenth February. In the heart's mouth
> an awakened shibboleth. With you,
> Peuple
> de Paris. *No pasarán.*

Yet in Celan's poetry there are many other *Schibboleths* that mark the end of a poem that is not an end. It is rather the rupture with which, although the constellation of that poem seems to close, another is opened. It opens with the star of that last word that is, instead, penultimate and stretches toward and promises itself to what is beyond and to come. They are the most disparate words of the most diverse languages, but they all possess messianic significance: *Wir, Heute, Alba, Ziw, Hoffnung, Esther, Immer, kumi ori, Sabbath, Mitsammen.*[219] These are words said "in one"—the pole and the end of the appeal of the *Schibboleth*. They do not ground anything. But they open up to the to-come of a community that is wandering like the Tent around which it constitutes itself and incessantly puts itself up and takes itself down, divides itself and gathers itself, crossing and mixing with all the other wandering communities of the mondialized world. These words, just as many Tents, as many stars, as many Schibboleths, messianically launched, open the way to a utopia yet to come.

NOTES

1. Paul Celan, "In rivers," in Selected Poems and Prose of Paul Celan (New York: W.W. Norton, 2001), 227.

2. See Gottfried W. Leibniz, Theodicy: Essays on the Goodness of God the Freedom of Man and the Origin of Evil, trans. E. M. Huggard (La Salle, IL: Open Court, 1990), 392.

3. This latter thesis is affirmed in particular by Baumgarten. See Alexander Gottlieb Baumgarten, Reflections On Poetry; Alexander Gottlieb Baumgarten's

Meditationes philosophicae de nonnullis ad poema pertinentibus (Berkeley, CA: University of California Press, 1954), 57.

4. Regarding himself, Celan writes that he is nourished "by the writings of Pëtr Kroptkin and Gustav Landauer." See Paul Celan, "The Meridian," in Selected Poems and Prose of Paul Celan (New York: W.W. Norton, 2001), 403. Celan also knows Landauer through Buber. See Buber, Paths in Utopia (Syracuse: Syracuse University Press, 1996) chapters "Kroptkin" and "Landauer," 38–57.

5. Gustav Landauer, Revolution and Other Writings: A Political Reader, ed. and trans. by Gabriel Kuhn (London: The Merlin Press, 2010), 113.

6. Ibid.

7. Ibid., 115.

8. See Ibid., 115.

9. See Ibid., 160, 114.

10. Ibid., 114.

11. Ibid., 115.

12. Ibid., 121.

13. Ibid.

14. Ernst Bloch, The Spirit of Utopia, trans. Anthony Nassar (Stanford, CA: Stanford University Press, 2000), 228.

15. See Ernst Bloch, Antizipierte Realität—Wie geschieht und was leistet utopisches Denken? In Universitätstage 1965: Wissenschaft und Planning (Berlin: Veröffentlichungen der Freien Universität), 15. On the concept of "anticipation" in the messianic sense, see also Franz Rosenzweig, The Star of Redemption, trans. William W. Hallo (Chicago: Holt, Reinhart and Winston, 1971), 234.

16. See Gustav Landauer, Revolution and Other Writings: A Political Reader, ed. and trans. by Gabriel Kuhn (London: The Merlin Press, 2010), 132. See also Ernst Bloch, The Spirit of Utopia; for Bloch, music, rather than poetry, is the utopian art par excellence.

17. "But after all poetry, too, often shoots ahead of us." Paul Celan, "The Meridian," 404. Translation modified.

18. Paul Celan, "[Letter to Hans Bender]," in Collected Prose (Riverdale-on-Hudson, NY: The Sheep Meadow Press, 1986), 26.

19. Paul Celan, "The Meridian," 409. Translation modified.

20. See ibid., 410.

21. Emmanuel Levinas, "Paul Celan: From Being to the Other" in Proper Names, trans. Michael B. Smith (Stanford: Stanford University Press, 1996), 44.

22. Paul Celan, "The Meridian," 407.

23. Ibid., 408.

24. Ibid., 401, 409.

25. See Chapter VI, §15 of this book.

26. Paul Celan, "Introductory Notes to the Translations of Blok and Mandelstam" Paul Celan Collected Prose, trans. Rosemarie Waldrop (London: Routledge, 2003), 61–64.

27. See Gustav Landauer, Revolution and Other Writings: A Political Reader, ed. and trans. by Gabriel Kuhn (London: The Merlin Press, 2010), 132.

28. See Paul Celan, "The Meridian," 402.

29. See ibid., 404.

30. Paul Celan, "Argumentum e Silentio," in Selected Poems and Prose of Paul Celan (New York: W.W. Norton, 2001), 78.

31. Paul Celan, "The Meridian," 409.

32. Paul Celan, "Below," in Poems of Paul Celan (New York: Persea Books, 1995), 113.

33. Paul Celan, "Silent strike," in Fathomsuns and Benighted (Manchester: Carcanet Press, 2001).

34. Paul Celan, "Cologne, at the station," in Selected Poems and Prose of Paul Celan (New York: W.W. Norton, 2001), 111.

35. On this I point, I refer the reader to John Felstiner, Paul Celan: Poet, Survivor, Jew (New Haven: Yale University Press, 1995), 217.

36. See Donatella Di Cesare, "Stimme" in Historisches Wörterbuch der Philosophie, vol. 10 (Basel and Stuttgart: Schwabe & Co Verlag, 1999), 217.

37. See Paul Celan, "[Letter to Hans Bender]," 25–26; Celan, "The Meridian," 413.

38. Paul Celan, "Tübingen, January," in Poems of Paul Celan (New York: Persea Books, 1995). On stuttering in Hölderlin, see Hans-Georg Gadamer, "Die Gegenwärtigkeit Hölderlins," in GW 9: Äesthetik und Poetik II (Mohr Siebeck UTB, Tubingen 1999), 41.

39. Paul Celan, "Stille!" in Gesammelte Werke in sieben Bänden, (Frankfurt: Suhrkamp, 2000), Bd. 1, 75. Translation modified.

40. Paul Celan, "World to be stuttered after," in Selected Poems and Prose of Paul Celan (New York: W.W. Norton, 2001), 337.

41. Paul Celan, "The Meridian," 406.

42. Emmanuel Levinas, "Paul Celan: From Being to the Other" in Proper Names, trans. Michael B. Smith (Stanford: Stanford University Press, 1996), 43.

43. See Stefan Mosès, "Quand le langage se fait voix. Paul Celan: Entretien dans la montagne" in Contre-Jour. Études sur Paul Celan. Colloque de Cerisy, ed. Martine Broda (Paris: edition du Cerf, 1986), 119.

44. Paul Celan, "Letter to Hans Bender," 26. My emphasis.

45. Paul Celan, "The Meridian," 408.

46. Ibid.

47. Franz Rosenzweig, "The New Thinking" in Philosophical and Theological Writings, ed. and trans. Paul Franks and Michael Morgan (Indianapolis, Ind.: Hackett Publishers, 2001), 125.

48. Jacques Derrida, "Schibboleth: For Paul Celan" in Sovereignties in Question. The Poetics of Paul Celan, eds. Thomas Dutoit and Outi Pasanen (New York: Fordham University Press, 2005), 2.

49. Paul Celan, "Speech on the Occasion of Receiving the Literature Prize of the Free Hanseatic City of Bremen," in Selected Poems and Prose of Paul Celan (New York: W.W. Norton, 2001), 395.

50. Jacques Derrida, "Schibboleth: For Paul Celan" in Sovereignties in Question. The Poetics of Paul Celan, eds. Thomas Dutoit and Outi Pasanen (New York: Fordham University Press, 2005), 15.

51. See ibid. This is how Derrida interprets vse poèty zgidy, "all poets are Jewish," the motto Celan presents in the poem "And with the Book from Tarussa" in Paul Celan: Selections, ed. and trans. Pierre Joris (Berkeley, CA: University of

California Press, 2005), 94. The quote, slightly changed, is from Marina Tsvetaeva who, in her "Poem of the End" from 1924, speaking of the old ghetto in Prague, wrote: "all poets are Jews" where nevertheless zhidy "Jew" has a negative value and is therefore used in an ironic way to signify "expulsed" or "excluded." See Marina Tsvetaeva, "Poem of the End" in Selected Poems (London: Penguin, 1994), 89.

52. Jacques Derrida, "Schibboleth: For Paul Celan" in Sovereignties in Question. The Poetics of Paul Celan, eds. Thomas Dutoit and Outi Pasanen (New York: Fordham University Press, 2005), 55.

53. Ibid. 37. My emphasis.

54. Paul Celan, "It's all different," in Selected Poems and Prose of Paul Celan (New York: W.W. Norton, 2001), 205–207.

55. Paul Celan, "The Meridian," 409. Translation modified.

56. See Paul Celan, "Stretto," in Selected Poems and Prose of Paul Celan (New York: W.W. Norton, 2001), 119–131. See Peter Szondi, "Reading Engführung" in Celan Studies, trans. Susan Bernofsky and Harvey Mendelsohn (Stanford, CA: Stanford University Press, 2003), 27–82.

57. Paul Celan, "The Meridian," 408.

58. Jacques Derrida, "Schibboleth: For Paul Celan" in Sovereignties in Question. The Poetics of Paul Celan, eds. Thomas Dutoit and Outi Pasanen (New York: Fordham University Press, 2005), 6.

59. Ibid.

60. Paul Celan, "The Meridian," 409.

61. Ibid.

62. Ibid.

63. Ibid.

64. Paul Celan, "Introductory Notes to the Translations of Blok and Mandelstam" Paul Celan Collected Prose, trans. Rosemarie Waldrop (London: Routledge, 2003), 61–64.

65. Paul Celan, "The Meridian," 409.

66. Ibid.

67. Ibid., 408.

68. See Jacques Derrida, "Schibboleth: For Paul Celan" in Sovereignties in Question. The Poetics of Paul Celan, eds. Thomas Dutoit and Outi Pasanen (New York: Fordham University Press, 2005), 53.

69. On this refer to Gerhard Buhr, Celans Poetik (Göttigen: Vandenhoeck & Ruprecht, 1976), 85–86.

70. Paul Celan, "The Meridian," 406.

71. Ibid., 408–409.

72. On the importance of Rilke for Celan, see Ulrich Fülleborn, "Rilke und Celan" in Rilke Heute. Beziehungen und Wirkungen, eds. Ingeborg Solbrig and Joachim W. Storck (Frankfurt: Suhrkamp, 1975), 49–70; James K. Lyon, "Rilke und Celan" in Argumentum e silentio. International Paul Celan Symposium, ed. A. Collin (Berlin-New York: de Gruyter, 1987), 199–213.

73. See Hans-Georg Gadamer, "On the Problem of Self-Understanding," in Philosophical Hermeneutics, ed. David E. Linge (Berkeley, CA: University of California Press, 1976), 57.

74. See Paul Celan, "The Meridian," 409.

75. The word must have been clear to Celan.

76. Paul Celan, "The Meridian," 408.

77. See Chapter III, §3 of the current work.

78. Paul Celan, "The Meridian," 409.

79. For this poem there is a concrete and easily reconstructable background: In 1955, Celan visited the mother of Gisèle de Lestrange, by then widowed, who had retreated into a cloister in Britain; the woman, a noble French Catholic, had never accepted the Jewish poet who had married her daughter. During the visit they spoke through a grille in the cloister. See John Felstiner, Paul Celan: Poet, Survivor, Jew, 147–148.

80. Wilhelm von Humboldt, On Language: On the Diversity of Human Language Construction and its Influence on the Mental Development of the Human Species, ed. Charles Taylor, trans. Peter Heath (Cambridge: Cambridge University Press, 1999), 235.

81. See Donatella Di Cesare, "Kleine Apologie der Übertragug ins Fremde" in Translation und Interpretation (Schriften der Académie du Midi), ed. Rolf Elberfeld et al (Munich: Fink, 1999), 67–74.

82. Paul Celan, letter dated August 2, 1948 in Bianca Rosenthal, "Quellen zum frühen Celan" in Monatshefte, 75/4, 1983, 402.

83. Paul Celan, "Speech on the Occasion of Receiving the Literature Prize of the Free Hanseatic City of Bremen," 395. See Chapter IV, §3 of the current work.

84. Martin Heidegger, On the Way to Language, trans. Peter D. Hertz (New York: Harper and Row Publishers, 1982) 124.

85. In a very questionable verdict Adorno had already in 1949 stated that poetry after Auschwitz or about Auschwitz was "barbaric." See Theodor W. Adorno, Prisms, trans. Shierry Weber Nicholson and Samuel Weber (Boston: MIT Press, 1981), 34. This verdict, commonly referred to Celan's Todesfuge, even if perhaps mistakenly, had saddened the poet. On the other hand, Adorno knew Celan for a long time and had promised to write an essay that never saw the light. See Theodor W. Adorno, Gesammelte Schriften, ed. Rolf Tiedemann (Frankfurt: Suhrkamp, 1974), vol. 2, 700.

86. Martin Buber, I and Thou, trans. Walter Kaufmann (New York: Scribner, 1970), 95–96.

87. Paul Celan, "Conversation in the Mountains," in Selected Poems and Prose of Paul Celan (New York: W.W. Norton, 2001), 398.

88. Emmanuel Levinas, "Paul Celan: From Being to the Other" in Proper Names, trans. Michael B. Smith (Stanford: Stanford University Press, 1996) 44. See also Stéphane Mosès "Quand le langage se fait voix: Paul Celan: Entretien dans la montagne," in Contre-Jour: Études sur Paul Celan: Colloque de Cérisy, ed. Martine Broda (Paris: Cerf, 1986), 121.

89. The expression "do you hear?," Hörstdu, is repeated innumerable times, in an obsessive way, in "Conversation in the Mountains," in Selected Poems and Prose of Paul Celan (New York: W.W. Norton, 2001).

90. See Hugo Huppert, "Spirituell. Ein Gespräch mit Paul Celan" in Paul Celan, eds. Werner Hamacher and Winfried Menninghaus (Frankfurt: Suhrkamp, 1988), 319.

91. See Celan's letter sent to R. Hirsch on July 26 1958 in Jean Bollack, "Paul Celan über die Sprache. Das Gedicht Sprachgitter und seine Interpretationen" in Paul Celan, 298.

92. Paul Celan, "Speech-Grille," in Selected Poems and Prose of Paul Celan (New York: W.W. Norton, 2001), 107. Maurice Blanchot, "The Last to Speak" in A Voice from Elsewhere, trans. Charlotte Mandell (Albany: State University of New York Press, 2007), 87.

93. See Paul Celan, "In Egypt," in Selected Poems and Prose of Paul Celan (New York: W.W. Norton, 2001), 37.

94. The concept of "limit" and "limit-situation" are developed in Karl Jaspers, Psychologie der Weltanschauungen. Berlin: Springer, 1919, 202.

95. See Karl Jaspers, Philosophy, trans. E.B. Ashton, vol. 2 (Chicago: University of Chicago Press, 1970), 177.

96. See ibid., 178. Translation modified.

97. See Martin Heidegger, "Comments on Karl Jasper's Psychology of World-views (1919/1921)," in Pathmarks, ed. William McNeill (Cambridge: Cambridge University Press, 1998), 1–38, (6–8).

98. See Karl Jaspers, Philosophy, trans. E.B. Ashton, vol. 2 (Chicago: University of Chicago Press, 1970), 178.

99. See Jeanne Hersch, Karl Jaspers. Eine Einführung in sein Werk (München: Piper, 1980), 29–30.

100. Celan and Jaspers express this in a similar way. See Paul Celan, "The Meridian," 407.

101. Karl Jaspers, Philosophy, trans. E.B. Ashton, vol. 2 (Chicago: University of Chicago Press, 1970), 178. Translation modified.

102. Paul Celan, "By Threes, by Fours" in Selected Poems and Prose of Paul Celan (New York: W.W. Norton, 2001), 143.

103. Paul Celan, "A Boomerang," in Selected Poems and Prose of Paul Celan (New York: W.W. Norton, 2001), 176.

104. Already for Leibniz language is an instinct; but so was it to be for many other philosophers, such as Herder, Humboldt, and Nietzsche. See Gottfried W. Leibniz, "Brevis designatio meditationum de originibus gentium, ductis potissimum ex indicio linguarum," in Opera omnia, ed. Louis Dutens (1730–1812), vol. IV, 2 (Geneva: Frères de Tournes, 1768), 187.

105. As for the concept of "life" and "vital" in their connection with living, I refer the reader to what I have already said in Chapter III, § 6. See Walter Benjamin, "The Task of the Translator," in Walter Benjamin: Selected Writings Volume I, 1913–1926, ed. Marcus Bullock and Michael W. Jennings (Cambridge, MA: Harvard University Press, 2004) 254.

106. Friedrich Nietzsche, "Ecce Homo," in Nietzsche: The Anti-Christ, Ecce Homo, Twilight of the Idols, and Other Writings, eds. Aaron Ridley and Judith Norman (Cambridge: Cambridge University Press, 2005), 99.

107. See Giorgio Agamben, Remnants of Auschwitz: The Witness and the Archive, trans. Daniel Heller-Roazen (Cambridge, MA: MIT Press, 1999), 68.

108. Yet those philosophers who brought Auschwitz into philosophical reflection opened up a new way. For example, see Steven T. Katz, Historicism, The

Holocaust, and Zionism. Critical Studies in Modern Jewish Thought and History (New York and London: New York University Press, 1992), in particular 105–273; see also Steven T. Katz, Post-Holocaust Dialogues: Critical Studies in Modern Jewish Thought (New York: New York University Press, 1983).

109. Emil L. Fackenheim, "The Holocaust: A Summing up after Two Decades of Reflection" in Argumentum e silentio, 286.

110. See Giorgio Agamben, Homo Sacer: Sovereign Power and Bare Life (Stanford, CA: Stanford University Press, 1998).

111. On this issue, see David Patterson, "The Muselmann and the Matter of the Human Being," in Open Wounds. The Crisis of Jewish Thought in the Aftermath of Auschwitz (Seattle, WA: University of Washington Press, 2006), 144–172.

112. See David Rousset, L'univers concentrationnaire [1965] (Paris: Hachette, 1993). Escaped from Buchenwald, Rousset writes this work about the Nazi lager that he considered as a system tied to the fundamental logic of economic and social capitalism. It is Bettelheim, who managed to save himself from Dachau and Buchenwald, who speaks of the "limit situation" or of the "extreme situation" in regard to the German Lager in 1943. On this concept, I also suggest Bruno Bettelheim, The Informed Heart (New York: The Free Press, 1960), 214–215. It is clear that the "extreme situation," by becoming commonplace, is the exception that coincides with the rule.

113. See Primo Levi, The Drowned and the Saved, trans. Raymond Rosenthal (New York: Vintage International, 1989), 88–104. On this refer to Donatella Di Cesare, "Zeichen als Spuren hermeneutischer Orientierung und der gute Wille zum Verstehen," in Kultur der Zeichen, ed. Werner Stegmaier (Frankfurt: Suhrkamp, 2000), 106–109.

114. Primo Levi, The Drowned and the Saved, 90. Translation modified.

115. Ibid.

116. See Victor Klemperer, The Language of the Third Reich: LTI, Lingua Tertii Imperii: A Philologist's Notebook, trans. Martin Brady (London; New Brunswick, N.J.: Athlone Press, 2000).

117. Primo Levi, The Drowned and the Saved, 95, 91.

118. Ibid., 92. On this see Chapter IV §5.

119. Ibid., 91.

120. Ibid. Translations modified.

121. Ibid.

122. Ibid., 92.

123. Ibid., 97 Translations modified.

124. Ibid., 94.

125. Ibid., 93.

126. Ibid., 102.

127. See Primo Levi, Other People's Trades, trans. Raymond Rosenthal (New York: Summit Books, 1989), 173–174.

128. See Primo Levi, If this is a man; and, The truce (Harmondsworth: New York: Penguin, 1979), 197–200.

129. Primo Levi, The Drowned and the Saved, 89.

130. See Chapter VI § 9.

131. Hans-Georg Gadamer, Truth and Method, trans. Joel Weinsheimer and Donald G. Marshall (New York: Continuum, 1989), 268. Hans-Georg Gadamer, "Language and Understanding," in The Gadamer Reader: A Bouquet of the Later Writings, ed. Richard Palmer (Evanston: Northwestern University Press, 2006), 190; Hans-Georg Gadamer, "On the Scope and Function of Hermeneutical Reflection," in Philosophical Hermeneutics, ed. David Linge (Berkeley, CA: University of California Press, 1976), 25.

132. Hans-Georg Gadamer, "Language and Understanding," in The Gadamer Reader: A Bouquet of the Later Writings, ed. Richard Palmer (Evanston: Northwestern University Press, 2006), 93.

133. See Plato, Theaetetus, 155d. See also Plato, Symposium, 210e.

134. Ludwig Wittgenstein, Philosophical Investigations, trans. G. E. M. Anscombe, 2nd ed. (Oxford: Blackwell Publishers, 2000), §123, 49.

135. On "atopia" see Plato, Symposium, 215a. On "atopia" as the troubling of the soul, see Plato, Phaedrus, 251e.

136. Plato, Sophist, 257b.

137. Plato, Sophist, 216c.

138. See Plato, Symposium, 215a.

139. Plato, Apology, 17b.

140. Plato, Apology, 17d.

141. Michel Foucault, "Of Other Spaces," Diacritics, Spring 1986, 24.

142. See Julia Kristeva, Strangers to Ourselves, trans. Leon S. Roudiez (New York: Columbia University Press, 1991).

143. See Erich Fascher, "Fremder" in Reallexikon für Antike und Christentum (Stuttgart: Hiersemann, 1972), vol. VIII, 309.

144. See Talmud ₆Sanhedrin 97a.

145. Paul Celan, "The Meridian," 407.

146. See § 6 of this chapter.

147. Paul Celan, "The Meridian," 408.

148. See also§ 3 of this chapter.

149. Paul Celan, "The Meridian," 408–409.

150. Ibid., 409.

151. See Martin Buber, I and Thou. With regard to Buber, Celan had read Hans Kohn, Martin Buber. Sein Werk und seine Zeit, Wiesbaden: Fourier, 1979. See John E. Jackson, "Die Du-Anrede bei Paul Celan" in Text und Kritik (53–54, 1977), 62–68.

152. Paul Celan, "Anabasis," in 65 Poems (Dublin: Raven Arts, 1985).

153. John Felstiner, Paul Celan: Poet, Survivor, Jew (New Haven: Yale University Press, 1995), 159.

154. Paul Celan, "Speech on the Occasion of Receiving the Literature Prize of the Free Hanseatic City of Bremen," 396.

155. On this, see Gershom G. Scholem, On the Mystical Shape of the Godhead: Basic Concepts in the Kabbalah, 1st American ed. (New York: Schoken Books; Distributed by Pantheon Books, 1991), 141–142.

156. See Chapter VI, §1.

157. Stefan Mosès, L'Éros et la Loi. Lectures bibliques (Paris, Le Seuil, 1999), 75.

158. See Paul Celan, "I have cut bamboo," in Selected Poems and Prose of Paul Celan (New York: W.W. Norton, 2001), 185. Paul Celan, "To night's order," in Selected Poems and Prose of Paul Celan (New York: W.W. Norton, 2001), 339. The image of sand returns continually in Celan's work, even in other contexts.

159. Paul Celan, "Da du geblendet von Worten," in Gesammelte Werke in sieben Bänden, Erster Band, 73.

160. But for Celan the Zeltmacher, the "tentmakers," are also victims of the Shoah. See Paul Celan, "In the air," in Selected Poems and Prose of Paul Celan (New York: W.W. Norton, 2001), 211–13.

161. Edmond Jabès, The Book of Questions, trans. Rosmarie Waldrop, II vols., vol. I (Hanover: Wesleyan University Press, 1991), 55–56. See also "The drawn curtains," 344: "'Dullness of words where God speaks. A dark which feels good. Drawn curtains . . .' Reb Rissel." On this, see Jacques Derrida, "Edmond Jabès and the Question of the Book," in Writing and Difference (Chicago: University of Chicago Press, 1978), 64–78.

162. Paul Celan, "Conversation in the Mountains," 397.

163. Paul Celan, "Eastersmoke," in Breathturn (Los Angeles: Sun and Moon, 1995), 205. It is interesting to note that in an early version of the poem, from 1965, Celan uses gerettete, "saved," in place of mitgewanderte, "wandered-along-with." The "saved" language recalls the language "not lost"—very positive adjectives even during his Parisian exile. See John Felstiner, Paul Celan: Poet, Survivor, Jew (New Haven: Yale University Press, 1995), 10

164. Paul Celan, "At the Assembled," in Breathturn (Los Angeles: Sun and Moon, 1995), 171.

165. See Paul Celan, "All those sleep shapes," in Poems of Paul Celan (New York: Persea Books, 1995), 345.

166. See Edmond Jabès, The Book of Questions, 63.

167. Paul Celan, "A Boomerang," 179.

168. See Jacques Derrida, Given Time: The Time of the King, Vol. I. Counterfeit Money (Chicago: University of Chicago Press, 1993), 27.

169. Paul Celan, "The Meridian," 410. My emphasis.

170. Jacques Derrida, "Force of Law, the Mystical Foundation of Authority" in Cardozo Law Review: Deconstruction and the Possibility of Justice. 11: 5–6 (1990), 920–1045.

171. Paul Celan, "Wo Eis ist," in Gesammelte Werke in Sieben Bänden, Erster Band, 96.

172. Jacques Derrida, Given Time: The Time of the King, Vol. I. Counterfeit Money, trans. Peggy Kamuf (Chicago: Chicago University Press, 1992), 100.

173. See Emmanuel Levinas, Discovering Existence with Husserl, trans. Richard Cohen (Evanston: Northwestern University Press, 1998), 171.

174. Paul Celan, "The Meridian," 410.

175. Ibid., 411.

176. Ibid.

177. Paul Celan, "Speech on the Occasion of Receiving the Literature Prize of the Free Hanseatic City of Bremen," in Collected Prose (Riverdale-on-Hudson, NY: The Sheep Meadow Press, 1986), 395.

178. Paul Celan, "The Meridian," 413.

179. Paul Celan, "Speech on the Occasion of Receiving the Literature Prize of the Free Hanseatic City of Bremen," in Collected Prose (Riverdale-on-Hudson, NY: The Sheep Meadow Press, 1986), 395.

180. Paul Celan, "The Meridian," 413.

181. Emmanuel Levinas, "Paul Celan: From Being to the Other" in Proper Names, trans. Michael B. Smith (Stanford: Stanford University Press, 1996), 40.

182. Paul Celan, "The Meridian," 404.

183. See ibid., 406.

184. Ibid., 410.

185. Ibid., 411.

186. Ibid.

187. Ibid.

188. See Theo Buck, "Muttersprache, Mördersprache," Celan-Studien I (Aachen: Rimbaud, 1993).

189. In Petre Salomon, "Briefwechsel mit Paul Celan, 1957–1962," in Neue Literatur, 32/II, 1981, 60–80, a letter from March 8, 1962, 65. It is hard to believe, beyond this and other testimonies, that Celan's utopia is nihilistic, because it is instead profoundly political.

190. Paul Celan, "The Meridian," 413.

191. It is the famous but anonymous phrase that one often encounters: "we do not want [. . .] to do the possible and desire the impossible?" See Gustav Landauer, Sein Lebensgang in Briefen, in collaboration with Ina Britschgi-Schimmer, ed. Martin Buber (Frankfurt: Rütten & Loening, 1929), vol I, 448. Celan, who owned this volume, had underlined this passage. See Lydia Koelle, Paul Celans Pneumatisches Judentum. Gott-Rede und menschliche existenz nach der Shoah (Mainz: Grünewald, 1998), 395.

192. Walter Benjamin, "Theses on the Philosophy of History," in Illuminations, trans. Harry Zohn, edited and with Introduction by Hannah Arendt (London: Pimlico, 1999), 253.

193. Paul Celan, "The Meridian." 408.

194. See Paul Celan, "In rivers," 61.

195. It is practice in the Hebrew world to leave a stone on the grave of the deceased.

196. Paul Celan, "Slickensides," in Breathturn (Los Angeles: Sun and Moon, 1995), 89.

197. "The desert is homesick for the sea," observed Reb Safad. "This explains why it fascinates us." Edmond Jabès, The Book of Questions, 270. Paul Celan, "Praise of Distance," in Selected Poems and Prose of Paul Celan (New York: W.W. Norton, 2001), 25;

198. Paul Celan, "Praise of Distance," 25.

199. Emmanuel Levinas, "Paul Celan: From Being to the Other" in Proper Names, trans. Michael B. Smith (Stanford: Stanford University Press, 1996), 45.

200. Paul Celan, "The Meridian," 412.

201. Ibid., 413.

202. This is precisely how Gerhard Buhr understands it, see Celans Poetik, 152.

203. In German, it is the same word: Tropen.

204. Paul Celan, "The Meridian," 411.

205. Ibid., 403, 405.

206. Paul Celan, "In the Air," 211.

207. Ibid.

208. Paul Celan, "What happened?" in Selected Poems and Prose of Paul Celan (New York: W.W. Norton, 2001), 187.

209. Paul Celan, "A Boomerang," 179.

210. Paul Celan, "Argumentum e Silentio," 79.

211. Paul Celan, "So Many Stars," in Speech-Grille and Selected Poems, 171.

212. Paul Celan, "Da du geblendet von Worten," 73; see also "A woodstar," in Speech-Grille and Selected Poems, 147.

213. Paul Celan, "Introductory Notes to the Translations of Blok and Mandelstam" Paul Celan Collected Prose, trans. Rosemarie Waldrop (London: Routledge, 2003), 61–64.

214. Paul Celan, "Speech on the Occasion of Receiving the Literature Prize of the Free Hanseatic City of Bremen," in Collected Prose (Riverdale-on-Hudson, NY: The Sheep Meadow Press, 1986), 396. Translation modified.

215. See this chapter, §6.

216. Jacques Derrida, Politics of Friendship, trans. George Collins (New York: Verso, 1997), 296–299.

217. Paul Celan, "Schibboleth," in Selected Poems and Prose of Paul Celan (New York: W.W. Norton, 2001), 75.

218. Paul Celan, "In One," in Selected Poems and Prose of Paul Celan (New York: W.W. Norton, 2001), 189.

219. Translations: We, today, dawn, light (in Hebrew), hope, Esther, always, rise! (In Hebrew from Isaiah 60, 1: "Arise, Jerusalem shine, for thy light is come"), Shabbat, together.

INDEX